Walking Dublin

PAT LIDDY

24 ORIGINAL WALKS IN AND AROUND DUBLIN

PASSPORT BOOKS
NTC/Contemporary Publishing Company

First published in 1998
by Passport Books, an imprint of
NTC/Contemporary Publishing Company
4255 West Touhy Avenue
Lincolnwood (Chicago), Illinois 60646
U.S.A.

ISBN 0-8442-9479-9

Library of Congress Catalog Card Number: 97-69675
Published in conjunction with New Holland (Publishers) Ltd

Commissioning editor: Jo Hemmings
Editor: Anna Bennett
Assistant editor: Rowena Curtis
Designer: Alan Marshall, Wilderness Design
Cartographer: ML Design
Indexer: Alex Corrin

Reproduction by Dot Gradation
Printed and bound in Singapore by Kyodo Printing Co (Singapore) Pte Ltd

Photographic Acknowledgments
All photographs by the author with the exception of the following:
Department of Arts, Culture and the Gaeltacht: Plate 31; Dublin Tourism: Plates 3, 6, 9, 17,
28, 38, 39; Maurice Joseph: Plate 25; Norma Joseph: Plate 18; Life File/Nigel Shuttleworth:
Plate 19; PictureBank Photo Library: Plates 4, 16, 22, 32, 36; Powerscourt Estate: Plate 34;
Peter Ryan: Plates 8, 24, 27, 29; Neil Setchfield: Plates 1, 5, 7, 10, 11, 21, 23.

Front cover: The campanile at Trinity College, photographed by
Adrian Baker, PhotoBank.

Walking Dublin

Contents

Preface

To put it quite simply, I have had a life-long passion to show off Dublin. Until recently it has been a vastly underestimated city in the context of its architecture, monuments, culture, literature, contribution to the arts, business and the sciences and in the sheer beauty, uniqueness and variety of its natural surroundings, especially in its proximity and accessibility to the sea, rivers and mountains.

In the past a significant leap forward occurred in Dublin's physical fortunes at least once in every century but never before on the scale experienced in the last ten years or so. Rehabilitation of old building stock has taken place on an unprecedented scale and huge areas previously derelict or underused have and are still being imaginatively redeveloped. City streets, parks and the environment in general have been massively upgraded and the process is ongoing. Most important of all, people are coming back in their thousands to live again in new city centre apartments.

It is very timely, therefore, that New Holland should commission this book and I am particularly gratified that its generous compass has allowed me the opportunity both to indulge my passion and to deal with the subject in this format more comprehensively than has ever been attempted before.

I am grateful to Jo Hemmings, Publishing Manager for New Holland, for sharing my vision and to Rowena Curtis and Anna Bennett for facilitating an efficient and always pleasant two-way communication between publisher and author. I must also express my deep appreciation to Gerry Barry and the staff of the Dublin Corporation Parks Department; to Kevin Dillon and his colleagues in the Dun Laoghaire and Rathdown Heritage Society; to Bill Kearney, Fingal County Council Parks Department; to Pauline Kelly of the Rathfarnham Irish Countrywomen's Association; to Paula O'Neill of the Powerscourt Estate; to Siobhan Daly of Dublin Tourism for her help in supplying some of the photographs; and to Ita Hackett for sharing her deep knowledge on the environs of the River Dodder. My thanks to the proprietors and staff of the countless businesses and institutions I contacted in my relentless pursuit of information. I cannot (dare not!) forget the help my three children, Anne Marie, Padraig and Brendan gave me in cross-checking my work, sorting my files and accompanying me on several walking expeditions. Finally, I owe a special debt of appreciation to my wife, Josephine, who, as always, provided me with unstinting support, helpful criticism and the input of zillions of bytes into the trusty P.C.

Pat Liddy
Dublin

Introduction

There is no better way to perceive the heart throb of a city, to tune into the spirit of its people and to attain an intimacy with its history and culture than by walking its streets and lanes, its highways and byways. This book invites you, whether visitor or citizen, to enjoy walks into the many and varied parts of Ireland's capital, from the historic city centre to the suburbs, from stunning settings around Dublin Bay to the embrace of wooded hills. Well-trodden tourist paths will be enlivened with fresh perspectives and surprises. Enthusiasts of James Joyce's *Ulysses* can follow in the footsteps of Leopold Bloom on the fateful day, 16 June 1904, in which the action of the novel takes place.

While Ireland's capital is a comparatively large city, with a population of over one million, it has never lost its sense of individuality. In fact, it has been said that Dublin is really only a series of interconnecting villages. As a result, each walk suggested here contains its own distinct flavour and unique appeal.

There has never been a better time to visit Dublin and to walk its streets. After years of neglect there is now a palpable pride in the city, renewal is happening everywhere, a universal interest in rediscovering the historic past is self-evident and the cultural and entertainment scenes have a vibrancy second to none.

The walks are laid out sequentially, which will allow you, after an appropriate break, to move straight on to the next walk if you wish. If a particular kind of walk is of more interest to you than another you may find the section 'Categories of Walks' useful to consult. Visitors to the city would be strongly advised to undertake a couple of the coastal or hill-climbing walks for both the magnificent scenery on offer and the invigorating exercise (don't worry, only average fitness is needed!). Some of these walks alone would be reason enough to visit Dublin and its surrounding area.

Each walk is preceded by a short description (Summary) and includes information on how to travel to and from the Start and Finish points (for details on public transport see page 12), the Length of the walk and the Time it takes (which is based on continuous progress and does not take into account any stops or visits), availability of Refreshment opportunities and the Best Time to undertake the journey. Pathway Status will advise if you should, for instance, wear trainers or if parts of the route are unsuitable for wheelchairs, Route Notes will give supplementary advice specific to that walk and, finally, Connecting Walks highlights the adjoining itineraries. Opening times and other useful details relating to places accessible to the public are given on page 162.

Detailed but easy-to-follow maps accompany each walk with the walking route clearly marked in blue. Places of interest are individually labelled and for a full explanation of all the symbols and abbreviations used on the maps see page 13.

Historical Background

No one knows how old Dublin really is. Its millennium celebration was held in 1988 but this date was based on a historical event in the old Viking town and never claimed to be the anniversary of the occasion when the first stake was driven into the ground. There were tiny farming and fishing communities living around present-day Dublin at least 5,000 years ago. Their society was sophisticated enough accurately to calculate the movements of celestial bodies and build one of Europe's most impressive burial tombs, Newgrange, only 30 miles (48 kilometres) from Dublin and older by at least seven centuries than the earliest Egyptian Pyramids.

Around the 1st or 2nd century AD five great slighe or roads were built by the Celts which passed through Dublin either near or directly across a ford on the River Liffey at a place known as Ath Cliath, or the Ford of the Hurdles. Situated near the present Father Mathew Bridge, this important river crossing was most likely serviced by a small settlement. When the Vikings arrived en masse in 841AD they settled at another Celtic cum Christian foundation, Dubh Linn (Black Pool), an ideal harbourage for shallow-draft boats, formed by a pool created where the River Poddle spread out before discharging into the Liffey. That site was located between modern Patrick Street and South Great George's Street.

The Vikings first erected a wooden stockade and then a stone defensive wall around their vulnerable little settlement and over the next few centuries their tenuous hold on the place they now called Dyfflyn was hotly contested. In 1170 the town was finally and brutally wrested from the Norsemen by the more effectively equipped Anglo Normans. From that point on Dublin remained firmly under the domination of the English Crown and Parliament until the terms of the Treaty in 1922 restored it and the 26 southern counties to an indigenous government.

Except for a street or two, Dublin had to remain behind thick stone walls and fortified gates until the end of the 16th century. By then the dangers of attack had receded through the successes of the Elizabethan conquest. Expansion was rapid in the middle of the next century and the city as we know it today began to take shape. During the administration of a relatively independent Irish Parliament, composed only of the Protestant ascendancy class, Dublin flourished as a European cultural and business centre. Subject to a visionary planning policy the magnificent Georgian squares, boulevards and terraces of mansions were built, first north of the Liffey and then, more extensively and successfully, on the Southside.

The English Parliament grew alarmed at the increasing success and autonomy of its Irish counterpart, a position not helped by the serious but relatively isolated revolt of 1798. Through cajoling, manipulation, bribery and threats the members of the Irish Parliament were persuaded to vote themselves out of existence and to accept the Act of Union of Great Britain and Ireland in 1800. The effect of this betrayal brought a downturn in the fortunes of Dublin and the island as a whole. It must be remembered that even during the Georgian period of ostentatious style, elegance and wealth there remained in the wings a sizeable proportion of the population who were treated as an underclass. These were mostly Roman Catholics who had virtually no rights or liberties as a result of the infamous Penal Laws enforced in earlier centuries. Now the removal of Dublin's primary position in the Empire brought even greater hardship and poverty to a class that was growing in population terms at an unprecedented rate.

Catholic Emancipation in 1829 allowed the restoration of religious and civil freedom to the majority but before full advantage could be taken of it the terrible tragedy of repeated famines during the 1840s, in which more than a million people in Ireland died, added a further setback to the economic well-being of the city. The late 19th century, however, brought with it a new spirit of hope and optimism and the city again benefited from a building boom, this time in the highly decorative Victorian style. The newly emerging middle and merchant classes, however, were growing further apart, economically speaking, from the labouring and unemployed sectors of society. While the former moved to the expanding suburbs the latter were left to a large extent to eke out an uncertain existence, living in miserable, over-crowded conditions in the once genteel town houses which now degenerated into decaying tenements. To exacerbate the problem of a deteriorating city centre the bloody insurrection of 1916 and the Civil War of 1922–23 devastated O'Connell Street, the city's showpiece thoroughfare. By the time an independent Irish government took office in 1922 the slums of Dublin were considered to be among the worst in Europe. The first priority was to rehouse as many people as possible, and an ambitious programme of public housing in the suburbs was initiated. It is to the credit of successive governments and Dublin Corporation that the seemingly hopeless task of providing dignified living conditions to tens of thousands of underprivileged families was accomplished in the face of a fragile economy.

It took longer for the city centre to recover. Dereliction was accompanied in the 1960s and 1970s by brash, unsympathetic and often inferior developments. Public outrage and a growing awareness of the uniqueness of Dublin's architectural heritage brought about a significant change in attitudes and exploitation of the city's remaining period fabric was more or less halted. By the late 1980s, rehabilitation, restoration and renewal became the norm in the majority of cases. Major steps were taken to improve the environment and the quality of the city's natural resources. A phenomenon new to Dublin, city centre apartment living, caught on from the 1990s and thousands of new residents have moved in. Over the next few years they will be joined by at least 20,000 more people who will be accommodated in the new schemes being planned in redundant areas of former dockland. Dublin, a century ago the world's envy with its innovatively run tramways, will once again hear the hum of electric streetcars when the ultra-modern LUAS light rail transport system comes on line by the start of the new millennium.

All in all, while many problems not uncommon to any major city still remain to be resolved, your witness to the progress currently being made in Dublin is a witness to history itself in the making.

Categories of Walks

Each category is not exclusive as every walk will obviously also cover other categories.

Walks of Historical Interest
Custom House Docks
Georgian Dublin
North City Centre
Oxmantown
Phibsborough to the National Botanic Gardens
South City Centre
Temple Bar
The Liberties
Viking and Medieval Dublin

Parks and Demesnes
Bray to Enniskerry
Griffith Avenue to Clontarf Castle
Phibsborough to the National Botanic Gardens
St Enda's Park to Marlay Park
The Phoenix Park

Literary Dublin
Famous Dubliners
Georgian Dublin
Ulysses Walk

Hill Walking
Bray to Enniskerry
Dalkey and Killiney Hill
Hell Fire Club
Howth

Walks of Urban Renewal
Custom House Docks
The Grand Canal (1st Part)
Oxmantown
Temple Bar
Viking and Medieval Dublin

Suburban Walks
Griffith Avenue to Clontarf Castle
Leafy Suburbs
Phibsborough to the National Botanic Gardens
St Enda's Park to Marlay Park

Coastal Walks
Bray to Enniskerry
Dalkey and Killiney Hill
Dun Laoghaire Coastal
Portmarnock to Malahide
Sutton Coastal

Panoramic Views
Dalkey to Killiney Hill
Hell Fire Club
Howth

Circular Walks
Custom House Docks
Dalkey and Killiney Hill
Georgian Dublin
North City Centre
South City Centre
Temple Bar
The Phoenix Park
Viking and Medieval Dublin

Exercise (brisk) Walks
Bray to Enniskerry
Dalkey and Killiney Hill
Dodder River Walk
Dun Laoghaire Coastal
Griffith Avenue to Clontarf Castle
Hell Fire Club
Howth
Leafy Suburbs
Portmarnock to Malahide
Sutton Coastal
The Grand Canal
The Phoenix Park

Waterways
Dodder River Walk
The Grand Canal

Castles
Dalkey and Killiney Hill
Dodder River Walk
Griffith Avenue to Clontarf Castle
Howth
Portmarnock to Malahide
The Phoenix Park
Viking and Medieval Dublin

Walks served by DART (within 10 minutes' walk of both start or finish)

South City Centre
Temple Bar
Viking and Medieval Dublin
Georgian Dublin
Custom House Docks
North City Centre
Leafy Suburbs
Dun Laoghaire Coastal
Dalkey and Killiney Hill
Howth

Walks in order of length (miles/kilometres)

mi	km	
2	3.2	Custom House Docks
2	3.2	Famous Dubliners
2	3.2	Oxmantown
2	3.2	Phibsborough to the National Botanic Gardens
2	3.2	St Enda's Park to Marlay Park
2	3.2	Temple Bar
2	3.2	Viking and Medieval Dublin
2¼	3.6	Georgian Dublin
2¼	3.6	South City Centre
3	4.8	Dalkey and Killiney Hill
3	4.8	Dun Laoghaire Coastal
3	4.8	Leafy Suburbs
3	4.8	North City Centre
3½	5.6	The Liberties
3½	5.6	Ulysses Walk
4	6.4	Bray to Enniskerry
4	6.4	Portmarnock to Malahide
4½	7.2	Dodder River Walk
5	8	Hell Fire Club
5	8	The Grand Canal
5½	8.8	The Phoenix Park
5½	8.8	Sutton Coastal
6	9.6	Griffith Avenue to Clontarf Castle
8	12.8	Howth

Public Transport in Dublin

Dublin is a relatively easy city to get around and has an excellent transport system provided by Dublin Bus and DART (Dublin Area Rapid Transit). Some routes to the outskirts may only have, say, an hourly bus service so enquire about times in advance.

Generally, public buses in Dublin are green double-deckers although there is an increasing number of specialised services using different bus sizes and colour schemes but still operated by the same transport company, Dublin Bus. Many routes are exact change only so you will need to carry enough small coins. Day tickets, weekly tickets and family tickets (also interchangable on DART services) are cost-saving options. Services operate between 06.20 and 23.30, with some late night options. Information from Dublin Bus, 59 Upper O'Connell Street, Dublin 1; (00 353 1) 873 4222.

DART Services: on average there is a DART train every 10 minutes between 06.30 (09.00 Sun) and 23.45. Tickets can be purchased at the DART stations and discounts similar to the buses are available. Enquire at ticket offices. For further information call (00 353 1) 836 6222.

Bus routes listed for walks	City-centre termini or pick-up points
3	O'Connell Street
5, 7, 7A, 8	Burgh Quay
10, 13	O'Connell Street
14A	D'Olier Street
15A, 15B	College Street
16, 16A, 16B, 19, 19A	O'Connell Street
22	O'Connell Street
25, 25A	Abbey Street Middle
31, 31A, 32, 32A	Abbey Street Lower
33, 33B	Eden Quay
36, 36A	Parnell Square West
38	Abbey Street Lower
41, 41A, 41B, 41C	Eden Quay
42	Beresford Place
44	Hawkins Street
45, 46	Eden Quay
47, 47A, 47B	Hawkins Street
60	Eden Quay
63	Eden Quay
66, 66A, 66B, 67, 67A	Abbey Street Middle
68, 68A, 69	Aston Quay
78A, 79	Aston Quay
83	College Street
84	Eden Quay
120	O'Connell Street
123	D'Olier Street or Cathal Brugha Street
130	Abbey Street Lower
134	Abbey Street Middle

Key to Route Maps

Each of the walks in this book is accompanied by a detailed map on which the route of the walk is shown in blue. Places of interest along the walks – such as historic houses, museums and churches – are clearly identified. Those that are open to the public appear in **bold type** (as in the text). Opening times are listed walk by walk at the back of the book, starting on page 162.

The following is a key to symbols and abbreviations used on the maps:

Symbols		*Abbreviations*			
	route of walk	AVE	Avenue	PL	Place
		BR	Bridge	QY	Quay
	railway line	CT	Court	S	South
		E	East	SQ	Square
	major building	FR	Father	ST	Saint
		LA	Lane	ST	Street
†	church	LWR	Lower	TER	Terrace
		N	North	UPR	Upper
	public toilets	PDE	Parade	W	West
		PH	Public House		
	wood		(Pub)		
▲	mountain				

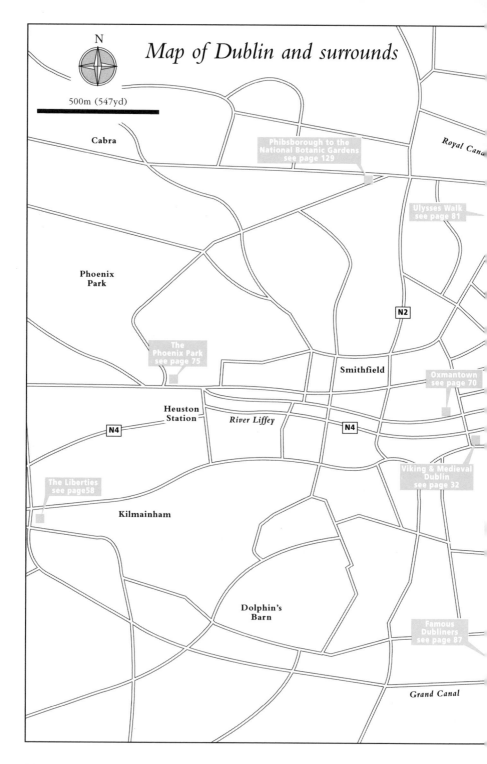

Map of Dublin and surrounds

N

500m (547yd)

Cabra

Phibsborough to the
National Botanic Gardens
see page 129

Royal Canal

Ulysses Walk
see page 81

Phoenix
Park

N2

The
Phoenix Park
see page 75

Smithfield

Oxmantown
see page 70

Heuston
Station

River Liffey

N4

N4

Viking & Medieval
Dublin
see page 32

The Liberties
see page58

Kilmainham

Dolphin's
Barn

Famous
Dubliners
see page 87

Grand Canal

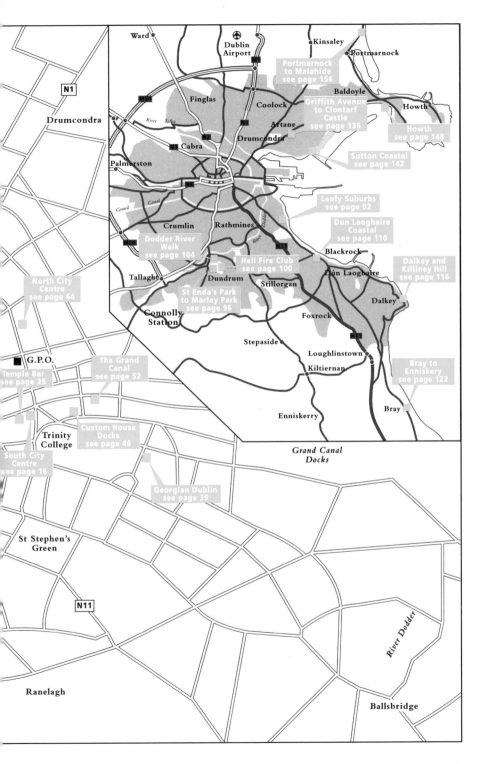

Ward

Dublin Airport

Kinsaley

Portmarnock

N1

Drumcondra

M50

Finglas

Coolock

Baldoyle

Portmarnock to Malahide
see page 156

Howth

River Tolka

N1

Artane

Griffith Avenue to Clontarf Castle
see page 136

Howth
see page 148

N2

Cabra

Drumcondra

Palmerston

Sutton Coastal
see page 142

Grand

Canal

Leafy Suburbs
see page 92

Crumlin

Rathmines

River Dodder

Dun Laoghaire Coastal
see page 110

M50

Dodder River Walk
see page 104

Blackrock

Dalkey and Killiney Hill
see page 116

North City Centre
see page 64

Tallaght

Hell Fire Club
see page 100

Dundrum

Stillorgan

Dún Laoghaire

Dalkey

St Enda's Park to Marlay Park
see page 96

Connolly Station

Foxrock

G.P.O.

The Grand Canal
see page 52

Stepaside

Loughlinstown

Kiltiernan

Bray to Enniskery
see page 122

Temple Bar
see page 25

Trinity College

Custom House Docks
see page 46

Enniskerry

Bray

South City Centre
see page 16

Grand Canal Docks

Georgian Dublin
see page 39

St Stephen's Green

N11

River Dodder

Ranelagh

Ballsbridge

15

South City Centre

Summary: The river Liffey physically divides Dublin into two halves but for some Dubliners the divisions go even deeper than this. Partisans on both sides of the river tend to extol the virtues of their own camp to the exclusion of the other. Southsiders might claim that they never visit the opposite shore unless they are travelling to the airport. Northsiders might say that they hate going southside as it is so easy to get lost there. Both claims need to be taken with a large pinch of salt. Nevertheless, the South City Centre still retains a perceived superior stylishness and a wealth of resplendent institutions. Here you can enjoy the museums, libraries and galleries, stroll in the parks (including the renowned St Stephen's Green) and side streets, lounge in refined hotels, classy restaurants and celebrated pubs, browse over monuments, street furniture and curiosities, linger in the august university precincts of Trinity College, and savour the elegant shops and that indefinable ambience that is Grafton Street.

Start and Finish:	Bewleys Café, Westmoreland Street (Sráid Westmoreland). Buses: all city centre services. DART Station: Tara Street. Multi-storey car park off Fleet Street.
Length:	2¼ miles (3.6 kilometres)
Time:	1¼ hours.
Refreshments:	You are spoilt for choice from fast food outlets to expensive restaurants. What will suit your taste and your pocket will be obvious to you at the time – most restaurants and hotels display their menus on their outside railings or in the lobby so it should not be too difficult to make a choice.
Pathway Status:	City and parkland paths. Ladies may wish to note that walking over the cobbles of Trinity College in very high heels can be a bit daunting.
Best Time to Visit:	Weekdays have one kind of charm, evenings another and Sunday morning has yet a third! Try all three but, of course, bear in mind the opening hours of the public institutions and St Stephen's Green.
Route Note:	This is a long walk and to avoid information fatigue you may prefer to break the walk into two parts, perhaps at some point around St Stephen's Green.
Connecting Walk:	Temple Bar.

Plate 1: *Bewley's Oriental Café on Grafton Street is a popular meeting place for Dubliners (see page 19).*

Plate 2: *Smart shops fill St Stephen's Green shopping centre (see page 20).*

Plate 3: *The Long Room Library at Trinity College (see page 24).*

Plate 4: The Three Fates Fountain, St Stephen's Green (see page 22).

Plate 5: The imposing West Front at Trinity (see page 24).

Plate 6: The famous Halfpenny Bridge is one of a number of bridges spanning the River Liffey and a fine place from which to view the city (see page 28).

Plate 7: *Temple Bar, filled with interesting shops and restaurants, has recently been 'reborn' as Dublin's 'cultural quarter' (see page 28).*

Plate 8: *The Brazen Head, claimed to be the oldest pub in Dublin (see page 35).*

Plate 9: *Dublin Castle is an intriguing mix of architectural styles (see page 38).*

Plate 10: *Foley's pub in Merrion Row (see page 45).*

Plate 11: *A Georgian door knocker in Merrion Square (see page 42).*

Plate 12: *Elegant Georgian doorways are to be seen throughout Dublin, attesting to the city's affluence in the 18th century (see page 42).*

Bewleys Café, the starting point of this walk, is a revered Dublin institution. Joshua Bewley, a Quaker from England, opened his first small tea and coffee shop in Dublin in the 1840s. This branch dates from 1916, and you will find another one later on in this walk in Grafton Street. Visit either for at least a cup of their own coffee or tea blends and a cake – they also have great value in the traditional Irish breakfast. Four doors away, at No 14, is Beshoff's fish and chip restaurant whose late founder, Ivan Beshoff, took part in the famous mutiny on the Russian battleship, *Potemkin*, in 1905.

Grafton Street

Head now towards College Green walking under the portico of the Bank of Ireland. Cross over to the centre island and, moving aside from the passing crowd, take stock of your surroundings. Looking back from where you have come you will see the full sweep and majesty of the Bank of Ireland, built in 1729 as the House of Parliament (see page 31). High up in the tympanum, the carving of the royal Coat of Arms still survives. The statues represent Fidelity, Hibernia and Commerce. No less than four eminent 18th-century architects were involved in building, extending and converting the Parliament/Bank of Ireland; Edward Lovett Pearce (1729), James Gandon (1785), Robert Parke (1797) and Francis Johnston (1803). Dame Street and College Green are dealt with in the Temple Bar Walk so next turn your attention to the facade of Trinity College. The college, founded in 1592, stands on the erstwhile grounds of the great Augustinian Priory of All Hallows, suppressed about 60 years previously by King Henry VIII. The present West Front of Trinity was erected between 1752 and 1759 and hardly deserves James Joyce's grudging description, 'a surly front, a dull stone set in the ring of the city's ignorance'.

Thingmotes, Cockles and Mussels

The Grafton Street end of College Green is graced by a fine group of Victorian shops and is called Fox's Corner after the famous tobacconist's James J. Fox, which was established here in 1881. During the Second World War Fox claimed to be the only shop in Northern Europe to keep a constant supply of Havana cigars. Just up from Fox's Corner is the fine facade (1891) of the Ulster Bank with its exquisite wrought-iron gates. Many banks set up their headquarters along Dame Street and College Green and you will shortly pass another splendid example, that of the former Northern Bank, now the National Irish Bank. Before leaving the island turn to face the statue of Henry Grattan fashioned in bronze by one of Dublin's most illustrious sculptors, John Foley. Grattan was a fiery orator and a highly respected party leader in Parliament. Despite all his efforts, however, he failed to prevent the Act of Union in 1800 and the dissolution of the Irish Parliament. The statue group and fountain behind Grattan is to another patriot, Thomas Davis. He and his fellows in the Young Ireland Movement sought to reverse the Act of Union, ultimately by violence, but he died before the miserable failure of the 1848 rebellion. Sculptor Edward Delaney also presents the trumpeting Heralds of the Four Provinces and the surrounding tablets illustrate the poetry of Davis and harrowing scenes from the Great Famine of the 1840s.

Walk up Church Lane past the National Bank (take a peek through the windows at the marvellous ceiling). Ahead is St Andrew's Church, now totally refurbished as the headquarters of **Dublin Tourism**. Its predecessor, which up to 1800 was the parish church to the Irish Parliament, was burnt to the ground and this worthy replacement was opened in 1873. At the top of Church Lane turn slightly to the right and cross to the church railings behind which you will see a marble column commemorating the soldiers of the 74th Dublin Company of the Imperial Yeomanry who died in the 1899–1902 Boer War. In Viking days a 40-foot (12-metre) mound called the Thingmote was erected here as an assembly point for councils and judiciary sittings.

Now head along Suffolk Street until you come to the corner with Grafton and Nassau Streets. Grafton Street was only a dingy lane until the early 18th-century when it was widened into a thoroughfare of fine residences. The only private house left now is at No. 1, the stately home of the Provost of Trinity College. Standing at the corner is Jeanne Rynhart's sculpture of Dublin's most famous character, Molly Malone (*'As she wheeled her wheel barrow, Through streets broad and narrow, Crying Cockles and Mussels, Alive, Alive O'*) . Her factual existence is doubted but her symbolic presence embodied in the city's unofficial anthem is real enough.

Consumerism with History and Style

At Wicklow Street note the stores at each corner with Grafton Street. Weir's Jewellers and Silversmiths, with its vintage curved glass and carved mahogany showcases, first opened for business in 1869. The partnership of John Brown and James Thomas was formed 21 years earlier, not in these premises opposite Weirs but in the very striking range of buildings across the road now occupied by Marks and Spencer's and beautifully restored by them. In 1995 Brown Thomas moved into their present abode, the erstwhile Switzers Department Store. McDonald's Restaurant in Grafton Street was the headquarters of the now defunct but once world-famous Irish Hospital's Sweepstakes, a charitable organisation which raised money by selling tickets for a draw based on the outcome of major horse races.

Enter Duke Street and observe a Dutch-style gable-fronted building in the reconstructed Marks and Spencer block. Called Dutch Billies (after King William of Orange), this style of architecture was prominent in pre-Georgian Dublin. The plaster-cast statue of a sailor using his sextant over the shop-front of Murray McGrath's was a one-time symbol for the Guild of Ship's Chandlers. On the opposite side is Davy Byrne's Pub, one of the important watering holes in James Joyce's novel *Ulysses*. Go into Duke Lane, left through the Royal Hibernian Way (site of the late, lamented Royal Hibernian Hotel) and into the street named after Joshua Dawson and laid down by him in 1707. His house was acquired eight years later for the Lord Mayor and the purchase price included the additional yearly rent of

Reading Room, Royal Irish Academy

6lb (2.7 kg) of refined sugar payable each Christmas. The Mansion House, which predates its counterpart in London, has remained there ever since. **St Ann's Church**, built in 1729 and refronted in 1868, is a vibrant religious and cultural centre. Dr T.J. Barnardo (1845–1905) the founder of the renowned children's charity, was a pupil in St Ann's Sunday School. Among the memorials inside St Ann's is a tablet to Felicia Hemans (1793–1835), poet and hymn writer, best known for her poem *Casablanca*, with the immortal lines 'The boy stood on the burning deck'. Following an 18th-century bequest, fresh loaves of bread are still provided on a daily basis on a shelf beside the altar for the needy to take away.

Nelson's Head

Between St Ann's and the Mansion House is the home of one of Europe's most respected learned societies, the Royal Irish Academy (established 1785). Scientific, historic and general scholarly research has been carried out here since 1852. Return to Grafton Street via Anne Street South and, passing by Bewleys Café, turn into

Johnson Court. Up this narrow lane is the entrance to St Theresa's Church, founded by the discalced Carmelites in 1793. Observe how the church is built away from the sight of Grafton Street. Until Catholic Emancipation in 1829 Roman Catholic churches could not directly face on to main or fashionable streets. Travel into the Powerscourt Townhouse Centre, an array of mostly craft shops, galleries and restaurants trading within what was previously the backyard of one of the city's foremost mansions, Powerscourt House (1774). You can walk right through the centre and come out via the house into William Street South. Just look up at the facade of the mansion and it is easy to be overawed by the level of personal wealth that could have afforded such architectural luxury. (See also Powerscourt Demesne on the Bray to Enniskerry walk.)

Proceed up William Street South passing the next building on the left, the **Dublin Civic Museum**. Built for the Society of Artists in 1766, it became the City Assembly House in 1791 to facilitate the Corporation meetings. From 1852 it served several other functions until it was acquired on behalf of the Old Dublin Society and Dublin Corporation to accommodate a vast array of artefacts and documents relating to the city's history. Even the head of Horatio Nelson, rescued from the rubble of Nelson's Pillar, which was ignominiously shattered by an explosion in 1966, is housed here. Chatham Street is home to one of Dublin's prime music schools, the College of Music. In front of you is the embellished facade of what was Mercer's Hospital, founded by Mary Mercer, which has been used as a student hostel, library and clinics for the Royal College of Surgeons since 1993.

A Saintly Green

Into King Street South, a little up to the left, is the Gaiety Theatre, home from 1871 to opera, musicals, pantomimes, plays, concerts and television shows, all in a wonderful Victorian setting. At the top of Grafton Street you are standing at the north-west corner of St Stephen's Green, named after a medieval leper hospital dedicated to St Stephen. (If your feet are weary you can take a circular horse and carriage ride from here around the Green.) To your right is the St Stephen's Green Shopping Centre, a lofty glass and steel retail palace and straight ahead is the Fusiliers' Arch, the formal entrance into the park. Cross the road and pass under the arch, noting the names of all the officers and men of the Dublin Fusiliers who died in the Boer War which are inscribed in the panels over the gates.

St Stephen's Green was originally an open tract of land used for grazing animals. It was taken in hand in 1663 and the central 27 acres (11 hectares) were enclosed by a wall to serve as an open space for the use of the citizens. The balance of about 30 acres (12 hectares) was sold off in building lots. In 1817 Sir Arthur Guinness, later Lord Ardilaun, paid for the remaining green area to be turned into a park. It is now creatively landscaped with ornamental lakes, pavilions, statues, rockeries and fountains, all under the care of the Office of Public Works. Take the west perimeter path and exit again at Lord Ardilaun's statue. Across the road is the Royal College of Surgeons, which was granted its royal charter in 1784. Today the college has an international reputation and students from over 50 countries attend courses here. Further up the street, between faceless office blocks, is the Unitarian

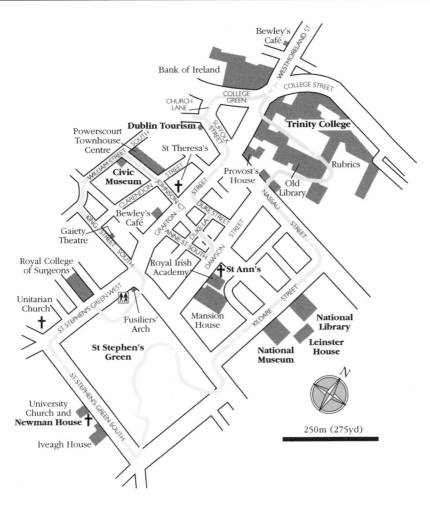

Church (1863), built for the descendants of non-conformist Protestant settlers who arrived in Dublin from England during the reign of Elizabeth I.

A Trio of Houses

Follow the railings of the park along its southside. There are three notable buildings along here, the first two being University Church and the adjoining **Newman House**. The church appears squeezed between two neighbours but once inside it opens out into a neo-Byzantine splendour. Built by John Henry, Cardinal Newman in 1856, it is said to have influenced the interior of London's Westminster Cathedral. Newman was rector of the first allowed Roman Catholic University in Ireland since the Reformation. Newman House comprises the two buildings next to the church which were acquired in the 1840s; the schools of Philosophy and Letters were begun in 1854. Both houses contain exquisite plasterwork and have

Iveagh House

recently been restored to their former glory. The crouching lion has gazed down on the comings and goings of such notables as writer James Joyce and poet and priest Gerard Manley Hopkins. The last of the trio is Iveagh House, a mid-19th-century combination of two houses owned by Benjamin Lee Guinness, another member of the famous brewing family. A new facade of Portland stone was erected in 1866 and a lavish interior, now one of the most sumptious in Dublin, was added. Rupert Guinness, the second Earl of Iveagh, presented the house to the Irish nation in 1939 and since then it has served as the headquarters of the Department of Foreign Affairs.

Museum Pieces

Re-enter the park at the next corner. The Three Fates Fountain was presented in 1956 by the people of Germany in recognition of Irish efforts to help relieve their appalling distress in the postwar period. Stay on the curving path until you arrive at the two splaying fountains at the park's central hub. From this vantage point it is easy to see how this park is an oasis in the middle of a bustling city. Students read, office workers take lunch, people stroll, old people linger, couples court and children play with their families and feed the ducks. Cross over the stone bridge following the path to the right, skirting along by the lake and the summer-house pavilion. Leave the park by the Famine Group Sculpture and the north-east exit outside which stands the uncompromising statue of Wolfe Tone (1763–1798), the United Irishman and ill-fated patriot (sculpted by Edward Delaney). The glory of this side of the Green is the Shelbourne Hotel, which was built in 1867 to the highest specifications of the day. In 1922 the Irish Free State Constitution was drafted in one of the hotel's function rooms. The four Egytian-style statues holding their torches represent Nubian princesses and their shackled slave girls.

Turn right into Kildare Street,which is essentially a street of government offices and state-run institutions. Just beyond the plaza containing the statue of William Conyngham, who was Archbishop of Dublin between 1884 and 1897, is the **National Museum** building designed by Thomas Deane and opened in 1890. This is the parent building of the museum but since 1997 its chronic shortage of space was ameliorated with the addition of facilities in the former Collins Barracks (see page 74). Exhibitions on display in Kildare Street include vast archaeological collections dating from the Stone Age up to the Middle Ages. The magnificent treasures dating from Ireland's Bronze Age and Gold Periods are the highlight. World archaeology is also well represented and incorporates an Egyptian room among others. Ireland's political and military history is another main feature.

Trendsetting Earl

In between the National Museum and its matching counterpart, the **National Library**, lies **Leinster House**, the seat of Dáil Éireann (Parliament) and Seanad Éireann (Senate). Once building work commenced on James Fitzgerald, Earl of Kildare's grand mansion in 1745, many of Dublin's titled and rich renounced the Northside and followed south of the Liffey in the Earl's wake. Lanes and fields gave way to fashionable avenues and squares. When Fitzgerald was created first Duke of Leinster he renamed Kildare House after his new title. In 1815 the third Duke of Leinster sold the house to the Royal Dublin Society (R.D.S.) who established a library, gallery and museum there. Those eventually evolved into the National Gallery, National Library and the National Museum of today. In 1922 the Government decided to purchase Leinster House and the R.D.S. moved out to its new home in Ballsbridge.

Going further down the street you will pass the **Royal College of Physicians of Ireland**, an organisation founded by Royal Charter in 1667 but only in a permanent home since 1860 when William Murray designed these premises. At the end of the street the still splendid exterior of the former Kildare Street Club (its impressive interior with a carved stone staircase and vaulted arcades, was insensitively ripped out by a developer in 1971) beckons visitors to either the Alliance Française or to the **Genealogical Office** (where you will receive help in researching family history), the Department of Manuscripts and the Heraldic Museum. Look closely at the base of the outside pillars and you will see carvings of monkeys playing snooker, hounds chasing hares and bears playing violins.

Hallowed Squares

Cross Kildare Street and walk by the shops on Nassau Street. Halfway along is Fred Hanna's Bookshop, which has been a celebrated mecca for bibliophiles for nearly 100 years. As well as stocking rank-and-file publications, it is also a famous source of second-hand, rare and antiquarian books. At the next set of pedestrian lights cross over and enter **Trinity College** through the Arts Building foyer and out into the quadrangle. A full tour around the 42 acres (17 hectares) of Trinity College is not within the scope of this walk; it requires and deserves its own excursion. There are regular tours on offer from the main gate or you can purchase a guide from the library shop which is directly opposite, beyond the Henry Moore sculpture.

By going around the Old Library (designed by Thomas Burgh in 1712) – in which are displayed some ancient treasures including the intricately illustrated 9th-century masterpiece, the Book of Kells and the so-called Brian Boru harp on which the harp emblem found on Irish coinage is based – you will come to Library Square. The red-brick building on the east side is the Rubrics, the oldest existing structure in Trinity (c.1700). Oliver Goldsmith had his chambers there. Walk towards the Campanile (1852, designed by Charles Lanyon) which occupies the spot where the College's predecessor, the medieval Augustinian Monastery of All Hallows, had its bell tower. The two seated figures flanking the campanile are Provost George Salmon and historian W.E.H. Lecky. The cobbled area is called Parliament Square on account of a subsidy received from the Irish Parliament to lay it down. On the right is the formal classicism of the Chapel (1798), almost mirrored on the opposite side by the Examination Hall (1785), both designed by William Chambers. Set behind and between the Chapel and the grey Graduates' Memorial Building (1899, designed by Sir Thomas Drew) is the lovely Dining Hall (begun 1758), designed by Hugh Darley and restored after a fire in 1984. The back of the West Front closes off the square. All these marvellous buildings are atmospherically set off by the cobbles, antique lamps and cast-iron bollards but nothing remains today of the buildings erected in 1592 when Queen Elizabeth granted her charter to the college. The land had been donated by Dublin Corporation who had earlier received the property of the suppressed monastery as a gift from King Henry VIII.

An Orator and a Poet

Walk through the vestibule of the West Front as far as the boundary railings and look back. Compared to the soft flowing curves of the Bank of Ireland, the limestone and granite facade of Trinity College is straight and austere but possesses a majestic solemnity as befits the institution. The statues on either side of the entrance are of two of the college's most famous alumni. On the left is Edmund Burke (1729–1797), essayist, orator and statesman and on the right Oliver Goldsmith (1728–1774), poet, playwright and novelist.

You are now probably more weary of mind than of body so a good brisk walk around all the squares and playing fields of Trinity might be one solution or else head for some refreshment in Westmoreland Street or Temple Bar.

Temple Bar

Summary: Temple Bar has become synonymous with urban regeneration, restoration and cultural growth. A mere decade ago it was a forgotten and run-down former dockland of narrow streets and forgotten alleys and the area was under threat of being turned into a major transportation centre. Then short-term low rents in semi-vacant buildings encouraged a bohemian flowering of artists, musicians, craftworkers and galleries. The place began to hum with a new activity and representations to government convinced the then Taoiseach (Prime Minister), Charles Haughey, to designate the area for special protection and development. Since 1991, not only has it become the cultural and entertainment quarter of the city (currently with 11 hotels and hostels, 14 music venues, 21 bars and 74 eating places!), but an influx of small businesses and apartments has increased the resident population from an original 200 to more than 1,000 today. In the evenings the whole place fairly throbs with activity and the principal streets are teeming with mostly young revellers. Temple Bar covers 28 acres (11.3 hectares) and is bounded by Dame Street, Fishamble Street, the South Quays of the River Liffey and Westmoreland Street. The area west of Parliament Street, although part of Temple Bar, is not included in this walk as it has been attached to the Viking and Medieval Dublin walk.

The history of Temple Bar is the history of Dublin itself. The Viking longphort (stockaded harbour) which grew into the town of Dyfflin was established near the western end of present-day Temple Bar. Dyfflin consolidated into the walled medieval city of Dublin which extended as far as Parliament Street. Apart from the building of Trinity College and a handful of residences, a street system and quayside walls did not come to Temple Bar until the 17th century. The quays were constantly jammed with brigs, barques and barquentines and day and night the cobbled streets rang to the cacophony of commerce and craftsmen, iron-shod hooves and wheels and to the raucousness of the taverns and coffee houses. The perennial problem of a tidal river and the advent of deeper draught vessels forced the removal of shipping further downriver in the late 18th century. Warehousing and merchandising became the main activities until they too disappeared to the suburbs in the 1960s.

Start and Finish: Temple Bar Hotel, Fleet Street (Sráid na Toinne = Street of Waves). Buses: all city centre services. DART Station: Tara Street. Multi-storey car park off Fleet Street.

25

Length:	2 miles (3.2 kilometres)
Time:	1¹/₄ hours.
Refreshments:	As the summary above shows, you certainly won't be short of a place of nourishment on this walk.
Pathway Status:	Street footpaths.
Best Time to Visit:	Any time. Business hours give one flavour (and entry to certain places), quieter Sundays impart a more reflective atmosphere and evening brings its own joie de vivre.
Route Notes:	The Stock Exchange and the House of Lords are only open during business hours. Meeting House Square may be shut in the evenings.
Connecting Walk:	South City Centre precedes this walk and it leads into Viking and Medieval Dublin.

To get to the starting point you may have already passed the well-known Palace Bar, a narrow-fronted traditional pub with a big heart, a literary history and a Victorian interior. The many public bars encountered on this walk will range from the genuine or pastiche Victorian to some hi-tech and ultra-modern versions.

Across the road the architecture of the multi-storey car park echoes that of the building it replaces, the site of Dublin's first power station (1892). Walk down Fleet Street and at the Oliver St John Gogerty pub, turn left up Anglesea Street. The street surface is laid, like most of Temple Bar's thoroughfares, with rectangular-shaped stone setts just as they were a century or more ago. A fine example of a highly ornate 19th-century wooden shop front is presented on the right by James Flynn, solicitors, at No.10. Opposite is the headquarters of the **Dublin Stock Exchange**, founded in 1799 and trading here since 1878. The wonderful old trading floor, quaintly archaic despite its supply of modern computer terminals, can be visited by the public during trading hours. A Mongolian barbecue restaurant illustrates how cosmopolitan culinary habits have become in Dublin. In Temple Bar alone you can savour not only the aforementioned Mongolian fare but also food from Italy, India, Turkey, France, America, Mexico, China and, of course, Ireland.

The Sign of the Crown
Turn right past Blooms Hotel (named after Leopold Bloom, the protagonist of James Joyce's *Ulysses*) into Cope Street and right again into Crown Alley, which most probably got its name from an 18th-century tavern called The Crown. It used to be common practice in Dublin parlance to call a street an alley; this was not a derogatory term but one used to describe a narrow street which led down to a river. Laid out in 1728, this street used to continue up to Dame Street but was truncated in 1972 by the erection of the Central Bank. The street had at least two large warehouses which have now, typically, been converted into bars and restaurants.

The new square at the end of the street facilitates street entertainers and the large red-bricked gabled building on the opposite side was Dublin's first purpose-built telephone exchange (1898). The failure to capture it and deny its use to the British authorities in the Insurrection of 1916 ensured the earlier defeat of the rebels.

Shopfront, Anglesea Street, Temple Bar

The Halfpenny Bridge

Enter the street called Temple Bar (which gives its name to the whole area) and turn right and left again into Asdill's Row. A surprise, even to most Dubliners, is the secluded apartment complex, Crampton Buildings, which stands around a courtyard off Asdill's Row. Built in 1890 by the Dublin Artisans Dwelling Company for poorly paid craftsmen and their families, the apartments are now privately owned. This short road exits on to Crampton Quay where you should turn left, cross the road, go to the centre of the Halfpenny Bridge and take an overview of Temple Bar. The bridge itself, one of the oldest cast-iron bridges in the world, was erected in 1816 to replace some very leaky ferries and derived its popular name from the toll exacted to cross it for the first 100 years of its existence. Now more or less a symbol of Dublin as a whole, the bridge was nearly replaced in 1913 when the Corporation declared, 'Wellington Bridge [as it was then known] is an unsightly structure... a suitable new bridge will be built.' The bridge now carries one of the heaviest pedestrian flows between the two sides of the city divided by the River Liffey.

Until the quay walls were built the river was several hundred metres wider along this stretch but its low depth and tidal variances made it unsuitable for shipping. The building of the quays between 1662 and 1816 did improve matters but as the average tonnage of vessels increased the docks had to move further east. It was this movement that left the 18th-century dockland of Temple Bar almost in suspended animation for the next 170 years. Straight ahead is Merchants' Arch, a passageway which suggests an entry into an enclave. The building the arch is part of is Merchants' Hall, built originally for the Guild of Merchants in 1822.

Multimedia and Ancient Wells

Cross back, enter under the arch and turn right along Temple Bar, a street whose name commemorates Sir William Temple (1555–1627) a notable public figure and property owner in the district. At the next corner on the right is the Temple Bar Gallery and Studios, an organisation founded in 1983 to support artists in their work. In this building, the largest complex of its kind in Ireland, 30 full-time professional artists have rented affordable studio space. Now take a left turn up Fownes Street. On this and other streets look out for old warehouses, many converted into apartments, which are still equipped with upper floor delivery doors and projecting beams to carry the lifting hooks.

The mix of old and new is emphasised at the corner with Cecilia Street by the modern Green Building, a specially commissioned environmentally friendly apartment block. Turning right into Cecilia Street you will notice Cecilia House, the former home of the first Catholic University School of Medicine, founded in 1855. This site is of even greater importance for Cecilia House was preceded first by the renowned Crow Street Theatre (1757–1820) and before that by the medieval Friary of Augustinian Friars (1259–1537). Some remains of the friary, one of the most notable foundations outside the city walls, were uncovered recently during rebuilding next to Cecilia House.

Walk past Crow Street, named after William Crow who, in 1597, bore the glorious title of Chirographer and Chief Prothonotary of the Court of Common Pleas. Turn

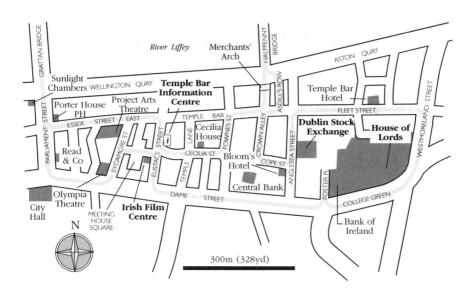

left into Temple Lane and right again on to the newly laid-out curved street where the modern building on the right contains the Temple Bar Music Centre. On the left is the Arthouse, an innovative centre to train artists in the use of multimedia technology. Continue into Eustace Street, pass the Ark – formerly a Presbyterian School and now a cultural centre for children – on one side and on the other, at No. 18 (a restored 18th-century residence), the offices of Temple Bar Properties and the **Information Centre**. Temple Bar Properties, a government agency, had the overall responsibility to encourage and monitor the public and private investment of close on £200 million to redevelop the area. At the end of the street is a 17th-century well discovered by workmen in 1991.

Parliamentary Boulevard
Now follow Essex Street East, (named after Arthur Capel, Earl of Essex and Lord Lieutenant 1672–1677), a road which, for centuries, was busy with dockland traffic. From its earliest days dedicated commerce was mixed with entertainment. Today offices, galleries, craft and design centres (e.g. The DESIGNyard) blend with theatre (The Project Arts Theatre), night clubs, pubs and hotels. Where the street curves to the left a side passage used to lead directly into the old Custom House (1707–1791) and its quay. The grandiose Bad Bob's Pub and Dolphin House were, in former days, respectively a wine and spirit merchants and the famous Dolphin Hotel.

Come out into Parliament Street and turn right at the Porter House (a pub with its own in-house brewery) and cross over to Grattan Bridge (1874) to survey the scene. Parliament Street was laid out in 1758 by the Wide Streets Commissioners to replace a narrow lane and provide a more sumptuous arrival from the North Quays to Dublin Castle and the Houses of Parliament. To make way for the road the developers forced the tenants of condemned houses to vacate their premises by removing their roofs in the middle of the night. The Clarence Hotel, owned by the U2 rock band, occupies the site of the old Custom House. The Poddle River, the main waterway of the medieval city, disgorges into the Liffey through an opening in the quay wall just above the Clarence Hotel. On the right of Parliament Street stands the remarkable Sunlight Chambers (1901) with its unique terracotta friezes advertising the uses of soap.

Non-Conformists
Engage reverse gear, walking back up Parliament Street until you reach Thomas Read & Co., Cutlers and Swordmakers, the oldest shop in Dublin (1670). Distinguished shops have always lined this street, serving the court at Dublin Castle and the honourable gentlemen of Parliament. Until recently Reads continued to forge swords, not for bewigged patrons but for officers of the Irish Army and some examples are still on view inside the shop. Next turn into Dame Street at the City Hall (see page 38) until you come to the Olympia Theatre (1879), a grand-dame of theatres resplendent inside with Victorian embellishments. Turn into Sycamore Street where Joshua Bewley opened his first coffee house in 1846 (see page 17) and where, in 1672, the Society of Friends (Quakers) erected their meeting house. Although Dublin had a large Roman Catholic population in the 17th and 18th century, all government was in the hands of the Protestant Ascendancy. Many non-conformist groups from Europe, notably Quakers, Huguenots, Palatines, Presbyterians, Methodists, Unitarians and others, were welcomed with open arms. These immigrants often brought in great business and craft skills. Catholics, on the whole, were deprived of many civil rights including freedom of worship and government positions. Halfway down enter the new and exciting Meeting House Square designed for use as a casual rendezvous point or as a formal open-air auditorium. The square is complemented by surrounding institutions such as the Dublin Institute of Technology School of Photography, the National Photographic Archive, The Gallery of Photography, and the Gaiety School of Acting.

Leave the square by way of the steps and archway into Eustace Street which will bring you past another cultural establishment, the **Irish Film Centre**, which houses the Film Institute of Ireland, the Irish Film Archive, cinemas, shops and bars and a number of independent film organisations. Beside it is the Quakers' Meeting House, which has operated from here since 1705.

Captured by Pirates
A left turn into Dame Street will bring you into a busy street whose architecture reflects the presence of many financial and insurance corporations that once had their headquarters here. Named after a medieval church, Mary del Dam, Dame Street was initially only a humble lane outside the city walls until it was widened after 1592 to connect the new Trinity College fittingly with the old city. The Central Bank, erected between 1972 and 1978, caused much heated controversy when it was built and since described by many as a fine building in the wrong place. A whole block had to be levelled to accommodate the structure but one building

that was removed was rebuilt again. Now facing west (it used to face south) into the Central Bank Plaza, the former Commercial Buildings were headquarters to the Dublin Chamber of Commerce from 1799 until 1964. The sculpture set into the side of the wall, showing a three-masted sailing ship, is a reminder that the chamber grew out of the Ouzel Galley Society which was founded in 1705 to arbitrate over a contentious insurance claim when a cargo ship, The Ouzel, captured by Algerian pirates in 1700 and recaptured by the crew five years later, limped back to Dublin. Another sculpture, entitled 'Crann an Óir' (Tree of Gold) by Eamonn O'Doherty, stands in the plaza.

House of Lords

The street now becomes College Green, a throwback to the days when there was an area of common pastureland in front of Trinity College. This will bring you, on your left, to a serene little street abutted on three sides by classical architecture. Foster Place is a cul-de-sac of banks. Firstly there is Allied Irish Banks, one time headquarters of the later incorporated Royal Bank and possibly the oldest (since 1797), continuously operating bank site in Ireland. Next, closing off Foster Place, is the Bank of Ireland Arts Centre which, as the overhead sculpture suggests, was the armoury or guardhouse for the Bank of Ireland, later becoming, until 1978, the offices of the Central Bank. On the east side is the curving classical elegance of the Bank of Ireland, originally built in 1729 to house the Irish Parliament. This was the first building in the world to be specifically designed as a two-chamber legislature. A quick visit, during banking hours, up the steps, past the sentry boxes and cannon guns (a legacy from the days when the bank had armed guards) and into the public rooms will be amply rewarding. Not to be missed is the unique **House of Lords**, preserved totally intact since its last sitting in 1800. In that year the Irish Parliament was cajoled and bribed into voting through the Act of Union which shifted direct rule from Dublin to London, thus ending a brief and culturally splendid de-facto independence from Britain. The two large tapestries (1733), woven by Dutch craftsman, John van Beaver, depict 'The Glorious Defence of Londonderry' and 'The Glorious Battle of the Boyne', two campaigns fought by William of Orange against James II in 1689–1690. Made up of 1,233 separate pieces, the chandelier dates from 1788 and the original carved oak mantelpiece is still in place. The Mace of the House of Commons (made in 1765 at a cost of £244-4s-11$^{1}/_{2}$d is the most substantial item to remain of that chamber as all traces of the old House of Commons, at the insistence of the British Government, were removed in 1803. The impressive Cash Office now occupies the site.

Leave the bank and move into Westmoreland Street laid out to replace Fleet Alley in 1801, the last scheme undertaken by the Wide Streets Commissioners. It is named after John Fane, Earl of Westmoreland and Lord Lieutenant 1790–1794. This will bring you back to Fleet Street and the completion of the walk.

Viking and Medieval Dublin

Summary: Very little is visible above ground of Viking and medieval Dublin although tangible evidence of this historical background exists in street patterns and names, in the remnants of the old city's walls, gates and towers and in the surviving sections of churches now incorporated into or standing alongside more recent buildings. Underground, however, the story is quite different. Large amounts of internationally important antiquities are still being uncovered by dedicated archaeologists. Vast quantities of artefacts and the foundations of a complete Viking neighbourhood consisting of houses, boundaries, paths, roads and harbour revetments were found along Wood Quay during the 1970s. Since then archaeological digs are a mandatory prerequisite before rebuilding is allowed on designated sites and worthwhile period buildings are no longer being destroyed at random but are being sensitively restored where at all feasible.

The fabric of this area's unique heritage is now being woven in several imaginative ways along your route which will help you to recreate the sense of a thousand years of history. The walk begins and ends at the western quarter of Temple Bar.

Start and Finish:	The Porter House, Parliament Street (Sráid na Feise = Street of Parliament). Buses: all city centre services. DART station: Tara Street. Multi-storey car park off Fleet Street.
Length:	2 miles (3.2 kilometres).
Time:	1¹/₂ hours.
Refreshments:	There is a wide choice of restaurants, hotels and pubs around the Start/Finish point. On this walk you could enjoy a traditional take-away from Dublin's most famous fish and chip shop, Burdocks, at No. 2 Werburgh Street.
Pathway Status:	Street pavements. Everywhere is accessible by wheelchair except for the steps leading up to the old walls.
Best Time to Visit:	Obviously, any time that suits you is good but if you want to savour a more medieval atmosphere try a Sunday for less traffic and the sounds of the bells from three different churches. Sunday services in St Patrick's Cathedral include excellent singing from the choir.
Connecting Walks:	Temple Bar is 5 minutes away and Georgian Dublin 15 minutes away.

Where better to start a walk around a once walled medieval city than at one of the entrance gates? Cross Parliament Street, a typical 18th-century avenue, into Essex Gate, a narrow little street which owes its origins to the medieval confinement of walls and closely packed housing. A bronze plaque on an upright stone pillar marks the assumed spot of Essex Gate, also known as Buttevant's Tower. (These name plaques appear wherever records show the existence of a gate or tower – look out for these as you go along.) The lower part and the foundations of Essex Gate will no doubt be the subject of excavation one day, as were those of Isolde's Tower which were unearthed along Essex Quay in 1995 and can now be seen through a special grill from the pavement.

Winding Streets and Legendary Theatres

A major excavation of Viking and Norman remains at the junction of Exchange Street Upper and Essex Gate was carried out between 1996 and 1997. On your right is Exchange Street Lower, a street which still follows the curve of the old walls. It was formerly called Blind Quay because it was out of view of the river. Next on your right is a building that mixes old and new. This is the **Viking Adventure**, a full-scale reconstruction of Viking Dublin peopled by live performers who will answer any questions you may have. In the evening there is a themed Viking Dinner. Grace Weir is the sculptor responsible for the magical panels which depict a Viking ship navigating with the aid of the heavenly constellations. The older part of this complex was built as the Church of SS Michael and John and opened in 1813. If you look up at the belfry you will see the first bell to have rung (in 1818) from a Roman Catholic Church in Dublin for nearly 250 years. The Penal Laws enacted against Catholics from the 16th century were lifted only in 1829.

The church was built on an earlier institution, the Smock Alley Theatre (its

City Walls

33

foundations were recently located). Opened in 1661, this playhouse was as famous for its unruly audiences as it was for the quality of its actors including the renowned Peg Woffington. The final curtain came down in 1790. Essex Street West was widened in the 1940s and, in the process, it lost its medieval curve. In common with most of the ancient streets and lanes it was called by various names during its long history including Stable Lane, Cadogan's Alley, Smock Alley and Orange Street. The house at the corner with Fishamble Street is reputed to be the longest inhabited family house in central Dublin and dates from at least the 17th century, although its exterior was 'modernised' in the 1720s.

Fishamble Street (now only half its original length) was laid down around the

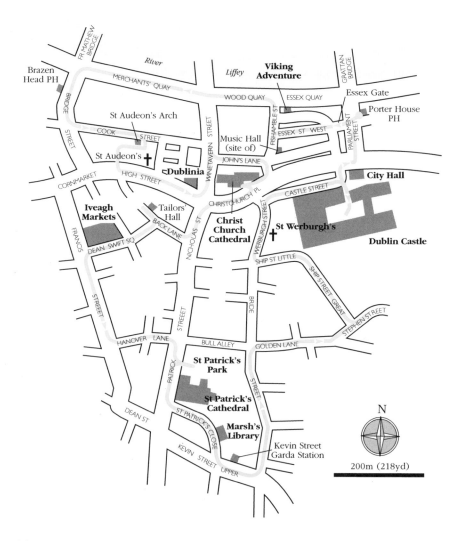

10th century. It was the main thoroughfare from the Viking port to High Street, the principal trading street. It derives its name from the fish stalls or shambles that lined the pavements. In the 18th century it had become a fashionable address and was further enhanced by the opening in 1741 of William Neal's Music Hall. A year later, on Tuesday 13th April, George Frederick Handel conducted the very first performance of his *Messiah* to a packed and rapturous audience in the Music Hall. The success of his visit to Dublin launched one of the most enduring and popular musical compositions and brilliantly relaunched Handel's own flagging career. The location of the Music Hall was just to the left of the hotel named after the composer. You may well want to raise a glass here to his honour and to that great event.

The large office complex along one side of Fishamble Street is the headquarters of Dublin Corporation, the Civic Offices. Nicknamed 'The Bunkers', the original development was received with dismay by most Dubliners. Amends have since been made by a superior frontage along Wood Quay, which is where you are now heading. Before you turn left into Wood Quay have a look at the front of the old SS Michael and John and at the intriguing sculpture of a rotting Viking longboat by Betty Maguire. Walk past the imposing frontage of the Civic Offices, cross over Winetavern Street and continue down Merchants' Quay. The church of St Francis is commonly called Adam and Eve's after a tavern through which the churchgoers entered, in the Penal Law days, to gain access to a concealed chapel. The next bridge you come to is Father Mathew Bridge (1818) and is the site of the fordable crossing which gave Dublin its Irish name, Baile Atha Cliath, the Town of the Hurdle Ford.

Ancient Walls and Bells
Turn left into Bridge Street and to what is claimed to be Dublin's oldest pub, the Brazen Head, which reputedly dates from 1198. The present building dates from 1668. Take the next left turn into Cook Street (many of the medieval streets were named after the predominant trade plied in them, e.g. Cornmarket, Haymarket, Fishamble Street etc.) Here you will find the most significant remains of the old town walls and one of its gates, St Audeon's Arch (1240). At its defensive peak, Dublin was protected by a massive ring of walls, a strong castle and up to 32 fortified gates and towers. Most of these installations were demolished in order to use the stone for other purposes but this inner wall survived hidden between later buildings. The wall was restored in 1975 by Dublin Corporation to celebrate European Architectural Year. Enter St Audeon's Arch and climb the steps up to the ramparts, the little park and a view over the North City. The lofty stone church is the Catholic St Audeon's (1846) and beside it is the Church of Ireland St Audeon's which is the city centre's oldest medieval parish church (c.1190) still in use today. The tower contains a set of bells dating from 1423. Leave the park by the High Street gate and proceed towards St Michael's Hill corner where the former Synod Hall stands, now the home of **Dublinia**, a striking recreation of the streets and life of medieval Dublin, and offering a panoramic view of the city from its tower.

Cross over to the Christ Church Cathedral side and walk down under the Synod Hall Bridge. Study the carvings on the wide footpath just below the entrance to

John's Lane East. They trace the outlines of two Viking dwellings, their outhouses and pathways based on a nearby archaeological dig. Watch out in other places in this part of the city for pavement carvings representing the various artefacts found in this and similar excavations. Turn back into John's Lane which is bordered by the sheer bulk of the cathedral. Next turn right and enter into the grounds of Christ Church. The stone ruins on the right are all that is left of a priory which was once attached to the cathedral.

Twin Cathedrals

Christ Church Cathedral was first founded in 1038 by the Norse King of Dublin, Sitric Silkenbeard and Donat, the first Bishop of Dublin. This wooden structure was replaced with a stone building in the 1170s by the Norman knight Strongbow and Archbishop St Laurence O'Toole. A very necessary restoration exactly 700 years later was funded by Henry Roe, a Dublin distiller. Like all great cathedrals it has a voluminous history which cannot even be attempted here. Best pay a visit, pick up an explanatory leaflet and don't forget to inspect the crypt, the oldest part of the cathedral which contains, among many other interesting items, the official ancient stocks (pillory) of the Liberty of Christ Church dating from 1670, a time when the Dean held civil jurisdiction over his own liberty (district).

Re-emerge on to Christchurch Place and cross over to Nicholas Street, passing the sunken Peace Park and the ruins of St Nicholas Within (the walls). Continue crossing over to the other side and head up Back Lane. Situated in an old factory, **Mother Red Caps Tavern and Market** is a haven for browsers and knick-knack hunters. Directly opposite and behind its ancient stone-arched entrance is the venerable Tailors' Hall. Now the headquarters of An Taisce (The Irish Heritage Trust), it was built between 1703 and 1707 for the Guild of Tailors, one of the ancient craft guilds founded in 1418, who relinquished it in 1873. Over a period of time it fell into serious disrepair until it was salvaged by voluntary efforts in 1966. Cut up to Dean Swift Square to see the **Iveagh Markets**, originally a fish and second-hand clothes market but now changed into a speciality food market. It was built by a Guinness foundation, the Iveagh Trust, in 1907. Look out among the carved keystone heads for the bearded, winking face with the impish grin – some say that it represents Lord Iveagh himself.

Brewing and Distilling Churchbuilders

You will next make your way via Francis Street and Hanover Lane to see some more great legacies of the Iveagh Trust. When you emerge through the archway into Patrick Street you will see the attractive red-brick apartments built in 1904 by the Iveagh Trust to house the poor. Cross into **St Patrick's Park** which was laid out by Lord Iveagh to replace the cleared-away slums. Flanking this park on Bull Alley is the impressive play and educational centre (now a vocational school) built by the philanthropic Lord Iveagh (Edward Cecil Guinness) in 1915 to give children an alternative to wandering the streets. The park also gives a sweeping view of **St Patrick's Cathedral**, a beneficiary of an earlier Guinness, Sir Benjamin Lee Guinness. He virtually saved the building from collapse in 1864–69. So much for

Christ Church Cathedral

the evil of drink – a brewer saved St Patrick's and a distiller rescued Christ Church! Return to Patrick Street and as you pass the cathedral note the medieval level of its entrance which is two metres lower than the modern pavement. As with Christ Church you must visit the interior at your leisure especially if the choir (founded in 1432) are in full voice at one of the services. In the 5th century St Patrick is reputed to have baptised some converts at a holy well near the entrance gate to the present park and a small wooden church was later founded in his honour. John Comyn, appointed Archbishop of Dublin in 1181 and not wishing to be subject to the city provosts or to the Priory of Christ Church, decided to build his own church. St Patrick's, begun in 1191, became a cathedral in 1213. Its most famous Dean was Jonathan Swift, author of *Gulliver's Travels* and an indefatigable champion of Dublin's poor. He was dean from 1713 to 1745 and is buried in the south aisle. At the back of the church is the medieval Chapter House door with a hole which was cut into it by the Earl of Kildare in 1492 when his enemy, the Earl of Ormonde, sought refuge in the Chapter House. In an effort to effect reconciliation, Kildare courageously thrust his arm through the hole and his rival eagerly clasped the proffered hand of friendship. This gave rise to the phrase 'chancing your arm'.

From Liliput to Moscow
Halfway up St Patrick's Close is **Marsh's Library** (1701), the oldest public library in Ireland. There is a great sense of antiquity within, not least from the collection of books which date from the 15th century. Original carved bookcases line the L-shaped library and three caged-in alcoves are provided into which readers used to be locked as a precaution against pilfering. On the right hand side of St Patrick's Close, behind a castellated wall, is the deanery of the cathedral. Next to the pave-

ment is a stone horse trough, a reliquary of more sedate times. Turn into Kevin Street Upper. The Garda Station inside the gate occupies the Episcopal palace of St Sepulchre, home of the Archbishops of Dublin from the end of the 12th to the early 19th century. The Dublin Metropolitan Police took possession in the 1830s.

Turn left into Bride Street and cross into Golden Lane. This corner is overlooked by some rather superb public housing. Note on the upper facades the carved circles containing scenes from *Gulliver's Travels*. Take the left fork into Stephen Street where in No. 67 John Boyd Dunlop founded the world's first pneumatic tyre factory in 1889. Turn into Ship Street which brings you to the back of Dublin Castle. Some of the original city walls continue out from the second archway over which Hoey's Court, the birthplace of Dean Swift, once stood. Turn right into Werburgh Street, named after the **church** dedicated to a Saxon king's daughter. The church's tall, elegant spire was ordered to be dismantled in 1810 when the authorities feared snipers might use it to fire into Dublin Castle. John Field, pianist, composer and creator of the nocturne was baptised here in 1782 (he died in Moscow in 1837). Lord Edward Fitzgerald is buried in the vaults and his captor, Major Sirr, ironically, lies close by in the graveyard. Two ancient fire pumps, dating from the days when volunteer firemen operated from parish churches, are preserved in the porch. Across the way is Burdock's famous fish and chip shop which seems to have a queue waiting outside day and night.

Dublin Castle

Turn right into Castle Street, which until this century was the main westward route out of Dublin. Halfway along you can peer in through the railings at the new extension to Dublin Castle which features a modern symbolic drawbridge and moat. When there are no big EU meetings the castle is usually open to the public. You may enter into the Upper Yard through the gates and an archway over which a statue of Justice looks on holding her scales. During the days of British Rule the cynical citizens used to say that Justice stood with her back to the city.

The scene that greets you may not at all look like a castle but two of the original towers still stand, one of which you will see if you go down into the Lower Yard. During recent excavations large segments of a tower and the walls were uncovered and these may be viewed in a specially lit undercroft area. Dublin Castle was the Crown's political, judicial and punitive centre for over 700 years and successive viceroys tore down most of the old castle and built elegant and comfortable surroundings. The **State Apartments**, now used for state occasions, are as sumptuous as those to be found in any European palace. The castle was first built in 1204 and was finally surrendered to the Irish Provisional Government on 16th January 1922. Also located here is the **Chester Beatty Library** (see page 94).

Return to Castle Street to see the last point of interest on this walk, the **City Hall**. Commissioned as a Royal Exchange by the Guild of Merchants, it was designed by Londoner, Thomas Cooley and was erected between 1769 and 1779. In 1851 it was taken over by Dublin Corporation and council meetings are held in the former coffee room of the guild members. Speaking of coffee or, indeed, something a little stronger you may now head for the suggested finish.

Georgian Dublin

Summary: In the last walk (Viking and Medieval Dublin) we saw that for centuries the city was confined within walls and their immediate neighbourhood. Only in the late 16th century was there any kind of a move eastwards towards the mouth of the River Liffey. The river itself was the main obstacle because of its marshy estuary but in time it was tamed by retaining quay walls and the marshes were filled in. By the early 1700s developers saw opportunities in these fresh fields and began tentatively, especially on the south side, to build grand new suburbs. They adopted the latest Georgian style in architecture which was ideal for building terrace after terrace of mansions suitable for the aristocracy and the affluent gentry.

Those developers who were attempting to sell their new properties on the Northside were thrown off course when the Earl of Kildare decided in 1745 to locate his splendid new mansion in the Molesworth Fields, a green field site just south of Trinity College. His example was followed by hundreds of others and the great Georgian avenues and squares blossomed forth in all directions south, east and west of Kildare (later Leinster) House.

Eighteenth-century developers created Georgian Dublin, 19-century developers enhanced it but mid-20th-century developers threatened to annihilate it. Generally speaking, however, this sorry trend affected relatively few areas. Dublin now treasures its Georgian past and while current fashion dictates that the vast majority of the houses are occupied as offices, it is not too hard to imagine, especially on the quieter streets, that you are back in a more refined era.

Start:	Westland Row (Rae an Iarthair = Row of the West). Buses: 1 and 3. DART Station: Westland Row. Very little on-street parking. Westland Row is only 8 minutes' walk from Grafton Street or O'Connell Bridge.
Finish:	Shelbourne Hotel, St Stephen's Green (Faiche Stiabhna = The Green of Stephen). City Centre buses from Westmoreland Street or D'Olier Streets. DART Station: Westland Row. Metered parking around St Stephen's Green or city-centre multi-storey car parks.
Length:	2¹/₄ miles (3.6 kilometres).
Time:	1¹/₄ hours.
Refreshments:	Several restaurants along the route are expensive. The self-service restaurant in the National Gallery is very reasonable.

Pathway Status: Street footpaths.
Best Time to Visit: Any time including the evening when floodlighting enhances many of the buildings but parks and institutions will be closed then. Sunday morning is good when the exclusion of commercial activity helps to recreate the atmosphere of a bygone age.
Connecting Walk: Both the Viking and Medieval Dublin and the Custom House Docks walks are about 12 minutes away.

Across from Pearse Station is the glass-fronted O'Reilly Hall, an innovation centre for Trinity College. The Liberator, Daniel O'Connell, was involved in the building of the **St Andrew's Church** and he presented it with two large paintings – the *Martyrdom of Thomas á Becket* and *The Crucifixion*. Walk up Westland Row on the left-hand side. On the far side is a terrace of houses now owned by Trinity College. Oscar Wilde was born in No. 21 in 1854. Further up, at No. 36 on your own side, are the premises of the Royal Irish Academy of Music, founded in 1848 and operating from here since 1871. The house was built in 1771 for the Marquis of Conyngham and has some good plasterwork ceilings by Michael Stapleton.

Georgian Splendour
Turn left into Fenian Street and right into Merrion Street Lower. The Davenport Hotel resides behind the facade of Merrion Hall, a one-time meeting place for an evangelical congregation. Further up, at the corner, is the American College, at No. 1 Merrion Square, the home to which the Wildes moved when they left Westland Row. Oscar Wilde's father, Sir William, was an eminent surgeon and his wife, Lady Jane (known as Speranza) was a noted poet. The plaque on the wall leaves you gasping at Sir William's achievements: 'Home of Oscar Wilde, poet, dramatist, wit. His father lived here – Sir William Robert Wills Wilde. Aural and Ophthalmic Surgeon, Archaeologist, Ethnologist, Antiquarian, Biographer, Statistician, Naturalist, Topographer, Historian, Folklorist – lived here 1855–1876'. Look over to your far right at Greene's Bookshop with its quaint outdoor bookstalls in Clare Street. The shop has been trading here since 1843.

As you walk along the north side of Merrion Square note, in the first place, the names of the occupiers of each house if only for your greater erudition. Halfway along stop and take stock. Merrion Square, as the name suggests, is a square (but, typically of Dublin, it is far from being a geometrically correct square) of terraced houses built around a park (officially **Archbishop Ryan Park**). The triumph of a Georgian terrace is its individuality contained within a prescribed uniformity. All the houses have the same basic design and number of storeys (usually four over a basement). The basement housed the kitchen and utility rooms, the ground floor was the reception area, the first floor contained the drawing room and other reception rooms and displayed the best decoration and furniture, on the next floor were the family and guest bedrooms and, finally, at the top of the house, the servants' quarters. Notice how the windows on the second and third floors get progressively shorter. There are often wrought-iron balconies outside the first floor windows

Plate 13: *Designed by James Gandon, the impressive Georgian Custom House building stands on the north bank of the Liffey (see page 48).*

Plate 14: *The hump-backed Huband Bridge was built in 1791 (see page 55).*

Plate 15: *A glimpse of the refurbished Custom House Docks area (see page 50).*

Plate 16: *A memorial to the poet, Patrick Kavanagh (1905–1967), who often frequented the banks of the Grand Canal (see page 55).*

Plate 17: *The courtyard of the Royal Hospital, Kilmainham (see page 62).*

Plate 18: *The famous O'Connell Bridge and Monument (see page 67).*

Plate 19: *The historic pillared portico of the General Post Office (see page 66).*

Plate 20: *The Parnell Monument, unveiled in 1911 (see page 69).*

Plate 21: *Many of the traders selling fresh fruit, fish and flowers in Moore Street are still supplied by horse and cart (see page 68).*

Plate 22: *The fine Four Courts, one of Dublin's grandest Georgian buildings, is the seat of the Irish Supreme and High Courts (see page 72).*

and if the internal lights are switched on you may be able to glimpse some stuccoed ceilings on the ground or first floor levels. While all the buildings are approximately the same height, there is sufficient variance between them to please the eye. Incidentally, at weekends, hundreds of paintings are hung by hopeful vendor-artists on the railings of Merrion Square.

In all of the several thousand Georgian houses in Dublin hardly any doorway is the same as another. They were designed to indicate the possible grandeur within and the more opulent the entrance the greater the anticipation of what lay behind the door. Classical adornments such as carvings, pillars and pilasters, lintels, pedi-

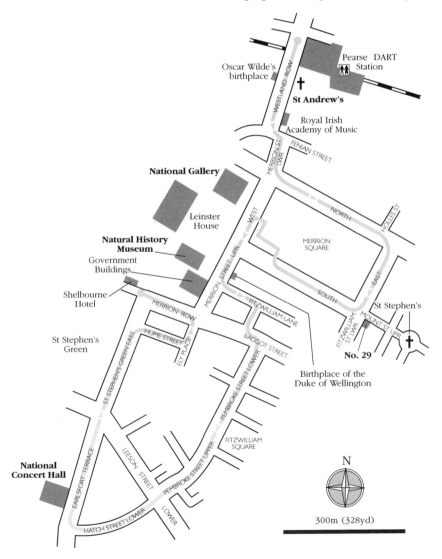

ments and porticoes were individually arranged and styled. Fan lights and side windows were often elaborately decorated with wrought iron. The doors themselves reveal endless combinations of panels (in size and number), of knocker design and of colour. When the idea of the Penny Post was first promulgated (1765 and again in 1810) householders initially refused to cut out slots for letter boxes in their elegant doors. Outside each doorstep is the humble footscraper, a useful object in the days of horse traffic and inadequate street cleaning.

The Pepper Canister

Start up again and head towards the crossing with Holles Street and the National Maternity Hospital, one of the city's three maternity hospitals (the others are the Coombe and the Rotunda). Founded initially in 1884 and re-established ten years later, the present building dates only from 1934–38. Its striking neo-Georgian facade is best viewed from Merrion Square East to where you now cross. Again, as a little aside, look down at the 18th- and 19th-century coal-hole covers in the pavement outside each house. Holes in the granite paving slabs had to be carefully hand-cut to receive the rims of the covers. To prevent the unwelcome intrusion of burglars the aperture was kept small. The name of the foundry is often inscribed on the cover. At one time such covers were common all over Europe but were largely destroyed in the bombing raids on the larger cities. When you reach the next corner, the view up Mount Street Upper presents an almost perfect Georgian streetscape. Closing off the vista is St Stephen's Church (1824), neo-Georgian on the outside, Victorian Renaissance on the inside. With the Dublin penchant for apt nicknames, the building is fondly known as the 'Pepper Canister'.

Standing on their Pedestals

Cross over to **No. 29 Fitzwilliam Street Lower**, which is a completely restored middle-class house built in 1794. The owners, the Electricity Supply Board, in association with the National Museum of Ireland, have recaptured the atmosphere and furnishings of a typical middle- to upper-class home of the period 1790 to 1820. The impressive length of Fitzwilliam Street and its onward extensions is spoiled by the modern office block but perhaps some day even this will be improved. Now make your way along Merrion Square South. No. 58 was the home of Daniel O'Connell, the writer Joseph Sheridan LeFanu lived at No.70 and three doors up is the headquarters of the **Irish Architectural Archive**. From a little further up the road cross over to the other side and enter the park. You will meet busts to Michael Collins and Henry Grattan before turning left at the next crosspath. Notice the different lamp standards along the paths. Dublin has always had a huge variety of vintage street lights and one example of each kind is placed along the park's pathways. Follow the curving path until you reach the back of the Rutland Fountain and then leave the park by an adjoining gate.

The Rutland Fountain (1791) provided fresh drinking water, not only to its elegant neighbours but also to the poorer classes. It must be remembered that many thousands of families lived in destitution only a stone's throw from all the Georgian grandeur. Opposite the fountain is one of the city's greatest treasures, the **National Gallery of Ireland**. In 1853 William Dargan organised and virtually paid for the Great International Exhibition, which was held in the grounds of Leinster House now occupied by the Gallery. This event inspired the collection of works of art on a more permanent basis and the gallery was opened in 1864 as a testimonial to Dargan, a unique privilege for a person who was still alive. His statue (sculpted by Thomas Farrell) was unveiled on the same day. The gallery houses works by many of the Old Masters and George Bernard Shaw enjoyed spending his youth here so much that he bequeathed the royalties from *Pygmalion* (the stage play original on which the musical *My Fair Lady* is based) to the gallery. Walk over to the gallery side of the road and make your way towards the railings of Leinster House. You might be tempted to think that this is the rear of the great house but it is actually the front – but so is the side which faces Kildare Street. The Earl of Kildare could not agree with his architect which side of the house should be the front so both sides were decided upon! The 65-foot (20-metre) high obelisk com-

St Stephen's Church

memorates Michael Collins, Arthur Griffith and Kevin O'Higgins, prominent figures in the emerging days of the Free State. Ironically, in the grounds of a republican Parliament, is a statue group honouring a royal personage, Prince Albert, the popular consort of Queen Victoria. Erected in 1871, it was crafted by Dubliner John Henry Foley who was also responsible for sculpting the statue of the Prince on the Albert Memorial in London's Kensington Gardens.

Continue to the next building, the **Natural History Museum** which houses an immense collection of the fauna of Ireland and the world in a wonderfully crowded Victorian manner. As well as being a museum it is also a very active research centre especially in entomology (the study of insects). The opening in 1857 was commemorated with a lecture delivered by Dr David Livingstone on his 'African Discoveries'. Another person connected with Africa stands on his pedestal outside the museum, Thomas Heazle Parke (1857–1893), Surgeon Major in the Royal Army Medical Corps.

Government Buildings is next on the agenda. This is the last major construction to have been commissioned by the British Government before Ireland obained self-rule in 1922. It is a magnificent complex built on the grand scale and best appreciated if you cross back again to the other side of the road. At your back is No. 24 Upper Merrion Street, the birthplace of Arthur Wellesley, Duke of Wellington.

A Meander past Mews and Muses

Leave the main streets now and turn into Fitzwilliam Lane. This is the other side of the Georgian coin, the back lanes. Behind the terraces were long gardens at the rear of which were the stables and coach houses. For the most part the gardens have been converted into car parks and the outhouses into mews apartments, workshops or offices. A short way up the lane turn right, emerge into Baggot Street and cross over to enter Pembroke Street. Fitzwilliam Square is to Dublin what Harley Street is to London, a place for doctors' consulting rooms. Continue through Leeson Street into Hatch Street Lower passing University Hall, which is an imposing neo-Gothic specimen built by the Jesuits in 1913 to house university students.

At Earlsfort Terrace turn right and view the long pile of University College Dublin, the centre portion of which is now the **National Concert Hall**. The Concert Hall is the only part to survive from the buildings erected for the International Exhibition of 1865. Note the fist-shaped hinges holding up the gates – they are also survivors as is the Winter Garden (now the Iveagh Gardens) to the rear of the Hall. Proceed past the modern office blocks and the Conrad Hotel until you reach the junction with St Stephen's Green on your left. Cross over and remain on the right hand side. No. 56 was the first site of St Vincent's Hospital founded by Mary Aikenhead on 23rd January 1883. The famous Loreto School and Convent, known as Loreto on the Green, have occupied Nos 53 to 55 since 1883. No. 51 is the headquarters of the Office of Public Works, a government department responsible, among other things, for the care of National monuments and state-owned property.

Hume Street may look Georgian but several of the houses are a pastiche and are a compromise in the wake of the celebrated demonstrations in 1969 protesting against the demolition of the real thing. The street itself dates from 1770. Hume Street Hospital (now only an outpatients' hospital) was built in 1911 to specialise in the treatment of skin cancer. Turn right into the backwater of Ely Place. The house of Dublin wit and writer Oliver St John Gogarty was demolished in 1971 to allow the building of the **Royal Hibernian Academy (R.H.A.) Gallagher Gallery**. The R.H.A. was established in 1823 and lost its permanent home in the rubble of the 1916 Rising. In 1971 a prominent developer and builder, the late Matthew Gallagher, financed the building of the new gallery but on his death the work was interrupted. The main structure is now complete but other facilities wait to be finished. Return up Ely Place to come out into Merrion Row where you will find a number of restaurants, Donoghue's Pub (birthplace of the folk group The Dubliners), a branch of the **National Museum** (housing Viking artefacts) and a tidy little graveyard (last resting place of many of Dublin's Huguenots). Dating from 1693, it is the oldest non-conformist Huguenot cemetery in Europe. You have now reached the distinguished Shelbourne Hotel where you can indulge in a traditional high tea or the refreshment of your choice.

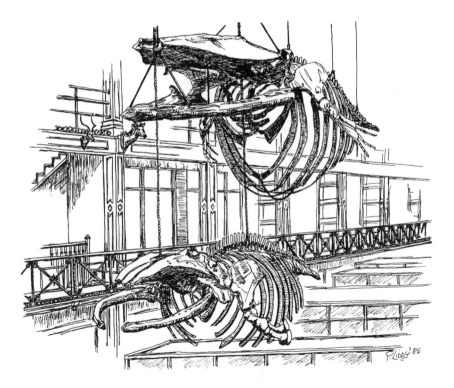

Natural History Museum

Custom House Docks

Summary: The walk examines the dockland area that replaced Temple Bar when the new Custom House and its adjoining dock basins were opened in 1791. Just as the Temple Bar dockland was 'beached' in the 18th century when accommodation for ships moved downriver, so too the Custom House Docks became irrelevant in the early part of the 20th century. In the era of ever larger ships the two dock basins, separated from the River Liffey by lock gates, were anachronistic and fell into disuse. Situated only a stone's throw from one of Dublin's architectural glories, The Custom House, the redundant docks cried our for imaginative development. Their time came at last with the announcement in 1987 that a proposed Financial Services Centre was to be built on the site. The designs were to take into account the preservation of the docks and certain other Georgian and Victorian engineering and architectural features. To make it a living quarter, a hotel, museum, pubs, restaurants, shops and apartments were also planned. Most of the ambitious scheme has now been realised but, except for those who work in the centre, it is still an area waiting to be discovered by most Dubliners.

Start and Finish: Mulligan's Pub, Poolbeg Street (Sráid Phoill Bhig = Street of the Little Pool). Buses: all city centre buses. DART: Tara Street. Car Park: Fleet Street.

Length: 2 miles (3.1 kilometres)

Time: 1¼ hours.

Refreshments: Apart from Mulligan's Pub and all the other city centre hostelries, there are several possibilities in the Custom House Docks including the real olde-worlde Harbourmaster's Pub. Unless you are having just soup and a roll, you will need to reserve a table if you want a full lunch.

Pathway Status: All roadside paths or open squares.

Best Time to Visit: Probably best during the day-time as the night-time life is relatively quiet in this part of the city.

Route Notes: There are no admission restrictions day or evening on any part of the walk except for Connolly Railway Station which closes at around 21.00 (earlier on Sundays).

Connecting Walk: From the previous walk, Georgian Dublin to the next walk, The Grand Canal.

This walk starts at one of Dublin's most famous pubs, the venerable Mulligan's of Poolbeg Street, founded in 1782, and still retaining the aged atmosphere of old wood, Victorian mirrors, gas lamps and a cosy snug. Two doors up from Mulligan's is the saddle- and harness-making firm of Greer & Son which was given the number 7A to avoid the last house on the street being numbered 13. Poolbeg Street, previously known as Shoe Lane, is one of the last of a warren of narrow lanes which used to lead off from the dockland of a vanished era.

Bridges and Railways

Leave Poolbeg Street turning left into Tara Street, once famous for its public baths and wash house, a very necessary institution in a city where only a few generations ago thousands of families had no bathrooms in their tenements or artisan dwellings. Cross Butt Bridge and pause for a couple of minutes in the centre. The view of the Custom House to the right is partially blocked by a railway bridge, itself too heavily proportioned but not lacking in some style although the ugly advertisements rather spoil it. Built in 1890 and called the Loop Line Bridge, this railway crossing is testament to the free-for-all railroad building of the last century. There were several railway companies serving the city, each with their own terminus, but no rail line served the city centre. When it came to joining two of these termini, Connolly and Pearse Stations, it could only be done above street level.

Beyond the Custom House is the Financial Services Centre, the North Wall Docks, the deep-water Alexander Basin and the open sea. The Liffey is a tidal river and its depth varies enormously with the movement of the tides. The 16-storey building on the left is Liberty Hall, headquarters of the Trade Union S.I.P.T.U., (Services, Industrial, Professional, Technical Union) and built in 1962. Since rejected by most Dubliners on aesthetic grounds, it signalled the first and last experiment of skyscraperism in what is predominately a low-level cityscape. Named after Isaac Butt, founder in 1870 of the Home Rule Party, the present bridge (1932) replaced an earlier swivel bridge.

Cross to Beresford Place on the railway bridge side. The bronze statue to James Connolly (unveiled 1996; sculptor Eamonn O'Doherty) commemorates a leading Trade Union official of the Irish Transport and General Workers Union (I.T.G.W.U.), an antecedent of S.I.P.T.U. Old Liberty Hall was the nerve centre for the detailed planning of the Easter Rising in 1916. Connolly led the Union's own small armed force, the Citizen Army, and a contingent of the Irish Volunteers under Patrick Pearse from Liberty Hall to seize the General Post Office on that fateful Easter Monday morning. Connolly was executed after the rising collapsed. The starry plough design behind the statue represents the flag of the Citizen Army.

The Custom House

A much more acceptable modern structure is the new Irish Life building at the corner with Abbey Street. Across the other side of Abbey Street is an older Irish Life complex. In its plaza a statue group, the Chariot of Life by Oisin Kelly, represents Reason controlling the Emotions and not, as one Dublin wit described it, the state of the country being like two runaway horses with no one guiding them! Under

The Chariot of Life

the bridge behind the railings of the Custom House stand twin pillars joined by a capstone. These are reminders of one of the three fires that have afflicted this wonderful building in its 200 years of chequered history. Mobs, opposing its construction for fear of losing business when the old Custom House would be closed upstream, harassed the site from the moment the first trenches were dug. The architect, James Gandon, considered it prudent to carry his cane sword with him at all times. He had the more serious problem of providing adequate foundations in the marshy sub-soil but eventually he solved it innovatively by using a novel form of raft foundation which brought him international acclaim. In 1789, eight years after the foundation stone was laid, a mysterious fire damaged the partially completed building but it was substantially finished by 1791. Another blaze nearly consumed the edifice in 1833 but its most cataclysmic event took place in 1921, during the War of Independence, when the I.R.A. set the building to the torch. It burned for days and was nearly beyond redemption but it was painstakingly restored, a process that was only finally completed by the Office of Public Works in the early 1990s.

A House for Buses
Notice where a couple of houses had to be demolished in Gardiner Street to make way for the elevated railway. Yann Renard-Goulet's sculpture in front of the north entrance to the Custom House is a bronze memorial to the I.R.A. men who died in the 1921 attack and represents Ireland comforting one of her dying sons. Over the entrance portico stand the statues of Europe, Asia, Africa and America, the four corners of the world from where the trading ships came. Cross to the centre island on Memorial Road opposite the A.I.B. block in the International Financial Services Centre (I.F.S.C.). On one side of the road is Busaras (literally Bus House), the bus terminal for provincial services and Dublin's first truly modern public building (architect, Michael Scott, 1953). The memorial on the traffic island is a sphere of chains enclosing a candle with an ever-burning flame and the writing around the plinth exhorts us to remember all those 'whom we failed to rescue from prison, who were tortured, who were kidnapped, who disappeared'.

With the assistance of the traffic lights walk to the Busaras side and proceed up Amiens Street passing Store Street and the Coroner's Court, a building that seems not to have changed internally or externally in the last hundred years. Ahead is Connolly Railway Station, displaying its marvellous Italianate frontage and towers. Built in 1844, it now has the distinction of being the only mainline station in Dublin to receive trains from outside the Republic, i.e. Northern Ireland.

A Dockland Reborn

Step across the road into **Connolly Station**. From the newly refurbished vestibule (due to open in June 1998) you will be able to ascend up to view the activity on the seven platforms. From there you can descend down the ramp or the escalators to gain access into the I.F.S.C. or the Custom House Docks, as the area is often called. Here funds, treasury, reinsurance and investment managers and market dealers ply their trade from morning till night. Pass the La Touche and Andersen Building until you arrive at the **Harbourmaster's Bar**. If you are not planning to seek respite in the bar do at least take a quick peek at the inside which is laid out like a 19th-century maritime provisions store. Go left of the bar to arrive at the Inner Dock where 333 apartments were completed in 1996.

The development of the Custom House Docks, begun in 1987, is one of the most exciting things to have happened in Dublin in its recent history. The I.F.S.C.

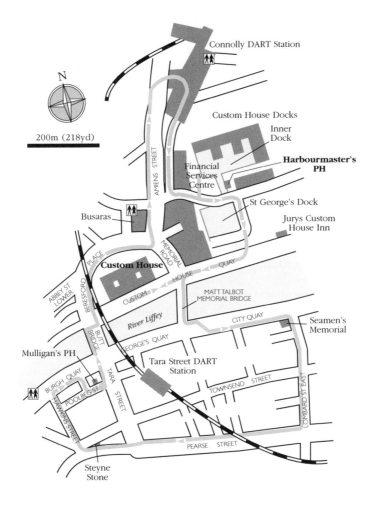

alone is set to provide over 6,000 jobs and is already managing funds worth $33 billion. More than 600 residents have moved into the apartments. The architecture is new, hi-tech and exciting and serves to complement the best of the old that has been retained. The water resources have become a central feature of the development. To cap it all the very success of the initial 27-acre (11-hectare) site prompted a threefold expansion and now a new Docklands Development Authority is turning its attention to the development of another 1,400 acres (566 hectares) downriver, on both sides of the Liffey.

Walk back again to the Harbourmaster's Bar and turn on to the new bridge and its wonderful set of three-branched lamps. The smaller dock is known as St George's Dock and on its east side is the preserved Stack A Warehouse, regarded as possibly one of the finest examples of 19th-century industrial architecture remaining anywhere in the world. The metal framework supporting the roof, for example, employs an ingenious and unique design and may be the earliest cast-iron roof in the world. This old tobacco warehouse was the only place in Dublin large enough to hold the 3,500 veterans of the Crimean War attending the lavish banquet held in their honour in 1856. On the far side of the warehouse is the new Jurys Custom House Inn. Head now towards the archway walking past an antique hard-operated crane. This archway originally formed the entrance off Amiens Street and was re-erected here as an effective focal point. Entrance to the docks is regulated by the lifting Sherzer Bridges (1912) which have been totally refurbished.

Along the refurbished quayside you will encounter a sculpture group representing a despairing file of ragged famine victims. You now might like to visit the **Custom House Visitor Centre** where some of the building's interior splendour can be examined while touring the various exhibitions on its fascinating history.

An Innovative Fire Station

From Custom House Quay make your way over Matt Talbot Memorial Bridge, taking in the magnificent outcome of the restoration on the Custom House and the exquisite sculptures of Edward Smith. As you walk on to City Quay, laid down in 1720, you will pass a statue to the Venerable Matt Talbot (1856–1925) who became well known after his death for his piety and self denial. Cross the road opposite the church of the Immaculate Heart of Mary (1863) when it is safe to do so as there are no traffic lights to help you. The Seaman's Memorial at the corner with Lombard Street commemorates the 13 Irish merchant ships and their crews lost in the Second World War, a high number considering the tiny size of the fleet and the neutral position of Ireland.

Turn up Lombard Street and continue to Pearse Street. Here the other end of the Loop Line connects into Pearse Station. The line from here was the first railway built in Ireland and opened in 1834. Follow into Pearse Street, named in honour of Patrick Pearse who was born here in 1879. The former St Mark's Church on the right was the church where Oscar Wilde was baptised. The fire station and its Italianate tower, at the Tara Street corner was originally built in 1907. At the time the station was hailed for its many innovations. When an alarm sounded, the men swished down the slide poles from overhead dormitories into the waiting car-

Custom House Coat of Arms

riages, the horses were automatically released from their stables and took up their positions, and when they were harnessed the door was opened by means of a lever over the driver's head and out swept the bell-clanging teams in a flurry of hooves struggling for traction on the cobbled streets.

The beautifully restored granite-fronted Pearse Street Garda Station was built in 1910 for the Dublin Metropolitian Police (DMP), a force that amalgamated with the Garda Síochána in 1925. Ireland is unique compared with many countries in Europe or the USA as it has only one police force. In the UK alone there are 40 separate constabularies, each with their own jurisdiction and management. On either side of the two front entrances are a pair of carved busts. One set represents the rank of inspector of the DMP and denotes the officers' exclusive entrance door. The second pair depicts rank-and-file constables and indicates their doorway. Next to the station stands the Steyne Stone, a modern reminder of the original stone placed here by the Vikings when they first arrived to Dublin in 837AD.

Turn into Hawkins Street past the diminutive bronze statue of a cinema usher and the mock Tudor front of An Bord Gáis (the Gas Board). At the end of the street is a memorial to Constable Patrick Sheahan who heroically lost his life in 1905 while trying to save the lives of men overcome by gas in the sewers underneath the street. Turn right into Burgh Quay and at No. 11 you will pass Lafayette Photography, said to be the oldest continuously operating photographic business in the world. It was founded in 1866 but the French parent company is long gone. You are now back at Tara Street and Poolbeg Street from where you started out.

The Grand Canal

Summary: A true Dubliner is said to be someone who is born between the two canals; the Royal on the Northside and the Grand on the Southside. Both canals originate almost opposite each other at the mouth of the Liffey and, with the river running through the centre, form an oval enclosure of the old city. The Grand Canal was the first one cut, work commencing in 1756. It stretches from Ringsend in Dublin to the Shannon River and beyond to Ballinasloe in Co Galway and together with all its branches the canal is 166 miles (265 kilometres) long. Once an important commercial artery, the canal is now primarily used for leisure boating and fishing. Its towpaths and linear parks provide a most pleasant walking environment and this particular walk is designed to show some of the canal's commercial and engineering heritage as well as to take you through a number of inner suburbs in its curving route to historic Kilmainham.

Start:	George's Quay (Cé Sheoirse). Buses: all city centre buses. DART Station: Tara Street. Parking only in city centre car parks.
Finish:	Kilmainham (Cill Mhaighneann = Church of Maighne). Buses: 19, 19A, 68, 68A, 69, 78A, 79, 123.
Length:	5 miles (8 kilometres)
Time:	2 hours.
Refreshments:	Along the route itself there is very little on offer except the occasional pub. It might be a good idea to take along a snack to sustain you until you reach Kilmainham.
Pathway Status:	Pavements and surfaced towpaths. The towpath along one section can be a bit muddy but you can always use the parallel pavement.
Best Time to Visit:	Daytime only on any day of the week.
Route Notes:	There are two museums and an interpretative centre on the way so if you want to visit them check their opening hours.
Connecting Walk:	From Custom House Docks to The Liberties.

Start this walk at George's Quay right at the exit from Tara Street DART station. Proceed past an attractive office block until you reach the Matt Talbot Memorial Bridge. This part of the route, until you reach the junction with Lombard Street, is dealt with in the previous walk, Custom House Docks. Continuing along City

Quay you will become aware of the empty crane rails along the quayside edge with only an occasional coaster or navy ship tied up alongside. Dublin is an extremely busy port but the vast majority of the shipping has been transferred to Alexandra Basin (named after Alexandra, Princess of Wales) further downriver. On a redbrick warehouse (beside Slattery's Office Supplies) just before Cardiff Lane (named after the owner of an 18th-century shipbuilding yard located here) are fixed the keystone heads rescued from the first O'Connell Bridge (then named Carlisle Bridge) when it was demolished in 1880. This is approximately the site of the old Marine School (1773–1872) which was officially known as the Hibernian Nursery for the Support and Education of Orphans and Children of Mariners.

A Future Being Built on the Past

The next mile (1.5 kilometres) of the walk is through an area that is going to see a huge transformation in the next few years. Major environmental improvements along with new apartments, housing, light industry and offices, leisure facilities (especially water-based ones) and other schemes are earmarked for both sides of the river. On your left side you will see a large and rusting box-like contraption with a vertical protruding shaft. This is the diving bell, manufactured in 1866, that was used during the construction of the North Wall Quay extension and other subsequent work carried out during the 19th century.

The length of quay you are on now is Sir John Rogerson's Quay, named in honour of the Chief Justice who had it built in 1713 as a business speculation. In the 18th and 19th century this was one of the most colourful areas of Dublin. Huge numbers of trading vessels and coal colliers crowded the quaysides, dockers swarmed everywhere, delivery vehicles choked the wharfs and military patrols in scarlet and buff uniforms policed the streets.

Docks, Locks and Blocks

By now you should have crossed over to the riverside where you will continue along the cobbles, passing the solitary crane, until you reach the end of the quay. Across the river is one of Dublin's primary concert venues, the Point Theatre, imaginatively converted from a railhead depot by Harry Crosbie, a local haulier and also well known for a business connection with the rock band U2. To the right of the Point is Alexandra Basin and, in the distance, the open sea. Now turn right into Britain Quay which overlooks where the Grand Canal, the River Dodder (see the walk devoted to this on page 104) and the Liffey converge. Grand Canal Docks, with their beautiful system of canal lock gates, (named the Camden, Buckingham and Westmoreland Locks) were opened in 1796. They were designed to hold 600 ships at a time but rarely held more than a few dozen. Their failure as a business may have helped preserve the docks and they are now set for a rich amenity harvest. Already some old and venerable ships and boats are anchored here for preservation purposes and already the first of a series of apartment blocks overlooks the 25 acres (10 hectares) of water.

Walk along Hanover Quay, turning left into Grand Canal Quay. Beyond MacMahon Bridge at the Pearse Street junction (be careful crossing here) is the

Huband Bridge

Waterways Visitor Centre, featuring exhibitions, an audio-visual show and a display of working models of engineering features connected with the history of Ireland's inland waterways along with information on available activities. The dock here is the second of the two Grand Canal Docks. Opposite to the Waterways Centre is the granite stone tower of a sugar refinery built in 1862. Its conversion to an Enterprise Centre won for it the international 'Europa Nostra' conservation award in 1984.

Reflections of New and Old
From this point the official Grand Canal Way walking trail begins and you will be more or less following this trail until you reach Kilmainham. The old stone warehouse on the left has been renovated to serve as offices and apartments. The railway line passes over a low bridge (8 feet [2¹/₂ metres] at its highest point) and once you emerge from under the bridge you will see what looks like an attractive arrangement of town houses which are own-door offices. The superbly designed office block at the corner with Grand Canal Quay has an intriguing figure climbing up the sheer face of the outside wall. Across the road from this building is the classical facade of another decommissioned hospital, Sir Patrick Dun's.

Again, cross with care over to Clanwilliam Place and enter the canal towpath through an opening in the wall. The next bridge at Mount Street was the scene of a battle in the 1916 Easter Rising when a handful of Irish Volunteers, strategically located in a couple of houses, inflicted scores of casualties on approaching British Army reinforcements. You will need to gain the road again to cross to the next section of canal along Warrington Place where office blocks give way to period housing. From here on this same pattern of walking along the canal bank but ascending to cross the road will, except in a few instances, prevail. Ahead the rustic little hump-backed stone bridge framing the cascading waters from the lock behind is the Huband Bridge, built in 1791 and named after a director of the Grand Canal Company. The view to the right is into Mount Street Crescent and to the not ungraceful shape of the rear of St Stephen's Church (1824).

Herbert Place will bring you to Baggot Street Bridge (Macartney Bridge). To the left are wonderful examples of the high period in Victorian architecture. To the right a graceful Georgian boulevard is punctuated by occasional modern office buildings. Further down, at the corner with Herbert Street, is the first **convent** of the Sisters of Mercy and halfway house for underprivileged girls built in 1824 by Catherine McAuley (1778–1841), the founder of the order. This order distinguished itself world-wide in the educational and medical fields. During the Crimean War the nuns laboured alongside the team formed by Florence Nightingale. Catherine McAuley's portrait adorns the Irish five-pound note.

Barges and Fly Boats

When you rejoin the canal cross over to the far side, carefully using the lock gate with the guard rails where a small monument announces that the Grand Canal is twinned with the Grand Union Canal in the UK. Nearby is a seat engraved to the memory of Patrick Kavanagh, poet (1905–1967), who often frequented this part of the canal. A little further up, and almost opposite a seated sculpture of Kavanagh, is a tying-up dock for barges. Thanks to the restoration work carried out by the Office of Public Works, the waterway is once again navigable for its entire length. The last commercial barge chugged its way from James's Street Harbour carrying a load of Guinness porter to Limerick in 1950. Now a myriad of barges and cruisers ply the canal but rarely come as far as the city limits. The pseudo-Georgian building on the corner with Leeson Street was built in the 1980s for the Investment Bank of Ireland.

At Leeson Street Bridge cross to the other side but instead of going down the canal enter into Adelaide Road. On the right is the magnificent Royal Victoria Eye and Ear Hospital which was extensively refurbished for its centenary year in 1997. Walk past St Finian's Lutheran Church and turn left into Harcourt Terrace. This is Dublin's last remaining Regency Terrace (on the right side only). The two co-founders of the Gate Theatre Micheál MacLiammóir and Hilton Edwards lived at No. 4. Directly across from it is the Film Censor's Office. Join the canal again at Charlemont Place and thence to Charlemont Mall. You have now arrived to Portobello or La Touche Bridge (1791). Cross Richmond Street South and walk to Portobello Place and to the front of Portobello College. This graceful building was built in 1807 as the Grand Canal Hotel serving the terminus for the passenger barges. In 1834 'fly boats' were introduced from here. This was a far superior and more comfortable way to travel than by road. Four horses at a gallop could pull a 90-passenger boat at an unbelievable 10 mph (16 kmh). The road you have just crossed leads to Rathmines where you can see from the bridge the green dome of Rathmines Church and the tower of the former Town Hall.

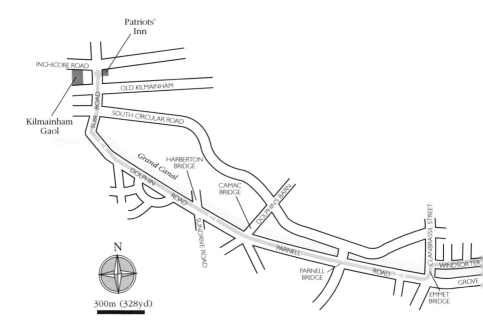

Patriots' Inn
INCHICORE ROAD
OLD KILMAINHAM
SOUTH CIRCULAR ROAD
Kilmainham Gaol
SUIR ROAD
Grand Canal
HARBERTON BRIDGE
DOLPHIN
ROAD
CAMAC BRIDGE
DOLPHIN'S BARN
SUNDRIVE ROAD
N
PARNELL
CLANBRASSIL STREET
WINDSOR TERRACE
PARNELL BRIDGE
ROAD
GROVE
EMMET BRIDGE
300m (328yd)

A Change in Beat

Continue on to Portobello Road. On your left is Cathal Brugha Military Barracks, known as Portobello Barracks in its British-controlled days. The road changes to Windsor Terrace before reaching Clanbrassil Street and its bridge is dedicated to executed patriot, Robert Emmet, who was arrested nearby. Change over to the left bank of the canal. Griffith College on the right occupies the former Griffith Barracks. Every barracks had a central clock tower but now, alas, the clock is gone too. You can walk under Parnell Bridge and continue up Parnell Road on a path which has been allowed to grow pleasantly wild. Parnell Road is named not after the great Parliamentarian and fighter for Irish liberties, Charles Stewart Parnell, but after his great-great-grandfather and director of the canal, John Parnell. The whole tenor of the canal changes somewhat from here. Buildings are set further away and the level ground dispenses with the need for lock gates. The stretch is also preferred by wildfowl.

The next bridge, Camac Bridge, ushers in the district of Dolphin's Barn, in medieval days called Dolfynes Berne and named after David Dolfyn, a knight hospitaller of the great Priory of Kilmainham. Dolphin Road used to be called 'Nettle

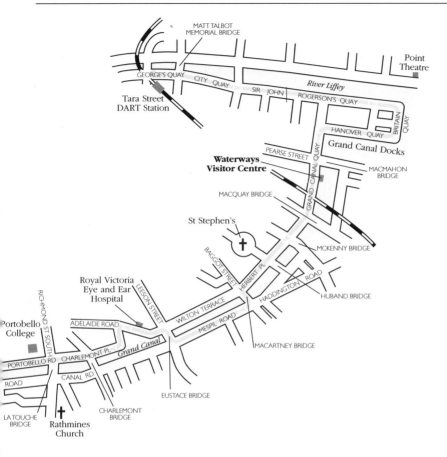

Banks', a reflection of the previously less cultivated canal banks. The scenery opens out further after the concrete bridge (1938) at Sundrive Road to reveal the large housing estates of the 1940s and 50s. Between the next two bridges a spur to the canal ran off to the right which directly served the Guinness Brewery. More accurately, this straight section was not a spur at all but was the original track of the canal ending at James Street Harbour (1759). There was always a need to connect the canal to the River Liffey so it was decided in the 1790s to build a circular line to Ringsend – the route you have just walked. The line to James Street was filled in some years ago and has been made into a linear path.

Ireland's Bastille

Walk up Suir Road to reach Kilmainham. At the junction with Old Kilmainham Road you will be able to see over to the left, on a hill over the Camac River, the sultry fortress of Kilmainham Gaol, Dublin's one-time Bastille (see the next walk). You can rest your weary feet in the Patriot's Inn before either getting the bus home or embarking on a very different walk to this one, The Liberties.

The Liberties

Summary: The Liberties were separate and independent districts in Dublin which, from medieval times right up to the early 19th century, were outside the jurisdiction of the Mayor and the city. They were initially attached to religious institutions but after the dissolution of the monasteries in the 16th century some of them were granted to favourites of the king. The Liberties were only finally abolished subsequent to the Municipal Corporations Act of 1841. This walk concerns itself with passing through parts of three of these Liberties; the Manor of Kilmainham, the Liberty of Thomas Court and the Liberty of Christ Church. They are all located just west of Dublin Castle. In Kilmainham, an ancient seat of the Vikings, you will see the world's second-oldest Military Hospital, Europe's best preserved 18th-century prison and the largest War Memorial in the British Isles. From there you will travel through what was once the most densely populated section of old Dublin, almost a city within a city. The aromas from the Guinness Brewery, once the world's largest, fill the air and tempt the palate.

Start: Patriot's Inn, 760 South Circular Road, Kilmainham (Cill Mhaighneann = Church of Maighne). Buses: 19, 19A, 68, 68A, 69, 78A, 79, 123. DART Station: none. Parking limited around the streets. Parking is available in the Royal Hospital for visitors only.

Finish: Jurys Christchurch Inn, Christchurch Place (Plás Teampaill Críost = Place of the Church of Christ). Buses: 50, 54A, 56A, 68A, 78A, 123. DART Station: Tara Street (15 minutes' walk). Car parking in Christchurch multi-storey car park, Werburgh Street.

Length: 3¹/₂ miles (5.6 kilometres).

Time: 1¹/₂ hours.

Refreshments: Plenty of pubs along the way and there are coffee shops in most of the museums. Weather permitting, a picnic beside the river of the War Memorial Park would be a nice idea.

Pathway Status: Street footpaths and parkland paths. Generally suitable for wheelchairs but parts of the route are fairly hilly or have steps. Kilmainham Gaol has lifts.

Best Time to Visit: Any time, bearing in mind park and museum times.

Connecting Walks: From the Grand Canal walk to the North City Centre walk.

Your starting point, the Patriot's Inn, has been the site of a tavern since 1793. It received its present name to remind us of the continuous procession of patriots who have been incarcerated in **Kilmainham Gaol** from its foundation in 1796 until its final closure in 1924. Make your way across the South Circular Road, past the still-used Courthouse to the grim facade of Ireland's Bastille. In fact, the building of Kilmainham Gaol was inspired by the fear of French revolutionary ideals spreading to these shores. This was a perfectly reasonable fear which ultimately found expression in the Rising of 1798. The leaders of the United Irishmen and the participants in the insurrection soon filled the dank solitary confinement and punishment cells. They were followed in quick succession by the losers in the revolts of 1803, 1848 and 1867. The repressiveness of the prison was brought into sharper focus during the events of the early part of this century. The leaders of the 1916 Easter Rising were executed by firing squad in the stone breaking yard and this single act did more than anything else to swing the population against the continuance of British rule. The War of Independence and the subsequent Civil War kept the jailers and executioners busy until the release of the final prisoner, Eamon deValera, future President of Ireland, on 16th July 1924.

The jail was abandoned and fell into decay. A voluntary group began the herculean task of restoration in 1960, only completed in the 1980s by the Office of Public Works. The result is the faithful preservation of the largest decommissioned but still intact 18th–19th-century prison in Europe. A tour around the dungeons, corridors and cells can still evoke a shudder and a sense of the building's tragic history. The jail also has a marvellous audio-visual display on its history and a modern museum presentation.

Kilmainham Gaol

Remembrance along Quiet Waters

Continue along Inchicore Road, noting to your left the low hall doors at the beginning of the terrace of houses. Either the houses have sunk a little or people were shorter a century ago! Cross over towards the remaining tower and steeple of a demolished church and turn up Memorial Road. At the traffic lights cross Con Colbert Road and enter the gates of the **Irish National War Memorial Park**. On the hill directly opposite is the Magazine Fort in the Phoenix Park. Take the steps down to the Memorial itself which commemorates the known 49,400 Irishmen who were killed on the battlefields of the Somme, Verdun, Marne and the other killing fields of the First World War. The War Memorial and Garden of Remembrance with their fountains, monuments, pavilions, sunken gardens and pools were designed by the renowned architect Sir Edwin Lutyens and opened in 1939 (ironically the year the even more calamitous Second World War broke out). The names and details of each soldier are recorded on special memorial books kept in one of the pavilions. Neglected for some years, the park, the largest war memorial in the British Isles, has been magnificently restored by the Office of Public Works and, in season, is spectacularly clothed in cascading flowers and roses.

Dragoons and Hussars

When you are ready to leave the gardens make your way over to the banks of the Liffey. The tidal effects do not reach here and it is particularly serene at this location. The far bank is lined with a number of rowing clubs and you may be lucky enough to see a rowing eight or four. Now make your way along by the line of the river until it curves away to plunge over a weir and leave the park through two sets

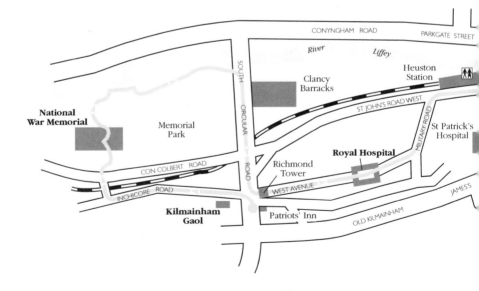

of gates to arrive on to the South Circular Road. Cross over to the far side and walk by the wall of Clancy Barracks, a wall low enough for you to see into the barracks itself. It was built in 1797 and in the mid 19th century the mounted garrison included the 5th Dragoon Guards (the Inniskillings) and the 10th Hussars. It was taken over by the Irish National Army in 1922.

Vikings and Knights
A rather complicated road junction lies ahead but after you ensure your safe crossing head towards the entrance to the **Royal Hospital**. Enter under the Richmond Tower (if this gate is closed you can still visit the Hospital by way of St John's Road and Military Road). Designed by Francis Johnston, this castellated gateway was completed in 1812 but not for this location. It stood instead at the corner of Watling Street and Victoria Quay but had to be removed to its present site in 1847 to relieve the traffic congestion caused by the opening of Kingsbridge (now Heuston) Railway Station a year earlier.

A view of the Royal Hospital up West Avenue is fairly dramatic. It would be as well to pause for a couple of minutes to reflect on the general history of the area and of the hospital. The Celts settled in Kilmainham about 2,000 years ago to take advantage of a ford across the Camac, the local river. The Vikings also established a community and their largest graveyard outside Scandinavia was found in Kilmainham. The monastery of St Maighne flourished until the arrival of firstly the Vikings and then the militarist Order of Knights Templar in 1175. They established a priory, almshouse and hospital which were taken over in 1310 by their successors, the Order of St John of Jerusalem, the Knights Hospitallers. This influential

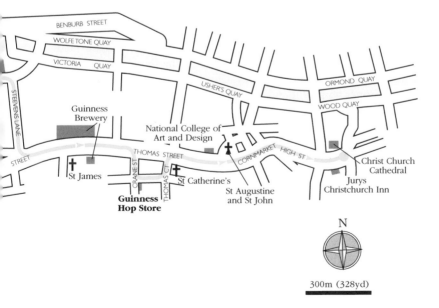

300m (328yd)

foundation, which controlled vast acreages of land including today's Phoenix Park, was suppressed around 1537. The next major development for the site came in 1680 when the Viceroy, James Butler, the Duke of Ormonde, under the aegis of Charles II, laid the foundation stone of the world's second oldest military hospital after that of Les Invalides in Paris and preceding Chelsea's Royal Hospital by a whisker. It was certainly inspired by the Paris hospital as the style of the building, designed by Sir William Robinson, is unmistakably French in influence.

Succour for Body and Mind

Intended as a home for up to 300 wounded, infirm or aged officers and men, it received its first residents in 1684. It functioned in its original role until 1928 when the remaining old soldiers were transferred to Chelsea. It then suffered inglorious neglect until wondrously rescued by the Office of Public Works in a detailed restoration carried out between 1980 and 1984, exactly 300 years after it was built. This treasure of a place, Dublin's oldest non-ecclesiastical public building, with its exquisitely decorated Great Hall and Chapel, has played host since 1991 to the Irish Museum of Modern Art.

In your immediate proximity there are three cemeteries associated with the Royal Hospital. On your right is the officers' cemetery and on your left, behind a wall, is that of the ranks, non-commissioned officers and civilians. Beside the latter is Bully's Acre, a graveyard that goes back more than a thousand years. Before the great Battle of Clontarf in 1014 the army of the victors under the High King of Ireland, Brian Boru, camped in its vicinity. After the battle Boru's slain son and grandson were buried in Bully's Acre. Other denizens of the graveyard include monks and knights of the monastery and priory.

When you reach the Royal Hospital building you can freely explore around the quadrangle, the formal French-style gardens, the artists' residences and so forth but there is an admission charge for entering the museum and exhibition proper. Take the east front exit on to Military Road and then to St John's Road. Heuston Station, on your left, was opened in 1846 to serve as the showpiece terminus for the Great Southern and Western Railway Company. Turn up Steeven's Lane, named after the former hospital founded by Grissel Steevens in 1720. The building, designed by Colonel Thomas Burgh, has a cloistered quadrangle not unlike that of the Royal Hospital. The full impact of this magnificent structure was only recently revealed when its new owners, the Eastern Health Board, cleared away some obstructing buildings. On one side of Steeven's Lane is the perimeter wall of the Guinness Brewery and on the other, just after the Eastern Health Board offices, is the institution founded by the writer of *Gulliver's Travels*, Dean Jonathan Swift. It is St Patrick's, one of the country's foremost psychiatric hospitals. It is to Dean Swift's immortal credit that he possessed an enlightened vision that allowed people with mental disorders to be treated as patients and not as criminals as they had been heretofore. You can see the facade of his original building, opened in 1757, from inside the entrance at the corner of Steevens Lane and Bow Lane.

Carefully cross to the traffic island on James's Street where stands an unusual relic from 1790, a fountain surmounted by an obelisk with vertical sun dials on each side.

Like so many other things that lay neglected for generations in this city it has been recently restored. Cross, again with caution, to the far side of James Street and walk to what is, literally, the City of Guinness.

First walk past the church of St James, famous for its resident choir, the St James Musical and Dramatic Society Choir. Across the road is the modern plant of the Guinness Brewery but the buildings that you are coming to on your own side are architecturally more evocative of a past industrial age. The gateway that leads into the headquarters of Guinness Ireland shows the founding date as 1759 along with the current year's date. Guinness was established by Arthur Guinness, a brewer's son, who opened his business in a disused brewery. Ale was the initial product but Arthur saw a better possibility in a darker brew made from roasted barley and popular with the porters at Covent Garden and Billingsgate in London, hence the name 'porter'. He then made a stronger brew and called it 'extra stout porter' which was shortened to 'stout'. The Guinness family built up the brewery into the largest in Europe and Guinness is now a major multinational company.

Windmills and Beam Engines
The onion-domed tower across the road was once Ireland's tallest windmill at 150 feet (46 metres) and first belonged to Roe's Whiskey Distillery. It is now owned by Guinness and might they not be persuaded some day to restore the sails? Take the next turn to the right, Crane Street, and walk up to the hugely popular **Guinness Hop Store** where you can enjoy the history, the contemporary story and the taste of Guinness. The surrounding cobbled streets just ooze atmosphere. Leave the Guinness complex by travelling up Rainsford Street (notice the rail tracks from the defunct internal Guinness railway system), into Thomas Court and around to the front of St Catherine's Church. Sadly, this wonderful old church, which dates from 1769, is currently without use and is decaying at an alarming rate. It was outside its Grecian Doric facade that the revolutionary, Robert Emmet, was hanged with several of his compatriots, in September 1803.

Now you are in Thomas Street, a street of not inconsequential shops which for generations have been central to an extremely self-reliant local population. Almost opposite Meath Street is an institution over 250 years old, the National College of Art and Design. It occupies the former Powers Distillery which has been imaginatively adapted. What could be retained from the distillery days, including a massive beam engine, was preserved. The red-coloured church with its soaring spire is the Church of St Augustine and St John (built 1862–1911) known colloquially as John's Lane, recalling the Penal Days when worshippers had to travel up a narrow lane to gain entrance into a secluded chapel. The architect was Edward Pugin and the sculptor of the 12 apostles in the tower niches was James Pearse, father of Patrick and Willie Pearse, leaders of the 1916 Easter Rising.

The last part of the walk will bring you into Cornmarket and High Street (see the Viking and Medieval Dublin walk) before reaching Christchurch Place and Jurys Christchurch Inn.

North City Centre

Summary: Great promise had been held out for this part of Dublin. While O'Connell Street, one of the widest boulevards in Europe, is considered to be the very centre of Dublin, a mere 300 years ago it did not even exist. Instead it was the mud flats of an estuary flooded by the River Liffey at high tide. The old walled city on the other side of the river was already 700 years old. When development did come, however, it spread quickly and extensively. Towards the end of the 17th century a narrow street, Drogheda Street, was laid down. It stretched from present-day Parnell Street to Abbey Street and was named after its developer, Henry Moore, Earl of Drogheda. Striving for immortality, he also incorporated his name and title into a number of other streets i.e. Henry Street, Moore Street (North), Earl Street, and even an Of Lane (now vanished).

In 1748 another developer, Luke Gardiner, Lord Mountjoy, tore down most of dingy Drogheda Street, widened it to its present impressive width and renamed it Sackville Street. He built grand mansions on either side and a promenading mall in the centre. In the 1770s the Wide Street Commissioners continued the street to the river front and opened a bridge across the Liffey in 1792. The character of the street then began to change from residential to commercial and over the next hundred years the fine old Georgian houses were either demolished or adapted for use as shops and offices. The name of the street was popularly changed from 1885 to O'Connell Street to honour the great 18th-century patriot Daniel O'Connell. Official renaming had to wait until Ireland gained its independence in 1921.

The Rebellion of 1916 and the Civil War of 1922 resulted in almost the complete destruction of the street which along with some insensitive development in the 1970s left only one survivor from Luke Gardiner's day, No. 42, part of the Royal Dublin Hotel.

Many other grand and interesting streets grew up around O'Connell Street but they did not thrive as much as their southside counterparts. This walk will visit places that perhaps deserved a kinder history but are now facing a better future.

Start and Finish: Gresham Hotel, O'Connell Street (Sráid Uí Chonaill = O'Connell Street). Buses: all services operating to O'Connell Street. DART Station: Connolly and Tara Street are 12 minutes' walk away. Multi-storey car parks in Parnell Street and Cathal Brugha Street.

Length: 3 miles (4.8 kilometres).

Time:	1½ hours.
Refreshments:	Relatively inexpensive restaurants are well spread out along this walk. There is hardly a street without at least one pub.
Pathway Status:	Street footpaths.
Best Time to Visit:	Any time.
Route Notes:	Henry Street is perhaps the most crowded street at peak times so exercise a little extra care over your belongings.
Connecting Walk:	Only five or ten minutes from all the preceding walks through to the following walk, Oxmantown.

Thomas M. Gresham first opened his hotel for business in 1817 and it became a very fashionable stopover for titled and wealthy visitors. The present building is a late-1920s replacement for the original destroyed in the Civil War in July 1922 following its occupation by Anti-Treaty forces under Cathal Brugha. Directly across the street, at No. 42, is the last remaining Georgian house on the street, the former Catholic Commercial Club and now part of the Royal Dublin Hotel. It has a fine staircase and plastered ceilings but it is awaiting full restoration. In the winter, the hardy London plane trees planted along the central island only loose their leaves in late November or early December, evidence of a slightly warmer ground temperature in O'Connell Street as compared to elsewhere. The birds which inhabit the trees all year round are pied wagtails who took up residence only about 50 years ago. They were probably encouraged to stay by the snug warmth provided by the thousands of Christmas light bulbs which are switched on from December to early January. The tall elegant lamp standards poking out from between the trees were especially commissioned for the city's millennium celebrations in 1988.

Streets Broad and Narrow

Moving down the street you will see the first in a line of statues. Father Theobald Mathew, dressed in his Capuchin habit, stands on his high plinth reminding us of his immense work in the early 1800s to wean Irish society away from its overindulgence in alcohol. Successful at first his work was negated in large measure by the tragedy of successive famines in the 1840s when people, in despair, turned again to drink. In the 1940s no fewer than seven cinemas operated on O'Connell Street but now there is only the Savoy which first opened in 1929 with *On with the Show*, the first full-colour film to be shown in Ireland. Across the road McDonald's Restaurant has restored for its own use another of the old cinemas, the Pillar Picture Theatre. Turn left into Cathedral Street and pause at its junction with Marlborough Street. At one side of the corner is St Mary's, the Roman Catholic Pro-Cathedral. The title pro-cathedral is applied because no Roman Catholic Archbishop of Dublin has asked the Pope to revoke the cathedral status first granted to Christ Church in the 12th century even though the church has been under the Protestant faith since the Reformation. On the other side of Marlborough Street is the headquarters of the Department of Education. The right-hand building of the matching pair was built in 1740 (architect, Richard Cassels) as the town mansion for the Earl of Tyrone. Set back into the grounds between the two buildings is the marble statue group *La Pietà*, a gift from the Italian people in recognition for humanitarian aid sent from Ireland to Italy after the Second World War.

Stamp of Approval
From Marlborough Street walk into Earl Street North where you will come to a bronze statue of James Joyce leaning on his walking stick (sculptor, Marjorie Fitzgibbon). A little to the right in O'Connell Street is the Anna Livia (the River Liffey) fountain, designed by Eamonn O'Doherty and unveiled in 1988. Underneath the six-pillared portico of the General Post Office, Patrick Pearse read out the Proclamation of the newly declared Irish Republic in April 1916. Within a few days the building was a smouldering wreck and Pearse and his fellow leaders were executed. Due to the wars still to come restoration did not start until 1924 and was magnificently completed five years later. Bullet holes can still be seen in the columns and in various parts of the facade. The G.P.O. first opened for business in 1818. The three statues, by Edward Smyth, are Mercury, messenger of the Gods, holding aloft a purse, then Hibernia (Ireland), holding her spear and harp, and Fidelity who holds a key to her bosom. The National Penny Postage was first introduced into Ireland in 1840 (a local post operated from 30 years earlier) and street post boxes appeared a decade later. A Dublin man, Henry Archer, was the inventor of perforated stamp sheets.

Proceed down O'Connell Street, past the great department store of Clerys. This present building dates from 1920 and replaced the one

General Post Office

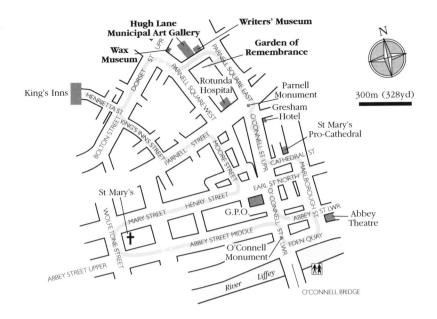

destroyed in 1916. Clerys or at least its predecessor, the New Palatial Mart, was the world's first purpose-built department store when it opened in 1852. Eason's book-store across the street owes its origins to the great English chain W.H. Smith. When Smith was appointed Chief Secretary for Ireland in 1886, to avoid a conflict of interest, he sold his Irish bookshops to his manager, Charles Eason. Now Eason's is the country's largest bookstore chain. The statue in the centre of the street with the outstretched hands is James Larkin, a trade union leader most famous for directing the city-wide lock-out strike of 1913 (sculptor, Oisin Kelly). Just beyond him is Sir John Gray, the work of Thomas Farrell. Gray was mainly responsible for vastly improving Dublin's water supply during the 1870s.

Shoppers' Paradise

As you walk along notice the granite kerbstones. Most of Dublin's city centre pavements are edged with granite as a matter of policy (aesthetically they are perfect but they are also hard-wearing and adaptable). Some of the stones have been in use for a couple of centuries. The name of the next street on the left, Sackville Place, is a reminder of when O'Connell Street was called Sackville Street. Turn left into Abbey Street Lower, continue along until you can cross into the lower end of Marlborough Street. At this corner is the Abbey Theatre, the National Theatre of Ireland. It was founded here in 1904 but the original building was burnt to the ground and was replaced with this current structure in 1966. The next turn right will bring you on to Eden Quay and to O'Connell Bridge (1880) which is unusual in that it is wider than its length. The O'Connell Monument occupies the central mall of the street and was unveiled in 1882 (sculptor, John Henry Foley). It shows Erin (Ireland) holding a copy of Daniel O'Connell's 1829 Act of Emancipation. The winged Victories (some with bullet holes from 1916) symbolise O'Connell's virtues of Courage, Fidelity, Eloquence and Patriotism. Behind O'Connell is a statue to another patriot, William Smith O'Brien.

Cross to the other side of O'Connell Bridge to head left into Abbey Street Middle. On the right, just after the Oval Pub, are the twin-domed offices of Independent Newspapers, Ireland's largest newspaper group. At the corner with Jervis Street is the new Jervis Shopping Centre, a development taking in the facade of the old Jervis Street Hospital. After Abbey Street Upper turn right into Wolfe Tone Street and up by St Mary's Church. It was built in 1697 to serve a newly made parish and a number of Dublin notables were baptised here, including patriot Wolfe Tone, world renowned mathematician Sir William Rowan Hamilton and the Earl of Charlemont. John Wesley preached from its pulpit and Arthur Guinness of brewing fame was married here. It is now a retail emporium, perhaps not its most dignified evolution.

Travel up Mary Street into Henry Street, an area which carries the sobriquet, National Shopping Centre of Ireland, such are the number of department stores trading along here. Household names such as Roches, Arnotts, Marks and Spencer, Pennys, Debenhams and Dunnes attract up to 100,000 people down this narrow street on a busy day. A different kind of retailing takes place in Moore Street. For generations street traders have sold their fresh fruit, fish and flowers from their makeshift stalls and are still supplied from the markets with goods delivered by horse and cart. O'Rahilly Parade, near the top right of Moore Street, is named after a member of the 1916 G.P.O. garrison shot here while leading a charge against the British barricades during the retreat from the burning post office.

Enter Parnell Street, turn left and briskly walk down as far as the Virgin Multiscreen Cinema, turn right up Kings Inns Street and emerge on to Bolton Street. Cross the road (use the lights further up or down if necessary) and enter Henrietta Street almost opposite. This was Dublin's first Georgian Street proper and it was laid out in 1721 by Luke Gardiner. Its residents were definitely from the gentry stock and included several bishops, barons, earls, generals and members of Parliament. Sadly, several of the houses, which, incidentally, are larger than the rest of Dublin's Georgian houses, were lost in less appreciative times and many of the remainder still need restoration. Initiatives, mostly private, have been taken to restore some of their palatial interiors. The street is closed off by the classical form, albeit the rear, of the Kings Inns, another Gandon masterpiece.

Return to Bolton Street, turn left and walk up to the next lights, then cross over to the **Wax Museum** whose labyrinthine corridors include an interesting parade of Irish and international historical figures. Behind the museum turn left into Parnell Square, a once elegant Georgian Square which fell on indifferent times but is now beginning to show a little lustre again. The magnificent town mansion of James Caulfield (1728–1799) 1st Earl of Charlemont, is now the **Hugh Lane Municipal Gallery of Modern Art**. Designed in 1763 by William Chambers, the house is a fine study in Neoclassicism. When the gallery took over in 1929 additional exhibition space, echoing the original interior, was built. The Gallery owes its origins to philanthropist and art collector Sir Hugh Lane who tragically died aboard the torpedoed *Lusitania* in 1915. Beside the gallery and forming a dual and complimentary cultural liaison with it is the **Writers' Museum** opened in 1991 in two restored Georgian houses. All the well-known Irish writers are represented here in paintings, photographs, manuscripts and displays of memorabilia. Next door is the imposing Abbey Presbyterian Church opened in 1864 and built entirely from funds donated by Alexander Findlater, founder of a grocery, wine and spirit chain.

A World First
Cross the road to visit the **Garden of Remembrance** laid out in 1966, the golden jubilee of the Easter Rising, to commemorate all those who died for Irish freedom. The bronze statue group (by Oisin Kelly) recalls a scene from Irish legend, the transformation of the Children of Lir into swans, thus symbolising that at certain moments in history people are utterly changed. On your way down the pavement you will pass a small upright column showing a severed link in a chain, a symbol of breaking the connection with England. The sculpture marks the formation of the Irish Volunteers in the Rotunda Gardens (behind the railings) in 1913. Next on your right is the Gate Theatre founded in 1928 by Hilton Edwards and Micheál MacLiammóir. A little further down and situated at the edge of the footpath is a

O'Connell Bridge lamps

beautifully designed old drinking fountain (for horses and people).

At the junction cross over to the traffic island on which stands the Parnell Monument and look back towards the Rotunda Hospital. Dr Bartholomew Mosse founded what is believed to be the world's first maternity hospital in George's Lane (now Fade Street) in 1745 and in 1757 moved his patients to this building. To fund his venture Mosse opened pleasure gardens behind the hospital and built the Rotunda Room (now a cinema) in 1764 and the Assembly Rooms (now the Gate Theatre) in 1786 to gain further income. The **hospital chapel**, although unfinished due to Mosse's untimely death, is Ireland's greatest masterpiece in the art of Rococo decoration. Charles Stewart Parnell was the father-figure of Ireland's nationalism in the 1870s and 80s and his monument, the work of Augustus St Gaudens, was unveiled before more than 100,000 people in 1911, illustrating the massive appeal of the statesman who had died 20 years earlier.

This walk is now concluded and with the vista of O'Connell Street spread before you the choice of your next port-of-call is entirely your own.

Oxmantown

Summary: The name Oxmantown is derived from Ostmen, or men from the east and refers to the Norwegian and Danish warriors and settlers who arrived in Dublin in the ninth century. When they settled around Wood Quay and High Street on the south side of the Liffey they also took the precaution of having a second but smaller defensive position north of the river. This was Oxmantown (Dublin's first suburb). When the Normans conquered the walled town in 1170 the Vikings were allowed to retreat to Oxmantown where they were eventually assimilated into the local population. Over the next four centuries this district, which commences a little over half a kilometre west from O'Connell Street, remained in relative obscurity and was dominated by the great Cistercian Abbey of St Mary.

In the 17th and early 18th century significant civic planning was promoted for Oxmantown but before anything substantial could take root the area was abandoned by the wealthy in favour of newer, fashionable areas. However, a number of important institutions did become established here including the Four Courts, the Blue Coat School, the Royal (now Collins) Barracks, Newgate Gaol, Arbour Hill Prison, the Garrison Church and the Fruit and Vegetable Markets and these have all made a substantial contribution to the history of Dublin. The wheel is now turning full circle with the inauguration of a new and imaginative civic development that is now taking place with Smithfield as its hub.

Start:	Ormond Quay Upper (Cé Urmhumhan = The Quay of Ormond). Buses: all city centre buses and a ten-minute walk from O'Connell Bridge. DART Station: Tara Street (15 minutes' walk). Use city centre multi-storey car parks.
Finish:	Ashling Hotel, Parkgate Street. Buses: 25, 25A, 66, 66A, 66B, 67, 67A. DART Station: none. Very limited on-street parking. Car park in Heuston Station.
Length:	2 miles (3.2 kilometres)
Time:	1¼ hours.
Refreshments:	There is little in the way of en-route refreshment opportunities except for a few pubs. The hotels at the start and finish are your best bet. Also check the newly emerging restaurants around Smithfield.
Pathway Status:	Pavements throughout.

Best Time to Visit: Mornings are best to experience the hustle and bustle of the area. Otherwise, check under Opening times (see page 162).

Route Notes: This walk does not pass by the front of the Four Courts so if you want to visit them (the public are allowed into most court hearings) make a side trip from Chancery Street.

Connecting Walk: From the previous walk, North City Centre to the following walk, Phoenix Park.

Your starting point, the Ormond Hotel, features prominently in James Joyce's *Ulysses* when a number of the characters converge on it for conversation and drinks. From the hotel turn left up towards Grattan Bridge. Ormond Quay was built by Humphrey Jervis in the 1680s and was a landmark construction for the city. Jervis had originally planned to build his houses and warehouses with their backs right up to the river but the viceroy, the Duke of Ormonde (after whom the quay is named), strongly urged that he reverse his plans and line the front of his scheme towards the Liffey with an open quay between them. Jervis agreed and thus set the future pattern of building along both sides of the river which allowed the Liffey to be integrated into the cityscape.

From an Abbey of Peace to Prisons of Infamy

Turn left again into Capel Street. This street has, in the main, changed little since Jervis laid it down in the 1680s. The houses on the east (downriver) side look the same now as when they were drawn for James Malton's famous views of the 1790s. There was a great deal more development taking place on the Northside in the late 17th century than on the more populous opposite shore. A generation later the tide would turn in the latter's favour. Since the 1970s Capel Street has suffered a blight of business closures and traffic congestion but is now making a comeback as a street of small shops including antique, craft, do-it-yourself and furniture stores. Mary's Abbey, your next destination, (second on the left) is named after the great Abbey of St Mary which was founded initially by the Benedictines from Savigny in France c.1139 and transferred to the Cistercians in 1147. The first Norman ruler of Dublin, Richard deClare FitzGilbert (Strongbow) granted to the monks vast tracts of land between the rivers Liffey and Tolka. For the next 500 years, apart from the tiny settlement of Viking-founded Oxmantown, the main development north of the Liffey was associated with St Mary's.

When the monastery was suppressed by Henry VIII in 1539 its buildings and lands were granted to the Earl of Desmond. In the next century the lands were carved up for development and stone from the buildings was reused, notably for the building by Jervis of the first Essex (Grattan) Bridge. Now on the next right walk into Meeting House Lane (named after a Huguenot and later a Presbyterian congregation who used to meet there). Behind a railings and gate (shut if you are outside the limited opening hours) is the entrance to the surviving **Chapter House** of St Mary's Abbey. During the days of the Abbey this building was often leased out for the meetings of the Privy Council, the King's representative body in Ireland. At a meeting of this august body on 11th June 1534, the acting Lord Deputy, Silken

71

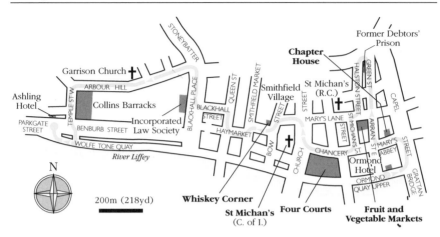

(so-named on account of his silk clothes) Thomas Fitzgerald, Earl of Kildare flung down his sword of office and started a bloody revolt which ended 15 months later with his execution in Tyburn in England.

Return to Mary's Abbey and turn right up Arran Street East into Little Green Street until you reach Green Street proper. The two 'Green' Streets were named after the green of St Mary's Abbey. St Michan's Park, on your left, was the site of one of Dublin's most notorious jails, Newgate Gaol. It was opened in 1780 and many patriots were imprisoned here, with floggings and hangings a common occurrence. The jail has been long since demolished but the thick lower part of two of the jail's corner towers are now integrated into the park walls. A courthouse was built (1792–97) next to the prison and it is still in use. It saw the famous trials of Wolfe Tone, Robert Emmet and the Fenian leaders. Adjoining the court is the grim Debtor's Prison where even the most eminent of citizens could be incarcerated for debts of as little as ten shillings. Continue around to Halston Street to see the front entrance of the old prison which is now being transformed into apartments.

The Four (actually Five!) Courts
St Michan's Roman Catholic Church is where a service is held for the legal profession at the beginning of each law term. Pass by Cuckoo Lane and facing you at the end of Halston Street are the Dublin Corporation **Fruit and Vegetable Markets**. It was opened in 1892 to centralise the scattered individual markets which owed their origins to those established by Jervis in the 1680s. The city's coat-of-arms may be seen over the main entrance. If the markets are open you may freely visit them and become absorbed into the hustle and bustle. Next walk down St Michan's Street along by the Fish Market and head up Chancery Street which runs along the back of the **Four Courts**. Built on the site of a 12th-century Dominican priory to a design of Thomas Cooley (who died a year before work started in 1786) and refined by James Gandon, this most splendid of buildings was opened to the four courts of Chancery, Common Pleas, Kings Bench and Exchequer in 1802. There was actually a fifth court, Judicature, which was overlooked in the arith-

metic. During the siege of the Four Courts in the Civil War of 1922–23 tremendous damage was caused, not so much by shelling but by an internal mine explosion set off accidentally. The resultant destruction ripped away the interior of the Public Record Office and countless important historical documents dating from as far back as the 12th century were lost forever. The courts were rebuilt in 1931.

Facing the Four Courts is the Bridewell Garda Station and detention centre. A bridewell gets its name from a house owned by Henry VIII situated near a holy well of St Bride in London. It was later turned into a house of correction and an overnight remand centre and such centres elsewhere began also to be known as 'Bridewells'. This one was built for the Dublin Metropolitan Police between 1899 and 1902. The Latin motto inscribed on the facade reads *Fiat Justitia Ruat Coelum* which roughly translates as 'Let Justice be done though the Heavens may Fall'.

Emerge now into Church Street, crossing over by the new Law Library (1994) until you come to **St Michan's** (Church of Ireland). Built by the Vikings in 1095 and dedicated to a Danish bishop, it remained the only parish church on the Northside for the next 600 years. It was extensively rebuilt in the 17th century. Handel is said to have played the organ in St Michan's while he was in Dublin during 1741–42. The orator Edmund Burke was baptised here and at the other end of the spectrum revolutionaries Oliver Bond and the Sheares Brothers were buried in the graveyard and vaults respectively. Some 17th-century bodies mummified by the drying effect of the vaults' limestone walls are on public view, not a most dignified last repose, so if you do go to visit them spare a thought for their hereafter.

Leave St Michan's and take a left into cobbled May Lane which leads to the old whiskey distillery buildings of John Jameson in Bow Street. The red and yellow

Fruit and Vegetable Market

bricked edifice on the corner is the former headquarters of Jamesons and is now the Research and Development Centre for Irish Distillers. The **Irish Whiskey Corner**, a thoroughly enjoyable visitors' centre, featuring an audio-visual presentation and exhibition of the history of Irish whiskey and a whiskey-tasting bar is around the next corner on the right. Whiskey was first invented in Ireland by monks and not in Scotland as is generally thought. It derives its name from the Gaelic *Uisce Beatha* (water of life). Turn right again past the Irish Distillers corporate headquarters in the converted spirit storehouse and out on to the expanse of Smithfield Market laid out at the end of the 17th century as the city's cattle market and currently undergoing a dramatic facelift through a major civic improvement scheme. Apartments, shops, restaurants, a theatre/art gallery and leisure facilities are being built. The tall chimney (1895), which is on the protected buildings list, is to be turned into a sky-top restaurant with outside lifts bringing patrons to the best view in Dublin. In keeping with the changes and the new-found pride in its status as a local community the district is now being called Smithfield Village.

Arbour Hill

Walk into Haymarket, up Queen Street and left into Blackhall Street which affords the best view of the headquarters of the Incorporated Law Society on Blackhall Place. It was built between 1773 and 1783 as the Hospital and Free School of King Charles II (it was established first in 1670) otherwise known as the King's Hospital or Blue Coat School on account of the boys' uniforms. The stunted central tower was to have been higher and more elegant but that version was abandoned due to a shortage of funds. Continue up Blackhall Place towards Stoneybatter, a name drawn from stony bothair or stony road. Turn left into Arbour Hill and you are now entering into what was a huge British Army complex of barracks, prisons, training grounds, military infirmaries, headquarters buildings and cavalry stables.

First to come into view, on the left, is the back of Collins Barracks. Commissioned as the Royal Barracks in 1704 it was then the largest in the world and could accommodate 5,000 troops. Until it was finally decommissioned in 1996 it was also the world's oldest barracks in continuous occupation. The buildings have now been modified and completely upgraded to house collections from the **National Museum of Ireland**. On the opposite side of the road is the former Garrison Church (1848) and **graveyard**. From an historic point of view this is one of the most hallowed sites in Dublin as towards the rear of the graveyard are buried the executed leaders of the 1916 Rising. Their bodies were buried in quicklime and on the 40th anniversary of their deaths a worthy memorial around their common grave was completed. Next door to the church is the one-time military detention prison but now used to house civilian prisoners. The subsequent road on the right once led to the cavalry stables and soldiers' married quarters. At the top of the lane is St Bricin's Military Hospital. Proceed down Temple Street West to come out at the Croppies Memorial Park. The park is named in remembrance of the executed Croppies (insurgents) of the 1798 rebellion who were buried nearby.

You can stroll down a short way to get a vantage point for viewing the front of Collins Barracks but the walk is now officially completed.

The Phoenix Park

Summary: During the 1670s, in an effort to impress and please the recently restored monarch, Charles II, the dignitaries of Dublin, led by the Viceroy, the Duke of Ormonde, walled in part of the former lands of the great Priory of the Knights Hospitallers of St John of Jerusalem. This new park was stocked with game for the King's exclusive pleasure but in time it devolved into the public domain and has since given recreation and relaxation to millions of visitors.

The Phoenix Park, named after Phoenix House, the first residence built within its confines, is a mere 1¹/₂ miles (2.4 kilometres) from O'Connell Street. It is Europe's largest urban walled park and comprises 1,752 acres (708 hectares) of grassland, lakes, ornamental gardens and wooded areas. It is home to an abundance of wildlife and also contains many historical sites and monuments. Within its demesnes live the President of Ireland, the United States Ambassador and the animals of the world's oldest zoo after that in London's Regent Park. Since its foundation it has witnessed monumental events of political and religious significance.

Start and Finish:	Ryan's Pub, Parkgate Street (Sráid Geata na Páirce = The Street of the Gate of the Park). Buses: 25, 25A, 26, 51, 51B, 66, 66A, 67, 67A. (Infirmary Road: Bus 10). DART Station: none. Car parking within park.
Length:	5¹/₂ miles (8.8 kilometres)
Time:	2¹/₂ hours.
Refreshments:	Ryan's Pub or the Ashling Hotel, Parkgate Street. Halfway through the walk you can visit the coffee shop situated in the Ashtown Castle Visitors Centre (open daily).
Pathway status:	Tarmac paths and grassy parkland.
Best Time to Visit:	All year but especially in early summer and late autumn for leaf colour. The park is open during daylight hours.
Route Notes:	Take waterproof footwear if the grass is likely to be wet. There are many park benches throughout, often located at places offering panoramic vistas. Generally suitable for wheelchairs if you keep to the pathways.
Connecting Walk:	This walk continues on from the Oxmantown Walk.

On arrival at Parkgate Street carefully cross to the Phoenix Park's main entrance; the two centre pillars were removed for the Eucharistic Congress in 1932 and finally replaced only a few years ago. Proceed up the left side of Chesterfield Avenue, which scythes a perfectly straight course through the park for its 2.6-mile (4.1 kilometre) length. Notice the flanking lamp standards, the oldest of which are possibly the last of their kind in Europe still to be lit by gas.

The elegant parade of trees include sycamore, horse chestnut, beech, oak, ash and lime. About 30 per cent of the land area in the park is planted with trees comprising mostly broadleaf but some evergreen conifers are to be found in the wooded areas. Ornamental species occur in the grounds of Ashtown Demesne, Áras an Uachtaráin (literally meaning the Residence of the President), the Ordnance Survey and the American Ambassador's residence. In ongoing tree conservation programmes an additional 20,000 standard trees are being planted.

Wellington Monument and Magazine Fort
Once you reach the open space on your left cross over (or under) the railings and head directly towards the monolithic mass of the Wellington Memorial Testimonial. Built between 1817 and 1861 it honours Dubliner Arthur Wellesley, Field Marshal and Marquess of Wellington, Irishman, former resident of Dublin and victor over Napoleon Bonaparte. The massive bas-reliefs, cast in bronze from captured cannon, include depictions of battle scenes from his campaigns in India and Waterloo. At 204 feet (62.2 metres) it is the tallest obelisk in Ireland or Britain. It was built on the site of the 18th-century Salute Battery where 12 guns were fired on days of jubilation.

Now head towards Wellington Road and turn left. On your right are a number of cricket and athletic grounds. On the opposite side, the panorama across the River Liffey is over the Kilmainham district which, with the Phoenix Park, was once part of the lands of the Great Priory of St John of Jerusalem founded in 1177. When you reach the bottom of the hill ignore the exit road to the Islandbridge Gate and take the road bearing left of the next hill (Thomas's Hill) from whose summit the Magazine Fort looms down. Grim and forbidding and surrounded by a moat, it was opened in 1735 to house the main munitions of the British garrison. It was handed over to the Irish Army in 1922 but has held no munitions since 1940. The hill was originally the site of Phoenix House (which gave its name to the park), the 17th-century residence of the Viceroys. Jonathan Swift wrote of the fort thus:

> Behold a proof of Irish sense;
> Here Irish wit is seen;
> When nothing's left that's worth defence,
> We build a magazine.

You can easily climb up to the fort and circumvent its granite walls but then rejoin the road again to walk along the Military Road otherwise known as the Corkscrew Road. The reason for this curious name will soon become evident.

St Mary's Hospital and the Fifteen Acres
Along this winding road, on your right, you will see two lodges, typical examples of the several lodges scattered around the park to house keepers and rangers. They were

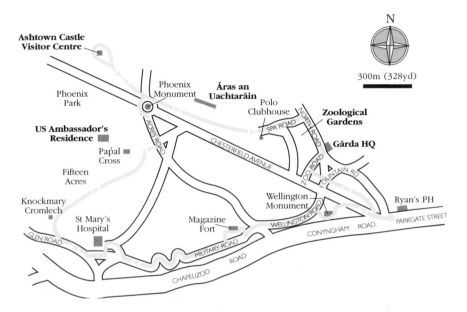

designed in the 1830s and 1840s by Decimus Burton, who was responsible during this period for laying down the park much as we find it today. At a point halfway through the 'corkscrews' there is a good view of the Liffey Valley and the once verdant countryside which is now somewhat swallowed up in urban expansion.

The road soon comes to a cross junction where you will take the right hand turn and walk up to and pass through the entrance gates of St Mary's Hospital, a large complex which plays a special role in the care of the elderly. The central building was designed very much in the barracks tradition of the day for the institution was originally founded in 1764 as the Royal Hibernian Military School. The monument standing in front of the main edifice is dedicated to 80 of the 'old boys' who perished in the First World War.

Leave the hospital by the steps outside the gateway, passing an archway which leads into residences laid out in military fashion and join the Military Road walking past the hospital perimeter and the Cara Cheshire Home. On the right between the Cheshire Home and a hilltop ranger's lodge you will see a path worn in the grass. Climb this path until you reach the top of the hill and over next to the railings of the lodge is the small but historically impressive Knockmary Cromlech. One skeleton discovered here was found to date from about 3500BC, making the burial chamber nearly 1,000 years older than the Pyramids of Egypt.

Now walk across the wide expanse of the Fifteen Acres – actually the area covers nearly 200 acres (81 hectares), its name being taken from an earlier enclosure of that same measurement – towards the large cross in the distance. This huge expanse of green sward and its surrounding woods are home to the Phoenix Park's herd of 450 fallow deer. They were introduced by 1671 when the Viceroy, James Butler, Duke of Ormonde, had the lands walled in and stocked with deer and partridge for the King's pleasure. You may catch a glimpse of either a doe or a buck (male) herd. Males and females stay apart except for the mating season which lasts for four weeks from mid October. Four varieties of deer are present here. These are Black (glossy black summer coat), Brown (rich chestnut brown summer coat), Common (in summer they are rich brown with white spots and a white rump) and Mentil (their summer apparel is ginger brown with white spots and a white rump). It is completely safe to walk as near as the docile but cautious creatures will allow but don't antagonise the antlered bucks during the mating season. Antlers, the fastest growing tissue known, are found only on bucks.

Deer are not the only mammals to be espied among the wildlife denizens of the Park. Other inhabitants include foxes, badgers, red and grey squirrels, rabbits (but no hares), Irish stoats, otters and bats including the pipistrelle, which at only 5 grams in weight, is the smallest bat in Ireland. The wood mouse, the long-tailed field mouse and pygmy shrews are ubiquitous and the brown rat is no stranger either.

For centuries the vast expanse of the Fifteen Acres has seen mammoth gatherings of one sort or another, from huge 18th- and 19th-century military demonstrations and mock battles to great protest meetings including one in May 1875 when thousands gathered to demand that pubs be closed on Sundays! Nationalist fervour was expressed by monster assemblies, and religious zeal found conveyance when hundreds of thousands gathered for the 31st Eucharistic Congress in 1932 when the world-famous Irish tenor Count John McCormack sang at his supreme best during the main High Mass. To cap them all, the largest multitude to gather in any one place in Ireland, if not in peace-time Europe, was on 29th September 1979 when Pope John Paul II said Mass before 1.25 million people. The 35-foot (115-metre) high, 40-tonne steel cross still bears witness to an organisational triumph. During that day the immense throng was divided by 40 miles of rope into 1,000-people corrals and was attended by 600 Gárdai, 12,000 stewards, 2,000 Eucharistic ministers and a 5,000-strong choir. Climb on to the artificial mound at the base of the cross and allow your imagination to recreate that enormous event.

The Great Houses

Regain the road (Embassy Road) and proceed towards the Phoenix Monument. The stately entrance to your left as you approach the junction is the gateway to the **American Ambassador's Residence**. Built on the site of an older house, the present structure dates from 1776, coincidentally the date of American Independence. Occupied since 1927 as an American diplomatic residence, the house was formerly home to the British Chief Secretary for Ireland.

You will now arrive at a major intersection. The Phoenix Monument in the centre of the road was erected by Lord Chesterfield in 1747. While the park was named after the original Phoenix House on Thomas's Hill, the name did not in fact relate to the mythological bird but to the Irish term *fionn uisce*, or clear water, referring to a nearby well. Further behind, the intricate wrought iron gates, attributed to Decimus Burton, lead to **Áras an Uachtaráin**. Apart from the legendary phoenix, the park does possess more than 60 different species of birds. In the open parkland, jackdaw, skylark, hooded crow, swallow, rook, swift, starling, goldfinch and mistle thrush may be found. Wooded areas will reveal the robin, blackbird, blue tit, wren, kestrel, long-eared owl, sparrowhawk and pheasant. By the lakes you may encounter herons, mallards, tufted ducks, mute swans, moorhens, coots, wagtails and little grebes.

At this juncture cross the road (with care) and walk up the signposted road to the **Visitor Centre**. While taking refreshment here you can absorb the history of the park and learn in greater detail about its flora and fauna. The Visitor Centre is situated in the former outhouses of the Under Secretary's Lodge which later became the Apostolic Nunciature. When this lodge was demolished some years ago the preserved stone structure of Ashtown Castle, which dates back at least to the 16th century, was revealed. Beside this castle is the Phoenix Park's tallest tree, a giant redwood, over 101 feet (31 metres) high, a native of the Sierra Nevada in California. Nearby is a tall chusan palm, the only palm tree which will grow successfully outdoors in Ireland.

Wend your revived self back to the main road and take to the grass and walk along the boundary of Áras an Uachtaráin. You will soon reach a break in the shrubbery where you will get a head-on but unfortunately restricted view of the front of the magnificent residence. The central section was built in 1751–52 with various extensions added on over the next century. The house became the Vice-Regal Lodge, or home to the Lord Lieutenant of Ireland, in 1782. Until it passed to the Irish Free State in 1922 it saw many courtly entertainments and the visits of kings and queens including Queen Victoria on no fewer than four occasions. In 1938 Dr Douglas Hyde took up residence as the first Irish President.

A Tragic Assassination

All along this stretch of the main road thousands of tons of turf and coal were stacked as emergency supplies during the Second World War, and wire was slung across the avenue to prevent aircraft from landing. On the footpath, at the point opposite Áras an Uachtaráin, on 6th May 1882 Lord Frederick Cavendish, Chief Secretary and Thomas Henry Burke, Under Secretary, were brutally assassinated by the Invincibles, a secret revolutionary society. The purpose of the killings was to rekindle conflict between England and Ireland but restraint prevailed and most of the perpetrators were captured and executed.

Walk diagonally towards the grand old wooden pavilion (1872) of the All-Ireland Polo Club and you might be able to watch a chukka or two.

Zoological Gardens

Continuing on from the Polo Grounds and passing the every-day entrance to Áras an Uachtaráin walk along the right hand side of Spa Road where you can peep through the railings to see the seal pool and other sections of the 22-acre (9-hectare) **Zoological Gardens**. Enter the back road and turn right, still walking along the railings of the zoo. On your immediate left but actually outside the park's boundary are the red-bricked buildings of McKee Barracks (formerly Marlborough Cavalry Barracks). The next complex is the national headquarters of the Gárda Síochána (Police). From 1839 until 1963 the grey stone buildings housed the police training centre which has since been relocated to Templemore, Co Tipperary. For anyone interested in the history of the police in Ireland there is a **Gárda Museum and Archive** here which can be visited by prior arrangement.

Turn right into Zoo Road until you reach the entrance to Dublin Zoo. The beautiful thatched Tudor-style gatehouse dates from 1832, one year after the zoo was opened. The roar of the famous lion who introduces M.G.M. films was recorded from a lion bred here. The imaginatively landscaped gardens contain a wide selection of animals, birds and reptiles. The zoo also contains a restaurant.

Next, walk straight across the road to the 'Hollow' with its Victorian bandstand. Emerge at Fountain Road and pass straight into the 22-acre (9-hectare) People's Gardens, a park within a park laid out in 1864 by the Earl of Carlisle and currently maintained in the authentic fashion of Victorian horticulture. Ahead is a bust of Sean Heuston, one of the executed leaders of the 1916 Insurrection. In 1842 three men, Charles Gavin Duffy, Thomas Davis and John Blake Dillon, sat under an elm tree there and decided to found a newspaper, *The Nation*, which later played a pivotal role in inspiring a newly awakened nationalism. Wander at will through the gardens but then regain the main path towards the Parkgate Street exit. Just before this exit, on the left, you will see another recently restored 18th-century building. Designed by James Gandon as a military infirmary, it became British Army Headquarters in 1913 and since 1922 has served as headquarters to the Irish Army.

Now leave the Phoenix Park and head for either the Ashling Hotel or Ryan's Pub with its wonderful Victorian (1896) interior. When you are ready, board a bus back to the city centre or a brisk walk of 35 minutes will also take you there.

Zoo entrance

80

Ulysses Walk

Summary: When James Joyce was writing his own epic novel he was shadowing Homer's tales of the wanderings of Odysseus (called Ulysses by the Romans). Odysseus roamed for ten years but the heroes of Joyce's *Ulysses* are only followed around the streets of Dublin for 18 hours, a short span of time that has gone down in literary history. This walk trails the footsteps of the most celebrated of the characters, Leopold Bloom, from when he first leaves No. 7 Eccles Street at around 8 a.m. until the late afternoon when he reaches the Ormond Hotel. For the sake of geographical continuity Bloom's mid-morning attendance at a funeral is ignored.

The action takes place on 16th June 1904, an anniversary that has since become known as Bloomsday. On that day Joyce fans perambulate and cavort their way around Dublin in the wake of Bloom and some of the other figures from the novel. You can undertake the walk on any day and still get the feeling of the occasion and discover just how much of Dublin Joyce would still recognise. It is probably more than you would assume after the passing of nearly a century. This walk, starting in Eccles Street, which is only 15 minutes on foot from the top of O'Connell Street, should interest everyone, from the most avid *Ulysses* reader to those who are just curious. It may even lead to your taking up this novel of novels for the first time.

Start: The site of No. 7 Eccles Street (Sráid Eccles). Buses: 3,11,13,16, 22, 36, 36A. DART Station: none (20 minutes' walk to Tara Street). Car parking in Eccles Street car park.

Finish: Ormond Hotel, Upper Ormond Quay (Cé Urmhumhan Uachtar = The Quay of Ormond Upper). Buses: 10 minutes' walk to all city centre services. DART Station: 15 minutes' walk to Tara Street. Car parking in several nearby multi-storey car parks.

Length: 3¹/₂ miles (5.6 kilometres).

Time: 1¹/₂ hours.

Refreshments: Along the route there is no end of choice but, as you are following the trail of Leopold Bloom, include a visit to Davy Byrne's in Duke Street (where Bloom had a Gorgonzola cheese sandwich and a glass of Burgundy).

Pathway Status: Roadside footpaths.

Best Time to Visit: Any time during daylight hours but mornings might be more in keeping with the book. Of course, if you can

	actually do the walk on the 16th June you will have the company of legions of enthusiasts.
Route Note:	If a place mentioned in Ulysses still exists but carries a different name the current appellation will be in parentheses.
Connecting Walks:	From the end of the North City Centre walk (see page 64) to the Oxmantown walk (see page 70).

Part 1. *Calypso* – 8.00–8.45 a.m. approximately

When you arrive in Eccles Street position yourself near the plaque dedicated to James Joyce at the entrance to the Mater Private Hospital. The precise spot of No. 7's hall door was more or less opposite to No. 76 on the far side. Leopold Bloom was making breakfast for his wife Molly and he himself fancied a grilled mutton kidney. Now follow Bloom as *he pulled the halldoor to after him quietly, more, till the footleaf dropped gently over the threshold, a limp lid.* Cross over to the other side, as Bloom did, and observe the footleaf, or hinged draught excluder, still affixed to the bottom of the doors on Nos 78 to 81. The *loose cellarflap* he nearly fell over is one of the coal hole covers on the pavement outside each house. Ahead is St George's Church whose *loud, dark tone of bells* he is accustomed to hearing every quarter of an hour. He turned the corner at Larry O'Rourke's (The Snug) and walked down Dorset Street passing over the pub's grating (now a steel trapdoor) from which floated up *the flabby gush of porter*. On the right he passed St Joseph's National School (St Raphael's House Garda Credit Union), a dark red-bricked building with five bays of windows. Finally Bloom reaches Dlugacz's window where he sees the last kidney for sale, a pork kidney which *oozed bloodgouts*. Dlugacz's never existed; it was the name of an acquaintance Joyce met after he left Dublin in 1904, so you can substitute one of the shops beyond the former school for the fictitious butcher.

Bloom returns home (you go back to The Snug and wait outside while you read on) to give Molly her breakfast and have his own precious kidney, nearly burning it in the process. The postman delivers a letter addressed to Molly from her lover, Blazes Boylan, and Leopold leaves to travel to town to see if there is a letter for him at Westland Row Post Office from Martha, a girl he's never met but with whom he shares a romantic correspondence.

Part 2. *Lotus-eaters* – 9.45–10.30 approximately

We do not know for certain how Bloom reaches Butt Bridge but we know from later references that he walked and his most direct route would be the inverse of the route taken by him and described by Joyce in a later chapter (*Ithaca*).

Cross the road by the traffic lights and walk along Hardwicke Place towards St George's Church (the Temple Theatre) one of the finest Georgian churches in Dublin, a Greek Ionic masterpiece designed by Francis Johnston in 1802. Apart from the church, a pub and the children's hospital there are no original buildings left in either Hardwicke Place or in its continuation, Temple Street. At the junction with Gardiner Place look to the right and you will see the buildings of Belvedere College, the school Joyce attended between 1893 and 1898. An important side trip that you can make now or later is a visit to the **James Joyce Centre**

St George's Church

just, a hop, step and jump away at No. 35 North Great George's Street (first right, then left and down three quarters of the way on the left). Here, in a superbly restored Georgian townhouse you will find manuscripts and memorabilia of the Joyce family and of the works of James Joyce including the actual door of No. 7 Eccles Street. Meanwhile, assuming you are still at the corner of Gardiner Place and Temple Street, turn left into Gardiner Place which, apart from some gaudy plastic hotel signs, is very much the same as Bloom would have seen it. Next right into Mountjoy Square, decayed in 1904 but recently restored, leads to Gardiner Street, a long Georgian boulevard. At least it used to be a Georgian boulevard but the upper half has simply vanished, replaced with an unworthy concoction of assorted buildings and derelict sites (at the time of publication but things are changing fast) with a railway bridge obstructing the view even for Bloom, to the Custom House.

Once past this bridge cross Beresford Place (see the Custom House Docks walk on page 46) and Butt Bridge. Bloom's plan at this point was to have a swim in the Tara Street baths but he changed his mind and decided to first collect his letter. Instead of going the direct route his journey meanders quite a bit, reflecting the confusions within his own mind. Proceed down George's Quay into City Quay. *Along Sir John Rogerson's Quay Mr Bloom walked soberly, past Leask's the linseed crusher's* (Nos 14 and 15, now a night-club), the postal telegraph office (No.18) and past

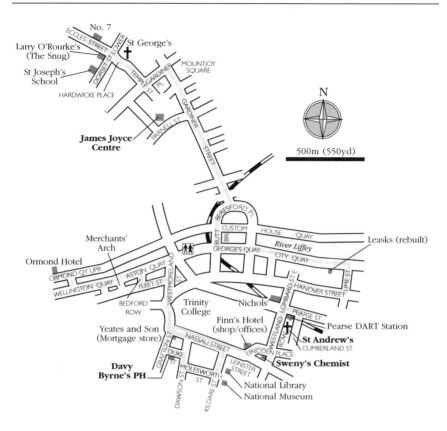

the sailors' home (The Sailors' Home and Shipwrecked Mariners Society) at No. 19 (Nos 17–19 are now rebuilt as offices). The *morning noises on the quayside* Bloom heard were the sounds of a busy dockland, now long gone, replaced by container traffic at a different location. His rambles next took him into Lime Street by Brady's Cottages (demolished, with modern apartments taking their place).

To arrive at Bloom's next mentioned position go along Hanover Street and then up the right hand side of Lombard Street East. The *frowning face of Bethel* (the Salvation Army Hostel at Nos 19/20) no longer frowns, its reincarnation is a garage. *And past Nichols' the undertakers* (Nos 26–31), not only is the building still there but so is Nichols' itself and probably not much changed since Bloom's shadow fell on it. Bloom then went across Great Brunswick (Pearse) Street and up Westland Row until *he halted before the window of the Belfast and Oriental Tea Company* (No. 6, now the O'Reilly Hall, Trinity College). *He turned away and sauntered across the road* to the post office (a newsagent's, part of the DART station).

Once he collected his letter he pocketed it and decided to pick a quiet place to read its contents. After his bad luck in bumping into an acquaintance, McCoy, he strolled back to Great Brunswick Street and turned right along the high station wall (the vehicle ramp and wall demolished to make way for Goldsmith Hall, a lecture halls and residence facility for Trinity College). There is no taxi rank here any longer much less hackneys whose horse power *regarded him as he went by, amid the sweet oaten reek of horsepiss.* He turned into Cumberland Street to read his letter surreptitiously. Meade's Timberyard, the ruins and tenements are now levelled to make way for another Trinity expansion. Going under the railway arch he tore up the envelope and reached the backdoor of All Hallows, otherwise **St Andrew's Church**. Cumberland Street itself, the vast and gloomy overhanging bridge and the slightly decrepit ancillary railway buildings have changed little since 1904.

Bloom entered the church by the back porch which, alas, is shut off today so unless the side passage is open you will have to retrace your steps around to the front entrance of the building. Enter the interior and savour the *cold smell of sacred stone.* St Andrew's, built between 1832 and 1841, was the first Roman Catholic Church to be built on a main street following Catholic Emancipation in 1829. Bloom's next port of call took him up Westland Row, past Conway's pub on the corner to **Sweny's Chemist** to have a prescription filled for his wife, Molly. Sweny's, on Lincoln Place facing into Westland Row, is still there in all its turn-of-the-century glory but then, as Bloom reflected, chemists rarely move. Buying a lemon soap for his own use (you can still buy similar soap here) he proceeds *cheerfully towards the mosque of the baths redbaked bricks, the minarets.* This description accurately fits the Turkish Bath Company of 6–15 Lincoln Place but this building was not in use by 1904 so it is more probably his destination was the Turkish and Warm Baths of 11 South Leinster Street. He notes, as you can, the gate of College Park (side entrance to Trinity College) and the porter's lodge. The last building on your right, Nos 1/2 Leinster Street, was Finn's Hotel, an establishment where Joyce's wife, Nora Barnacle, worked as a chambermaid. The name is still painted on the gable end facing into the college grounds. Across the road, at Nos 10/11, is the site of the baths (now a dark bricked and soulless-looking office block).

Part 3. *Lestrygonians* – 13.00–14.00 approximately

After his bath Bloom takes a tram to Sandymount, accompanies Dignam's funeral to Glasnevin Cemetery and on his return to town visits his place of employment, the *Freeman's Journal.* He decides he needs to get a copy of an advertisement from the *Kilkenny People* and makes his way to consult it in the National Library. You will next meet Bloom at the corner of Nassau and Grafton Streets after he has just passed *Trinity's surly front.*

The Provost's House, at No. 1 Grafton Street, is still there fulfilling its original function. Turn left into Grafton Street (see the South City Centre walk on page 16). The window of Yeates and Son, instrument makers, at No. 2 Grafton Street, no longer sells field glasses but mortgages. You might indeed need a mortgage to buy Bloom's old Goerz lenses, which cost him six guineas then. *He went on by la Maison Claire,* court milliner at No. 4 (now a fast food-restaurant). He next passed Adam Court, also still there, a laneway unrecognised by most citizens. In general terms, Grafton Street, *gay with housed awnings* has little changed since Joyce's time, except for the shops themselves and the fact that traffic is now excluded. His *dallying* before the windows of Brown Thomas would today have to be done on the opposite side of the road. The original premises, magnificently rebuilt in the same style, now house Marks and Spencer.

Turn into Duke Street. It was in Bloom's mind to have lunch at No.18, Burtons Hotel and Billiard Rooms (long gone but the building still stands), but changing his mind he settles for **Davy Byrne's**, the *moral pub* at No.21. This celebrated establishment still trades in all its Victorian glory. Perhaps you might emulate Leopold in his luncheon selection of a Gorgonzola cheese sandwich with mustard, washed down with a glass of Burgundy. After his lunch and discourse with Nosey Flynn, Bloom continues up Duke Street. The business of William Miller, plumber (No. 17) is gone, so too is that of Gray's Confectionery (No.13). John Long's Bar (No. 52 Dawson Street, on the left corner with Duke Street) is now a delicatessen and restaurant. The wonderful little bay window of the Reverend Thomas Connellan's Bookstore, wherein his books could be viewed, today displays the delicious cakes of the Tea Time Express (No. 51B Dawson Street).

Bloom helps a blind man across Dawson Street opposite to Adolphe Drago's, perfumer and hairdresser (No. 17, rebuilt for Sun Alliance). He then carries on up Molesworth Street noting the Stewart Institution for Imbecile Children (No. 40, demolished, European Parliament), Doran's Public House (No. 10, demolished, Jones Lang Wootton) and the Freemason's Hall (No. 17/18), still in its original use. He now crosses Kildare Street, veering right towards the National Museum to avoid Blazes Boylan and then he enters the **National Library**. If it is within opening hours you can do the same (see the South City Centre walk on page 16).

Part 4 – *Wandering Rocks and Sirens* 14.55–16.30 approximately

When Bloom leaves the library he heads for Fleet Street, presumably walking down Kildare Street, left into Nassau Street, down by Trinity College, across to the Bank of Ireland and into Westmoreland Street (see the Temple Bar walk on page 25). If he is on a similar but separate course to Stephen Dedalus, Bloom will turn into Bedford Row to examine the bookstalls there. He is looking to borrow a book for Molly. Not satisfied, he turns left on to Crampton Quay and left again under Merchants' Arch and then finds what he needs at a bookshop there. Most likely Francis Fitzgerald's (No. 1 Merchants' Arch).

His journey now takes him back to the riverside and a stroll up Wellington Quay. *He went by Moulang's Pipes* (No. 31)... by Wine's Antiques (No. 35, now a piano showroom)... *by Carroll's Dusky Battered Plate* (No. 29, jeweller, demolished and rebuilt), his *dark eye read Aaron Figatner's name* (No. 26, jeweller, a bar) and *Prosper Loré's Huguenot name* (No. 22, milliner, the Wellington Hotel). *By Bassi's Blessed Virgins*, a statue maker only recently gone (No. 18A and No. 14)... *by Cantwell's offices* (No. 12)... *by Ceppi's Virgins* (No. 8/9, another statue maker)... *the Clarence* (No. 6/7, still the Clarence Hotel but the interior recently rebuilt). From here on the block is largely intact.

Bloom crosses Essex Bridge (Grattan Bridge) and calls into Daly's, tobacconists (No. 1 Ormond Quay Upper, rebuilt, Bank of Ireland) to buy some vellum paper to write his reply to Martha before calling into the Ormond Hotel. Your duty could well demand that you follow him there.

Famous Dubliners

Summary: For its size Dublin has produced more than its share of famous citizens and residents. The city often likes to boast that no fewer than four Nobel prizes for Literature have been awarded to its progeny or citizens: George Bernard Shaw, William Butler Yeats, Samuel Beckett and Seamus Heaney. Of course there have been legions of other writers besides. Countless Dublin poets, painters, musicians, medical practitioners, soldiers, politicians, scientists and entrepreneurs have also made their mark on the domestic and the international stage. Many of these great names you will meet throughout all the other walks but on this itinerary you will specifically encounter a very varied coterie of Dublin's distinguished offspring and adopted sons and daughters. The walk starts in an inner city suburb on the banks of the Grand Canal only a short bus ride from the centre of Dublin, then twists and coils its way to within a stone's throw of Trinity College.

Start:	Portobello College, South Richmond Street (Sráid Risteamain Theas = The Street of Richmond South). Buses: 14, 14A, 15A, 15B, 47, 47A, 47B, 83. DART Station: none. Car parking: only two-hour disk parking.
Finish:	Adams Trinity Hotel, Dame Lane (Lána an Dáma = Dame Lane). Buses: a few minutes' walk to all city centre bus routes. Car parking at Trinity Street car park.
Length:	2 miles (3.2 kilometres)
Time:	1¼ hours.
Refreshments:	You will be passing a couple of good pubs but for restaurants you will have to wait until you are near the end of the walk.
Pathway Status:	Roadside pavements.
Best Time to Visit:	Any time but watch the visiting hours of the three museums on the trip.
Connecting Walks:	Either as a diversion from the Grand Canal walk (see page 52) or leading into the Viking and Medieval Dublin walk (see page 32).

From Richmond Street South head around to the front of Portobello College, a building that started life as Portobello House (1807), one of five hotels built on the Grand Canal between Dublin and the River Shannon. Jack B. Yeats, one of Ireland's most illustrious painters, lived here from 1950 until his death in 1957, during the period when Portobello House served as a nursing home. Turn right into Richmond Row and when you reach the end turn left into Lennox Street, both streets named after Charles Lennox, Duke of Richmond and Lord Lieutenant of Ireland 1807–1813. No. 6 (three houses up on the right) was the birthplace in 1905 of John McCann, a playwright and twice Lord Mayor of Dublin. Further along, No. 28 was the home of sculptor John Hughes (1865–1941) who had an eminent career in Ireland, Plymouth, Paris and Florence. He sculpted the Victoria Memorial which stood in front of Leinster House from 1906 until it was removed, for patriotic reasons, in the 1920s. It was subsequently sold to an overseas buyer.

Literati, Thespians and Politicos
Your next turn to the right will bring you to **No. 33 Synge Street**, the birthplace of a giant figure among the literati of the world, George Bernard Shaw (1856–1950). Shaw spent the earlier part of his life here and his later work was influenced by the characters visiting his modest middle-class existence. His mother, a mezzo-soprano of some talent, often held musical evenings in the house and George learned to appreciate music there. One of his most popular plays was *Pygmalion,* on which the musical *My Fair Lady* is based. He was awarded the Nobel Prize for Literature in 1925

George Bernard Shaw's Birthplace

for his play *Saint Joan*. The house was in a grave state of dereliction until it was rescued by voluntary effort and since 1993 it has been restored as a typical Victorian household and now houses the Shaw Museum.

Retrace your steps back into Lennox Street, then turn left up Kingsland Parade and right into Walworth Road. Halfway up on the right-hand side, at No. 4, is the **Jewish Museum**. A synagogue was opened here in 1918 in a pair of converted houses and continued to serve the local community until migration of the congregation to the suburbs and elsewhere forced its closure in the 1970s. Now fully restored as a museum, it charts the extraordinary history of Jewry in Ireland. Further along is No. 1, the birthplace of Barry Fitzgerald (1888–1969), born William Joseph Shields, a civil servant turned actor, making his debut in Hollywood at the age of 49. He appeared in memorable films such as *Going my Way, How Green was my Valley* and *The Quiet Man*.

Two more streets, left into Victoria Street and right into St Kevin's Road, will bring you to Bloomfield Avenue. A right turn will bring you to No. 33, the home of Ireland's first Chief Rabbi, Isaac Herzog and his son, Chaim Herzog, recent

President of Israel. Continue on, passing on the left, the former Jewish school, now offices and on the right, St Kevin's Church, now converted into apartments. Go around the corner on to the South Circular Road and head towards the traffic lights and cross the road to Heytesbury Street. On the left side, No. 33 (for the third time) was the birthplace of Cornelius Ryan, author of *The Longest Day*, *The Last Battle* and *A Bridge Too Far*. Cross the street facing Ryan's house and turn right into Synge Street. The school on the right is an Irish Christian Brothers foundation and has many eminent past pupils. Among the role of honour were the aforementioned Cornelius Ryan and Chaim Herzog (many Jewish boys were educated here). Others included were Gay Byrne, Irish radio and television personality and host of the world's longest running chat show (Radio Telefís Éireann's *The Late Late Show*); Cearbhall Ó'Dálaigh, past President of Ireland; Cyril Cusack, actor; Eamonn Andrews, broadcaster; Noel Purcell, comedian, stage and film actor, and Jack MacGowran, stage, television and film actor.

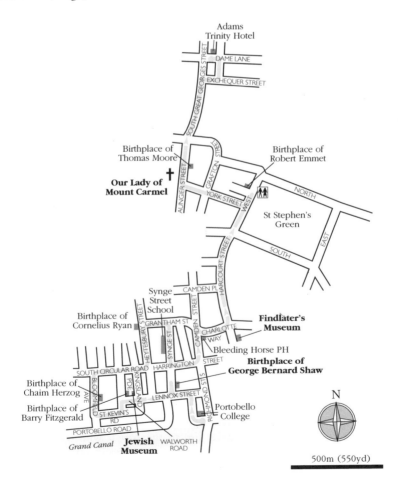

Masters of Horror
Two more left turns will bring you into Camden Street. Stop approximately opposite the Bleeding Horse pub (founded in 1649). From here, on the left side of Lower Camden Street, are two addresses of well-known people although the buildings have changed a good deal since the time of their illustrious occupants. If you wander down to have a look you will need to return to this spot again. Charles Robert Maturin (1782–1824) was born at No. 57 (now a centre for the Simon Community), whose work was admired by Sir Walter Scott, Balzac and Oscar Wilde among others. His medium was the Gothic novel and his best-known work today is *Melmoth the Wanderer*. With two other Dublin authors, Joseph Sheridan le Fanu (*The House by the Churchyard*) and Bram Stoker (*Dracula*), Maturin forms a trilogy of pioneering writers of the supernatural and the grotesque. No. 71 was the home of Joseph Holloway (1861–1944) whose lifetime's collection of theatrical memorabilia and his own personal journal of 221 volumes form a valuable collection, stored in the National Library, of life in the heyday of Dublin theatre.

Cross at the Bleeding Horse (to which the poet James Clarence Mangan was a frequent visitor) to walk up Charlotte Way and into Harcourt Street. The stone building with the portico is the former Harcourt Street Railway Station, now functioning as offices and warehouses. However, in the 21 vaults under the station, built 140 years ago as bonded warehousing for Gilbeys Wine Merchants, are the haunting premises and wine cellars of **Findlater's**, a wine and grocery firm (the grocery part is now gone) that was started in 1823 by the legendary Alex Findlater. An intriguing museum, open to the public, is located in one of the vaults. Moving down Harcourt Street, No. 61 (the Harcourt Hotel) was George Bernard Shaw's last domicile in Ireland before he left for London in 1876. On the opposite side of the street, further down, are four more addresses of note. No. 22 (the Russell Court Hotel) was the residence of Leonard McNally (1752–1820), a successful playwright and barrister who was the defence counsel for the ill-fated revolutionary Robert Emmet at his trial in 1803. It only emerged after McNally's death that he had betrayed Emmet in the first place and had been an agent of the Government working from within his membership of the United Irishmen since 1798. Clonmell House, at No. 17, was built in 1778 for the Earl of Clonmell. In 1908, the house, then in the ownership of Dublin Corporation, was provided to Sir Hugh Lane who was setting up the new Municipal Art Gallery (now located in Parnell Square). No. 6 was the residence from 1854 of John Henry, Cardinal Newman, the first rector of the new Catholic University formed by the Irish hierarchy in the same year. Two doors down, No. 4, a house saved from demolition but now blocked up, was the birthplace of Edward Henry Carson (1854–1935), the founder of modern unionism in Northern Ireland.

St Valentine's Day
Walk straight on to St Stephen's Green West. Just after Glover's Alley, at No. 124, is the birthplace of Robert Emmet. Return to the corner with York Street and proceed up a thoroughfare very different from its nobler residential days. In buildings long gone lived Richard Cassels (1690–1751) architect of Leinster House and

Portobello College

the Rotunda Hospital; James Clarence Mangan (1803–1849) No. 6, poet (*Dark Rosaleen*); Charles Robert Maturin No. 37; James Stephens (1880–1950) No. 30, poet and novelist (*The Charwoman's Daughter*) and William Stokes (1804–1878), physician, international achievements in medicine. Eamon deValera secretly trained a unit of the Irish Volunteers in the basement of No. 41 before the 1916 Easter Rising.

Facing the exit of York Street on to Aungier Street is the Church of Our Lady of Mount Carmel, known popularly as Whitefriar Street Church. Beneath a side altar lie the remains of a world-famous saint, especially remembered on 14th February: St Valentine. (He was not an Irishman, never visited Dublin in life, but in death was sent as a gift by Pope Gregory XVI in 1835.) Turn left, pass No. 21 Aungier Street, currently being restored with the claim that it is Dublin's oldest house in its original form (1680), and you will come to a pub at No. 12. This is the birthplace and home for the first 20 years of his life of composer and poet Thomas Moore (1779–1852). Together with Edward Bunting, he contributed greatly to the revival of traditional Irish airs. One of his most famous melodies is *The Last Rose of Summer.*

Continue down South Great George's Street, turn right into Exchequer Street, left into Dame Court and in through the Adams Trinity Hotel in Dame Lane to gain entrance to one of the most extraordinary and colourful bar interiors in Dublin, the Mercantile Bar. This former banking hall might be a good place to reflect on the lives of those you have just briefly encountered, many of whom lived lives of pecuniary deprivation.

Leafy Suburbs

Summary: For the last 250 years the majority of the wealthier segments of Dublin society have chosen to live on the city's south side (ie south of the River Liffey). Ballsbridge and its environs, a distance of only about 2 miles (3 kilometres) from the city centre, top the list of desirable addresses. This is a gentle walk which will bring you through a number of luxuriant roadscapes and past some of the most expensive mansions in the city. A couple of the roads, notably Ailesbury Road and Merrion Road, are known as Embassy Land because of the amount of foreign embassies located there. You will also encounter a number of well-known institutions.

Start:	Sydney Parade Avenue (Ascal Parád Sidni). Buses: 3, 5, 7, 7A, 8, 45. DART Station: Sydney Parade. Except at weekends on-street parking may be very restricted.
Finish:	Jurys Hotel or the Berkeley Court Hotel, Ballsbridge (Droichead na Dotra = Bridge of the Dodder). Buses: 5, 7, 7A, 8, 45. DART Station: Lansdowne Road. Provided you patronise a hotel there may be available spaces in its car park.
Length:	3 miles (4.8 kilometres).
Time:	1^1/$_4$ hours.
Refreshments:	There are a number of pubs and restaurants in Ballsbridge including the Horseshow House and the not inexpensive Rolys and Coopers. Most of the hotels are also concentrated in Ballsbridge.
Pathway Status:	Footpaths all the way.
Best Time to Visit:	Summer and early autumn to appreciate the tree cover.
Route Notes:	A straightforward walk on essentially level terrain.
Connecting Walk:	None.

Take a left hand direction after coming out of the DART station and proceed up Ailesbury Road turning left again into Merrion Road and then crossing over to go up Nutley Lane. The large but featureless hospital complex is St Vincent's Hospital which moved to Elm Park from St Stephen's Green in 1970. Just after the hospital is Elm Park Golf Course. Nutley Lane only became a fully-fledged road in 1947. At the top of the road is Montrose, the headquarters of **Radio Telefís Éireann**, the state broadcasting service. The Irish television service opened from here on 1st January 1961. To the left on the main avenue in Montrose is a Georgian mansion,

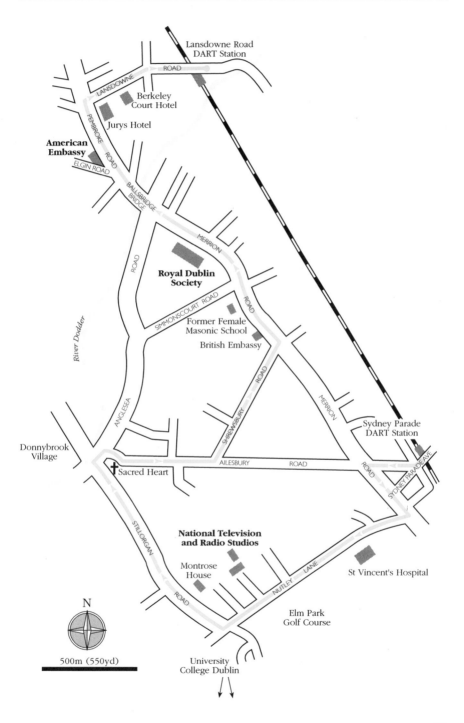

Montrose House, which dates from at least 1750. The owners a century later were the whiskey distilling family, the Jamesons. A relative of theirs married Giuseppe Marconi, the father of Guglielmo (born in 1874), the inventor of wireless telegraphy. Turn right into Stillorgan Road. Across from here and spreading out in a south-easterly direction from Stillorgan Road is the vast campus of the country's largest university, University College, Dublin, known simply as UCD. (Feel free to make a voluntary sidetrip to view the campus and then return to this spot.)

A Sense of Tranquillity

Follow Montrose's low boundary wall until you reach the Church of the Sacred Heart, Donnybrook and the junction with Anglesea Road which skirts along by the River Dodder. The village of Donnybrook was founded around a church about 750AD but it mainly owes its fame to the notorious Donnybrook Fair, founded in 1204, which after centuries of rowdyism was finally suppressed in 1855. One of the city's bus garages is on the left and as you make your way around to Ailesbury Road you will pass an obelisk dedicated to the memory of a past Lord Mayor, Alderman Arthur Morrison.

A sense of tranquillity will greet you when you arrive into tree-bedecked Ailesbury Road. However, it was not always so tranquil here. Before the road was laid, excavations revealed the bodies of 600 people believed to have been massacred by the Vikings. Many of the fine residences have been turned into foreign embassies which can be identified by their flags or by name plates on the railings. Halfway down turn left into Shrewsbury Road which is still predominately residential. No. 20 was the home, until its move to Dublin Castle in 1997, of the illustrious Chester Beatty Library, one of the world's greatest collections of Oriental and biblical manuscripts, papyri, miniatures, scrolls and Far Eastern jades. The benefactor was Sir Alfred Chester Beatty (1875–1968), a wealthy New York mineralogist who amassed a personal fortune which he used to build up his unique collection.

A Royal Society

When you reach Merrion Road turn left where you will next see the modern and somewhat incongruous British Embassy building. Almost next to the embassy is a red-bricked Victorian building which was built in 1882 to house the Masonic Female Orphan School. Once past Simmonscourt Road you will come to the main buildings of the **Royal Dublin Society** Showgrounds. The Society was founded in 1731 to promote 'husbandry, manufactures and other useful arts and sciences'. It was responsible for developing what in 1877 legislation became the National Library, the National Museum, the National College of Art and the National Botanic Gardens. The R.D.S. left its Leinster House headquarters in 1923 and moved to the present location in Ballsbridge. The showgrounds are used extensively for exhibitions, fairs, concerts, lectures, conventions and the world-famous Horse Show held annually in August. Directly across the road from the R.D.S. is the headquarters of Allied Irish Banks. At the corner with Anglesea Road is the old Town Hall (1879), a reminder that from 1863 until 1930 this district was self-administered by the Pembroke Urban District Council.

Royal Dublin Society buildings

Ball's Bridge

Next again is a high-quality office and apartment development built on the grounds of the defunct Irish Hospitals Sweepstakes organisation. As this was the main route between Dublin and its medieval port of Dalkey, a bridge of some kind must have been erected here from the earliest days over the River Dodder. The present elegant structure dates from 1904. Where the Herbert Park Hotel and its surrounding apartment blocks now stand was the site of a 17th-century dwelling called 'Ball's House', which evidently gave its name to the bridge and subsequently to the district. Situated at the junction between Elgin and Pembroke Roads is the rotunda form of the **American Embassy** and despite its futuristic design actually dates from 1964. The surrounding walls and railings have only been recently added as a security measure.

Cross over to Lansdowne Road and seek your provisioning in Jurys or The Berkeley Court Hotel before returning to the city by bus or by DART from Lansdowne Road Station.

St Enda's Park to Marlay Park

Summary: Dublin is fortunate in the number of its public parks, large and small, many of which are laid out around sites of great historical interest. Two such parks, in the southern suburbs of Rathfarnham (about 5 miles [8 kilometres] from the city centre), are the start and finish of this walk, St Enda's and Marlay Park. St Enda's is famed as the location for the school founded by two of the leaders of the 1916 Rebellion, Patrick and Willie Pearse and it is now a National Historic Property. Marlay Park has an 18th-century Georgian mansion whose outhouses have been converted into a well-known craft centre. This park is also the gateway to the finest and longest mountain wilderness walk in the country – the Wicklow Way, which is all of 82 miles (132 kilometres) long.

Start:	St Enda's Park, Rathfarnham (Ráth Fearnáin = Ring Fort of the Alders). Bus: 16. DART Station: none. Car park in the grounds of St Enda's, off Sarah Curran Avenue.
Finish:	Marlay Park, Rathfarnham. Bus: 47B. DART Station: none. Car park in Marlay Park, off Grange Road.
Length:	2 miles (3.2 kilometres).
Time:	1¹/₄ hours.
Refreshments:	There is a coffee shop both at the Pearse Museum and at the Marlay Park Craft Centre.
Pathway Status:	Park and road footpaths.
Best Time to Visit:	Any time but note opening hours.
Route Notes:	The usual cautions apply to small children when you are walking beside any rivers especially if they are in spate.
Connecting walk:	This walk connects with the next one, Hell Fire Club or with the Dodder River Walk (see page 104).

Walk into **St Enda's Park** from Sarah Curran Avenue which is named after the daughter of the celebrated 18th-century defence lawyer and neighbour of St Enda's, John Philpott Curran. She was also romantically involved with Robert Emmet, the executed leader of an ill-fated rebellion in 1803.

An Educational Experiment

The layout of the park remains much the same as it was in the 18th and 19th centuries and it has been skilfully restored by the Office of Public Works. Take the west walk, a path bordered by lime and immature yew trees, to the Whitechurch Stream. Stay on the path by the stream until you come to a stone bridge which you should cross and then a stroll on the right bank path will bring you to the ornamental lake constructed by a former owner, William Woodbyrne. This secluded area supports a wide variety of wild plants including flag, willow and various grasses and provides shelter for nesting birds. Take the signposted path to the **Pearse Museum** and the wonderful new landscaped courtyard complex at the rear of the main house. Here you will find a Nature Awareness Centre and tea rooms which dispense lovely home-made scones and cakes which may be taken in the courtyard beside a playing fountain. Live music, traditional and classical, is often played in the courtyard. Next move to the house itself and, if you wish, visit the museum which comprises an excellent collection of memorabilia, audio visual shows and displays associated with Pearse and the Easter Rising of 1916.

Gentle Teacher, Determined Revolutionary

In the 1780s a Dublin dentist, Edmund Hudson, built the mansion on grounds known as the 'Fields of Odin'. Hudson was an important contributor to the early recording of ancient Irish literature. In later years the name of the estate was changed to 'The Hermitage'. Various owners came and went until 1910 when Patrick Pearse leased it for a boys' school he had founded two years previously.

Pearse was a romantic and idealistic individual himself and had some very far-seeing ideas on how schools should be run. He broke with the current system of education (Pearse called it the Murder Machine), believing in a more open method that took cognisance of each boy's personal ability. Subjects went beyond the staple diet of the day and included drama, poetry reading, woodwork, nature study and sport. He was passionately convinced that any revival in the country's 'Irishness' started with instilling into children a love of Irish culture and social values. Corporal punishment was outlawed from the start. Teaching was carried out in both Irish and English. Pearse named

St. Enda's

his school after St Enda of Aran, a monk who abandoned the life of a soldier to teach in the seclusion of the Aran Islands. In the meantime, in contrast to the gentility of his teaching methods, Pearse immersed himself in preparations for an armed rebellion and saw blood sacrifice as the only way to achieve national identity.

The school had only mixed success principally because of incessant financial problems. Then, in April 1916, classes were interrupted when a detachment of Irish Volunteers, led by Patrick Pearse, marched out from St Enda's to do battle with the Forces of the Crown. By May, Patrick, his brother Willie, and teachers Thomas McDonagh, Con Colbert and Joseph Mary Plunkett had been executed for their part in the Easter Rising. Fifteen of their former pupils also took part in the fighting and were dispatched to a prison camp. The dream was over. For the next five years the British Army occupied the school but then handed it back to Pearse's family who started up classes again. In 1935 lack of support sadly forced the final closure. When Margaret, Patrick's sister, died in 1969 St Enda's was bequeathed to the state.

Leave the museum by the main road to the front noting a fine bust by John Behan facing the house. Before you reach the main gate take the inside wall path which will bring you to a star-shaped lodge nicknamed Emmet's Fort, where it is said Sarah Curran and Robert Emmet often met to avoid the gaze of her disapproving father who lived just across the road. Exit the park now by the side gate to the corner of Grange Road and Taylor's Lane. Straight across off Grange Road is the Hermitage housing estate where the ruins of Curran's house, the Priory, now stand in an open green space. Carefully cross Taylor's Lane and proceed towards Marlay Park past the Grange Golf Course and the Three Rock Rovers Hockey Club (named after a local mountain) and enter **Marlay Park** heading in the direction of the main house.

Gateway to the Hills

The Georgian mansion is an 18th-century reconstruction over an older house. The Harold family occupied the land from the 13th to the 17th century and the district became known as Harold's Grange (grange meaning a country house with farm buildings). The Taylor family succeeded to the property in the early 1700s and they built the present building. A few decades later it was much enlarged and improved by the next owner, the Huguenot David La Touche, who founded a Dublin bank and from which his family grew very wealthy. La Touche spent a large fortune on landscaping the grounds adding waterfalls, lakes, bridges and pathways. He married Elizabeth Marlay and promptly named his estate after her. The last La Touche left Marlay in 1872 and the next two owners sold off large tracts of the land for further development. In 1972 Dublin County Council bought the house and the remaining 86 hectares (214 acres) and opened a Regional Park in 1975.

From the front of the house (which is now being restored) there is an exceptional view of the surrounding mountains and you would almost think that the park led directly into their foothills. In one way it does; the famous long-distance Wicklow Way starts its journey from this spot and winds its way through the Dublin and Wicklow mountains to Clonegal in Co Carlow, an average trek of 12 days. Our journey, you will be relieved to hear, is considerably shorter! Walk down the path past the eight-stone circle and into the woodland ahead taking a shaded route skirting the Little Dargle River. Most of the trees are over a century old and, as is typical in Irish estates, include the old favourites such as beech, sycamore, oak and lime.

Go around the lakes and turn left where a grove of bamboo adds an exotic air and turn left at an old romantic-looking lodge awaiting restoration. This route will bring you near the children's playground and a miniature railway (which runs on Saturday afternoons in the summer). At the end of this walk you will arrive back at the rear of Marlay House where you can visit the craft centre. The coffee shop will attend to your basic needs. Return to the main gate and take the number 47B back to town or move straight on to the next walk.

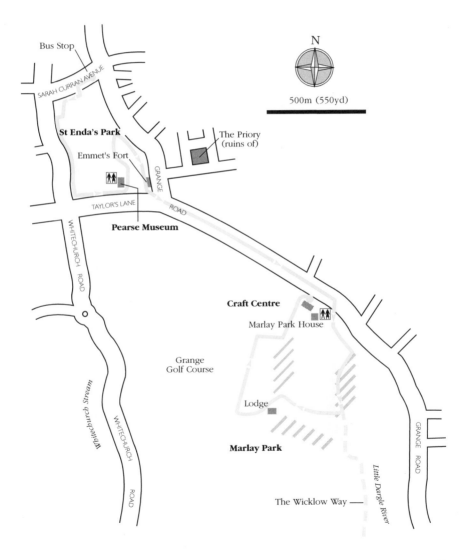

Hell Fire Club

Summary: While in one sense this is a very ancient area of Dublin with many pre-historic remains, the purpose of this walk has more to do with undertaking an invigorating exploration into the countryside and along forest trails culminating in a spectacular hilltop view of the city than about seeking out the relatively inaccessible historic sites. Even so, the unusual, the interesting and even the macabre will be offered up for your delectation. This trail is one of two walks in this book (the other being the Bray to Enniskerry walk on page 122) that will bring you on to the mountains rising from the southern suburbs of Dublin. The distance from the centre of Dublin is about 5 miles (8 kilometres).

Start: Marlay Park, Rathfarnham (Ráth Fearnáin = Ring Fort of the Alders). Bus: 47B. DART Station: none. Car parking available in Marlay Park.

Finish: Sean Doherty's Pub, Rockbrook (Sruthán na Carraige = Brook of the Rock). Bus: 47A (infrequent weekdays but with an almost hourly service at weekends).

Length: 5 miles (8 kilometres)

Time :   2$^{1}/_{2}$ hours.

Refreshments: Killakee House Restaurant (a fairly pricey establishment situated just before the climb to the Hell Fire Club) and, at journey's end, Sean Doherty's Pub. There are picnic opportunities on Mount Pelier Hill.

Pathway Status: Narrow country paths and a mixture of surfaced and rough forest and hill paths.

Best Time to Visit: Any dry day unless you are togged out for wet weather. Each season has its own charms.

Route Notes: Not suitable for wheelchairs. Take along a walking stick if you wish, a pair of binoculars and some light refreshment.

Connecting Walks: St Enda's to Marlay Park precedes this walk and a short bus ride from the finish will bring you to the start of the following walk, the Dodder walk.

Leave Marlay Park and walk past the Grange Golf Course before turning left up Whitechurch Road. A view of the mountains including the peaks of Kilmashogue, Two Rock, Tibradden, Glendoo, Killakee and Mount Pelier now come into view. Keep left at the roundabout. On the right the Whitechurch Stream gurgles on its inoffensive way unless swollen by mountain rains or melting snows. Presently you will come to the entrance of the Monrovian Cemetery. The Monrovians were founded as an evangelical Protestant denomination in Herrnhut, Saxony, in 1727 but were based on an older sect founded in Bohemia in 1458. The headstones all lie flat on the ground, men are buried on one side, the women on the opposite. Missionary Monrovians first came to Ireland from Greenland in 1746 but their church ceased to exist here in 1980. Whitechurch Church is the successor to a much older church that was once called 'the Church in the Marches' – the Marches being the name ascribed to the border lands of the Pale.

Next join the Tibradden Road which has on both sides, but not just visible from the road, a standing stone site. Its junction with Edmondstown Road is a bit confusing but turn left at this intersection which still continues on as Tibradden Road (follow the road sign for Glencullen). At about $^1/_2$ mile (800 metres) from the crossing you will reach a cemetery. Turn right here (a cul-de-sac sign marks the road), and walk until you reach a fork in the road. Keep to the right going through an open gate between a couple of farmhouses. You are now on a fenced right-of-way which will take you another $^1/_4$ mile (400 metres) to a forest gate. Go in through this opening, cross a bridge over the River Owedoher and take the main path which will bring you into Massey Wood, the one-time estate of Lord Massey. This small wood has a very balanced mixture of broadleaf and conifer trees and a couple of good clearance areas provide a respite from the overhead canopy. At the first fork take the wider left hander and at the next crossroads turn right which will bring you to the Killakee road.

Murder and Hauntings
Turn left and continue as far as the Killakee House Restaurant. The house was built in the early 18th century as a dower house of the Massey Estate and today is a collection of stone buildings surmounted by a small tower at one of the corners. It had strong connections with the Hell Fire Club, the ruins of which still

The Hell Fire Club

loom above Killakee House on top of Mount Pelier Hill. The perpetrators of the outrageous goings-on in the Club (see below) often lodged in the house and it was said that here they murdered a dwarf who had a deformed body and an unusually large head. To add to this bloodshed five IRA men died in a gun battle at the house during the period Countess Constance Markievicz, a participant in the 1916 Easter Rising, lived here. All this violence seemed to transcend into the supernatural sphere when a series of spine-chilling hauntings were reported by dozens of people during the 1970s. Then, in 1977, during some reconstruction, a shallow grave revealed the skeleton of a dwarf with a disproportionately large skull. He was accorded a full Christian burial and from then on the paranormal activities ceased.

Devilish Happenings
Turn left up the road for a few metres and cross over to the entrance of **Hell Fire Wood**. Follow the road leading up from the car park through the plantations of mostly Norway Spruce and Sitka Spruce. You now face a bracing climb along a zig-zag route (it will take about 20 minutes) which for the most part will be through forest. At about the point when you pass a little pond on the right the trees cease on your left and a glorious panorama of distant, softly rounded hills comes into view. You are now nearing the top of Mount Pelier (1,275 ft [389 m] high) and when you come to a T junction take the right hand turn. This will lead directly to the gaunt and massive ruins of the infamous Hell Fire Club. Built around 1725 as a hunting lodge for William Connolly, Speaker of the Irish Parliament, the pile was purchased by the notorious Hell Fire Club in 1735. The Club was founded in the 1730s by young bucks from the nobility and officer corps. They usually met in city centre taverns where they held evenings of drunkenness, licentiousness, blasphemous toasts and devil worshipping. There are ghoulish legends associated with their meetings on Mount Pelier. On one occasion a stranger who was admitted to play cards with them was seen to have cloven feet. On another night a priest happened by in a storm and was admitted. The cleric noticed a fiendish looking cat taking its place at the table. Believing it to be a reincarnation of the devil, the priest grabbed the cat and attempted to exorcise it as he flung the animal against the wall. Before the enraged gathering could react the cat was torn apart and a demon was ejected which then shot through the roof smashing it in the process.

Whatever the truth about such stories the roof was indeed badly damaged in a storm. It was repaired by vaulting it with stones robbed from a nearby Neolithic passage tomb, a further sacrilege. The house was abandoned altogether after that. For all its unseemly history the old building commands one of the most striking views of Dublin Bay, the city and the neighbouring Wicklow Mountains.

When you have fully absorbed the panorama (and any picnic you might have taken with you) descend the hill and retrace your steps until you reach the Edmondstown and Tibradden crossroads. This time continue on straight for a few minutes until you arrive at **Sean Doherty's Pub and Restaurant**. This homely mountain tavern has provided shelter and hospitality for more than 250 years. When your mission at Doherty's is complete take the 47A bus back to the city.

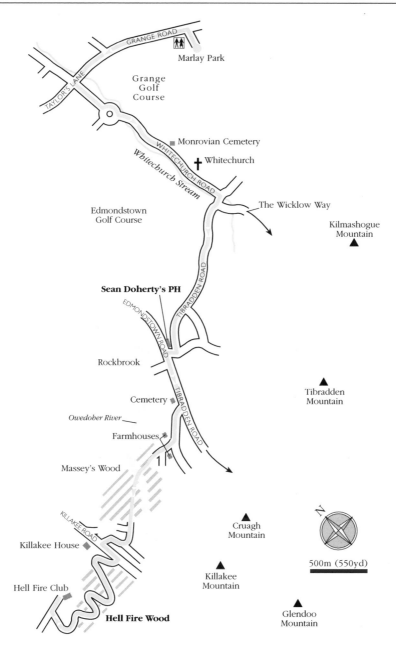

Dodder River Walk

Summary: Rivers have always been important to Dublin. The Vikings made their way up the Liffey and berthed their boats in a pool formed by a tributary, the Poddle River. This pool, Dubh Linn or the Black Pool, gave Dublin its name. The Poddle was the city's main fresh water supply for centuries. The Dodder also provided water to the many communities that sprang up around it and powered their mills. In 1244 it was connected to the Poddle by a canal to augment that river and in 1886–88 it was dammed to supply water to the new townships of Rathmines and Rathgar. If the Dodder is benign and beneficial in its easy flowing moods, swollen with the mountain run-offs from heavy rains it was savage and unmerciful before modern engineering controlled it. Now it provides a most pleasant walking opportunity along almost the complete length of its 15-mile (24-kilometre) course from Kippure in the Wicklow Mountains to where it joins the Liffey at Ringsend. Our part of the journey is only from Rathfarnham Castle to Ballsbridge.

Start:	Rathfarnham Castle, Rathfarnham (Ráth Fearnáin = Ring Fort of the Alders). Buses: 16, 16A, 16B, 47, 47A, 47B. DART Station: none. Car park beside the Castle.
Finish:	Herbert Park Hotel or Jurys Hotel, Ballsbridge (Droichead na Dotra = Bridge of the Dodder). Buses: 5, 7, 7A, 8, 45, 46, 63 and 84. DART Station: Lansdowne Road. Limited parking in the hotel car parks for patrons only.
Length:	4 ½ miles (7.2 kilometres).
Time:	2 hours.
Refreshments:	To pace yourself nicely you could use the Tea Rooms in Rathfarnham Castle, the Dropping Well Bar and Restaurant in Milltown and any number of establishments in Ballsbridge.
Pathway Status:	Roadside paths, grass parkland and riverside pathways.
Best Time to Visit:	Pick a dry day for preference.
Route Notes:	Wear comfortable shoes or trainers to cope with the varied terrain. Only gentle hills will be encountered. Take note that much of the route will be away from roads.
Connecting Walk:	From either the St Enda's Park to Marlay Park walk (see page 96) or the previous walk, Hell Fire Club, by a short bus ride. This walk leads into the next one, Dun Laoghaire Coastal, via a quick DART connection.

Plate 23: *Davy Byrne's, the 'moral pub'. Celebrated in James Joyce's* Ulysses *(see page 86), it remains a literary haunt today.*

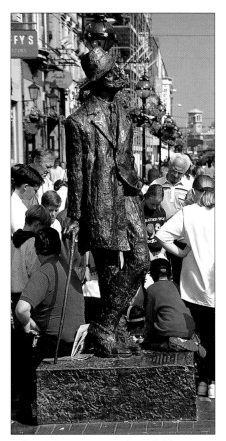

Plate 24: *The Wellington Memorial in the Phoenix Park (see page 76).*

Plate 25: *James Joyce chronicled his native city in the pages of* Ulysses *(see page 81).*

Plate 26: *The charming thatched gatehouse at Dublin Zoo (see page 80).*

Plate 27: *A plaque marks the home of the poet, WB Yeats (1865–1939) (see page 87).*

Plate 28: *No 33 Synge Street was the birthplace of the playwright George Bernard Shaw (1856–1950) and now houses the Shaw museum (see page 88).*

Plate 29: *Established in 1892, Ryan's in Lower Camden Street (see page 90) is one of Dublin's numerous atmospheric Victorian pubs.*

Plate 30: *At the top of Mount Pelier stand the ruins of the infamous Hell Fire Club (see page 102). From here a superb view extends across Dublin to the Wicklow Mountains.*

Plate 31: *The illuminated battlements of Rathfarnham Castle, built in 1585, the starting point for the Dodder River Walk (see page 105).*

Your first stop is at **Rathfarnham Castle**. There has been a fortification in Rathfarnham since at least c.50BC on a rise over the nearby River Dodder. In the 12th century the lands were granted to a Norman, Milo de Bret, and his family held them for 300 years. The present castle was built in 1585 by the Protestant Archbishop of Dublin, Adam Loftus. During the Confederate Wars the castle was occupied by a Parliamentary garrison until it was ousted by Royalists in 1649. The latter also lost it shortly afterwards when they were defeated at the Battle of Rathmines. The battlements and curtain wall have long disappeared and the castle itself was in danger of following suit when it was sold by the Jesuits in 1985 but it was thankfully rescued by the Office of Public Works, who have now nearly finished a massive programme of restoration. Leave the Castle and cross Rathfarnham Road and travel up Church Lane, by-passing Rathfarnham Village, until you can carefully cross Springfield Avenue and over to the path along by the Dodder.

Millraces and Holy Hours
The river is normally quiet and low but if there has been a spell of recent heavy rain or if the mountain snows are melting, it could be a raging torrent. On your left is Bushy Park which, like many of the parks in this city, is a remnant of a great 18th-century estate. Cross Rathfarnham Road where, next to Pearse Bridge (1952), there are some cottages which replaced those swept away in the flood of 1931. Continue along the Lower Dodder Road where perhaps you will find some people fishing. There is a weir (and remains of an old millrace) along this stretch, the first of many, indicating that our walk will generally be on a downward gradient.

A little further on, to your right, is a triumphal arch called Ely Gate, a one-time gateway serving Rathfarnham Castle and built c.1770 by Henry Loftus, Earl of Ely. There is a pedestrian bridge at this point over the Dodder which you should now cross so you can take the river path. On a rise to the right is Mount Carmel Hospital, to the left is the former grazing ground for the once famous Jersey cows of the Bewley's Café group of restaurants. Walk under Orwell Bridge on the far side of which you will find evidence of the millrace which served Waldron's Calico printing works. Just beyond here another millrace started at Orwell Weir. The pathway eventually brings you to a road called Dartry Cottages. At the top of this road was a cloth manufacturing company (you can still see the cavity for its mill wheel) which was followed by the Dartry Dye Works. A survivor of the dye works is the red bricked building facing Dartry Road with the date 1895 on it.

Next proceed down Milltown Road on the low wall side and as you reach a curve you will see the dramatic Nine Arches Bridge built for the now defunct Harcourt Street to Bray railway line in the 1850s. You can loop down to the river again and back up to the Dropping Well pub and restaurant. Established in 1847 when the famine was at its height, the bar (which catered for the 'victims' of alcohol) also had an adjoining morgue to cater for the victims of starvation. At the turn of the century the new owner, P. H. Meagher, for £50, in a specially erected boxing ring, regularly took on any customer who fancied his chances. In the 1920s the pub was also apparently responsible for Kevin O'Higgins, the then Minister for Justice, introducing the so-called Holy Hour, a law which compelled all pubs to close every day for an hour between 2.30 and 3.30. It seems that O'Higgins was having a quiet pint on a Saturday when dozens of workers arrived, just released from work, and stayed all afternoon squandering, in his view, their week's wages on drink. He determined (unsuccessfully in the event) to restrict the temptation. Some of the rooms here offer panoramic views of the river so there need be no break with the Dodder if you decide to stop for some refreshment.

Packhorse Bridge
Immediately after the Dropping Well cross over Classon's Bridge (named after Classon's Saw Mills) and walk along the river on the high ground. To the left of the Nine Arches was Milltown Railway Station. This line was closed down in 1959 but there are plans to use the bridge again for the proposed light rail (tram) network. Walk under the eight arch of this graceful structure and, on the far side, only the equally elegant chimney now remains of the Milltown Laundry, another firm which at one time depended on the power of the millrace. Move down to the riverbank path again where the river curves to the north until you arrive to an antique stone bridge that was, until a new bridge was built to replace it, the main crossing over the Dodder between Milltown and Dundrum. Believed to be the oldest bridge over the Dodder, 17th-century Packhorse Bridge has jutting-out sections in the parapets which were constructed to allow space for pedestrians to get out of the way of approaching carts on the very narrow passageway. Forty years ago, where the modern bridge and park is today, there were cottages, gardens, pigs, sheep and cattle and the inevitable pub (originally it was a coach inn and was in the hands of the locally renowned Hackett family for four generations).

Once over Dundrum Road descend again to the right hand bank of the Dodder and walk between it and the stone wall of the old Clonskeagh Castle on your right.

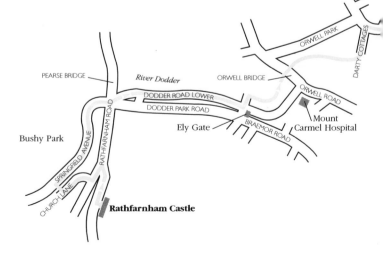

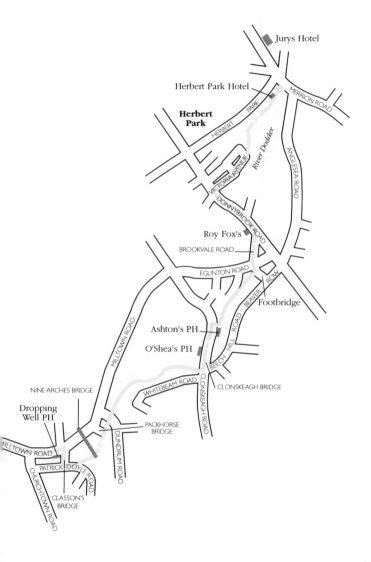

Jurys Hotel

Herbert Park Hotel

**Herbert
Park**

HERBERT PARK

MERRION ROAD

VICTORIA AVENUE

River Dodder

ANGLESEA ROAD

DONNYBROOK ROAD

Roy Fox's

BROOKVALE ROAD

EGLINTON ROAD

BEAVER ROW

Footbridge

MILLTOWN ROAD

Ashton's PH

O'Shea's PH

BEECH HILL ROAD

WHITEBEAM ROAD

CLONSKEAGH ROAD

CLONSKEAGH BRIDGE

NINE ARCHES BRIDGE

Dropping
Well PH

PACKHORSE
BRIDGE

MILLTOWN ROAD

DUNDRUM ROAD

PATRICK DOYLE ROAD

CHURCHTOWN ROAD

CLASSON'S
BRIDGE

N

500m (550yd)

Across the river, through the trees and shrubbery, you may be able to discern an attractive mix of old and new cottages. At Clonskeagh Bridge you will temporarily leave the river and walk down Clonskeagh Road. Take a quick peep into O'Shea's Pub, otherwise known as Clonskeagh House (established 1893). Its stone and mosaic floor interior is very different to most conventional Irish pubs yet it provided the inspiration for Paddy Moloney to arrange the music for the first album of his world-famous traditional folk group, The Chieftains. Smurfit Paper Mills produce brown paper for packaging from recycled raw materials. Occupying the site of an earlier iron works, the paper mills was founded in the late 1930s and was one of the first ventures of Jefferson Smurfit, now Ireland's largest multi-national company (nearly 26,000 employees world-wide).

Donnybrook and Herbert Park

At Ashton's Pub take the steps down to the river where there is the most spectacular weir yet, especially so when the river is in spate. At the footbridge, withdraw from the river once again and via Brookvale Road come out on to Donnybrook Road. Donnybrook Castle was demolished in 1798 to make way for a house which was purchased in 1837 by the founder of the Irish Sisters of Charity, Mother Mary Aikenhead, for use as a home of refuge and later as the Magdalen Laundry. Donnybrook owes its origins to another holy woman called Broc who founded a church there about 750AD. The old graveyard marks its site. The memorial gate to this cemetery commemorates one Thomas Chamney Searight and was erected by his colleagues of the Dublin Stock Exchange when he died in 1890. The grounds of the Bective Rugby Club across the road comprise part of the land given over annually for over 500 years to the notorious Donnybrook Fair until riotous behaviour forced its closure in 1859.

If hunger and thirst need to be satisfied you can divert into any number of Donnybrook's pubs and restaurants or buy some fruit from the famous Roy Fox's, a store which has wonderful outdoor displays of everyday and exotic fruit and vegetables, and which is very popular with foreign embassy staff. Make your way up Victoria Avenue and into **Herbert Park**. Turn left along a wooded path and right to enter under the domed centre of a pergola. This will bring you out to a large artificial duck pond. The Dublin International Exhibition of 1907 was sited on what is now Herbert Park. All the countries of the British Empire were represented and even a complete Somali village was recreated. All that remains of the great event is the pergola (made from leftovers of the veranda of the Fine Arts Building), the pond which was built as part of the popular Canadian waterchute exhibit and the bandstand. The Earl of Pembroke, land owner of the most of the surrounding district, granted what is now the park to the Pembroke Urban District Council in 1911. The Earl named the 33-acre (13.4-hectare) park after his father, Sidney Herbert.

Walk straight down past the pond and the shelter and go through the gates into what was once the premises of bakers Johnston, Mooney & O'Brien and now a wonderful new plaza bordered on one side by apartments and on the other by the Herbert Park Hotel which offers to guests a fine view of the park and the River Dodder which joins us again at the end of our walk.

Nine Arches Bridge

Dun Laoghaire Coastal

Summary: The coming of the railway in 1834 from Dublin to Kingstown (Dun Laoghaire) initiated the growth of towns and residential communities along the line. However, Dun Laoghaire was already by then well established as a packet station and today is the gateway to Ireland for the many visitors using high-speed and conventional ferries from Britain. This walk will start from Blackrock, 4 miles (6.5 kilometres) south-east of Dublin and, except for short intervals, the sea will be in constant view. You will experience the contrasting seclusion of quiet coves and the bustle of a busy ferry port. Towards the end of the walk, a Martello Tower with a Joycean connection peeks down upon a mostly male-only swimming preserve.

Start: Blackrock (An Carrig Dubh = The Black Rock). Buses: 7, 7A, 8. DART: Blackrock Station. Very limited parking near the station; parking for customers only at the two major shopping centres.

Finish: Sandycove (Cuan an Ghainimh = The Cove of Sand). Bus: 8. DART: Sandycove Station. Some parking along seashore and side streets.

Length: 3 miles (4.8 kilometres).

Time: 1¹/₂ hours.

Refreshments: There is a wide choice of pubs and restaurants in Blackrock and Dun Laoghaire while the latter has all the hotels. They are mostly located away from your actual route so you will have to make a small diversion to visit them.

Pathway Status: Roadside paths and concrete seashore pathways. Only occasionally unsuitable for wheelchairs and these stretches can be avoided with small diversions.

Best Time to Visit: A dry day is obviously best and a sunny day brings out the colour associated with coastal towns and harbours. Avoid cold days with an easterly wind unless you are well wrapped up.

Route Notes: If you can, allow time on this walk to wait for the arrival or departure of one of the gigantic HSS (High Speed Ship) ferries. They create such a big wash that signs on a nearby rocky foreshore warn people to steer clear of the waterline until 20 minutes after the ship has passed. Bring binoculars if you have them although there are coin-operated telescopes on the pier.

Connecting Walk: A 20-minute walk or a short DART journey will bring you to the next walk, Dalkey to Killiney.

When you come out of Blackrock Station turn right on to a path parallel to the railway taking the next left and immediate right again into **Blackrock Park**. Meander around the park and its duck pond at will but then leave by a path and some steps which will take you past a Tudor-style pavilion and out through a small gateway on to Rock Hill. Blackrock received its name from a large black rock outcrop along the seashore. Opposite to you now is Roches Stores and the Frascati Shopping Centre.

Turn left into Main Street walking past the other big local centre, the Superquinn Centre, thus arriving into the heart of Victorian Blackrock. Before the town grew up with the coming of the railroad, Blackrock was the seat of several great country mansions including Frascati House, Blackrock House, Maretimo and Newtown House and was a popular bathing resort for the privileged classes in the 18th century. The rolling estates virtually disappeared under the spreading urbanisation of the next century. Walk as far as the stone cross fixed to a modern plinth. This is an ancient stone and carries the effigy of a human face. It may date from the early Christian period but in the 18th century it marked the extent of Dublin and the Lord Mayor and the Corporation came as far as this cross when he annually asserted his authority within the boundaries in a pageant-like procession known as 'Riding the Franchises'. The immediate buildings around here date from at least 1835 (for example the Bank of Ireland) and the splendid Town Hall was opened in 1865. It is not too hard to imagine at this spot what the town's Victorian ambience might have looked like.

The High Seas, Friend and Foe
Return to Bath Place and proceed down again towards the DART Station. On the other side of the station you will notice the Blackrock outdoor public baths, more popular 100 years ago before the advent of indoor heated pools. Now make your way along Idrone Terrace. This is a very well proportioned terrace of 27 houses with the central block carrying the grand name of Idrone Sur Mer. As you approach the end of the terrace look ahead towards the railway and see the twin-towered pedestrian bridge, a fanciful little temple and a bathing place. These were all built by the railway company as part of the price to Lord Cloncurry to pass through his lands.

You will next come into Newtown Avenue where you will turn left passing the church of St John the Baptist. Halfway along Newtown Avenue is an entrance stone with the name *Maretimo* engraved on it. This is all that remains of Lord Cloncurry's mansion. Nearer to the bend in the road is Blackrock House, the 18th-century summer residence of the Lord Lieutenant. After Newtown House take the next left into Seapoint Avenue and continue on for about 400 metres before turning left again (opposite Belgrave Road) down a narrow lane and over a railway bridge which leads down to Brighton Vale. From the seaward side there is a full panoramic view of the city, the docks, Howth, Dun Laoghaire Pier and shipping in Dublin Bay. On the rocks you may be lucky enough to see a cormorant preparing to dive for dinner. If the sea is peaceful on the day of your visit remember that, at times, the Irish Sea is one of the most treacherous in the world. In the days of more vulnerable sailing ships it was not uncommon for a score of ships to be wrecked in one night. Just a short distance off shore and during a raging blizzard in 1807, two troopships, the *Prince of Wales* and the *Rochdale*, were wrecked killing 380 soldiers and members of their families. Further out to sea, on 10th October 1918, just a month before the end of the First World War, U-boat 132 put two torpedoes into the mailboat *RMS Leinster* with the loss of 500 lives.

At the end of Brighton Vale you will come to an old gun battery emplacement which has now been turned into a little promontory park complete with a sculpture. A Martello tower holds court over the whole scene. Sit here a while, if you will, to take in the views. Seventy-four Martello towers were planned to defend the Irish coast from French invasion in Napoleonic times. Of these, 27 were built to cover the eastern coastline either side of Dublin. They were erected over a ten-year period starting in 1804. The idea for the towers arose from a British naval action against a similar tower at Cape Mortella in Corsica in which the small garrison at the tower inflicted heavy damage on two ships and forced their retreat. Impressed by their defence capability, the British authorities ordered similar towers to be built around the coastlines of Britain and Ireland. They had 18- or 24-pounder cannon mounted on rails on the parapeted roof and in some cases extra batteries were positioned beside the tower. The walls were at least 8 feet (2.5 metres) thick. With the odd exception, most of the Martello towers still exist although several of them have been converted into homes or cafés.

500m (550yd)

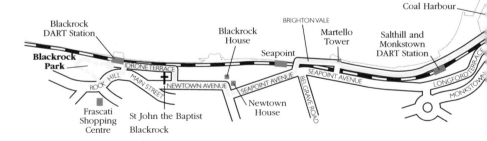

An All-Embracing Harbour

Now cross down to the lower path. This is one of several places along the route where hardy swimmers can be found, even in mid-winter, taking a quick dip. This walk is along by the railway wall but it will be necessary at the next footbridge to enter a gap in the wall and walk by the line itself (don't worry, you are protected by a wire fence), passing Salthill and Monkstown Railway Station. The well-designed buildings on a stick of land to your left are not clubhouses or some other elegant establishment but simple, everyday sewage pumping stations. Keep going straight on, passing under a road bridge, until you come to a little harbour within the main port of Dun Laoghaire. This is the Coal Harbour and, dating from 1767, it represented the first attempt at building a safe anchorage in Dun Laoghaire. Sweeping out from the left side of this harbour is the curving arm of the West Pier built between 1820 and 1827 and almost 1 mile (1.3 kilometres) long.

The Dún of Laoghaire

Now you are entering Harbour Road and at the next junction, on the right, the offices of Bord Iascaigh Mhara (the Fisheries Board) mark roughly the spot of the 5th-century dún or fort of King Laoghaire. (Dunleary was the original anglicised version until the harbour town was renamed Kingstown in 1821 only to revert back again in 1920 to the pure Irish version Dun Laoghaire). Below the wall on the harbour side is a small barracks belonging to an Slua Muirí (Irish Naval Service). Next to this is the depot for the Commissioners of Irish Lights, an organisation that has had the responsibility of looking after buoys, beacons and lighthouses around the coast of Ireland since 1867. The first of the yacht clubs is now approached. The

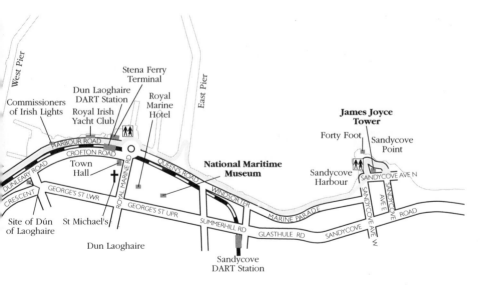

Royal Irish Yacht Club commissioned their eight-columned clubhouse in 1851. As soon as the harbour was built pleasure yachts began to use it and in 1828 the first recorded regatta took place. The next nautical building is the magnificent new **Stena Ferry Terminal** opened in 1996. It cost £22 million to build and handles the new HSS (High Speed Ship), the world's largest high-speed ferry.

The World's Oldest Ship's Longboat

From the vantage point of the terminal's attractive plaza look over at the town itself. The Railway Station, (1854, designed by J. S. Mulvaney), like all buildings erected in the last century next to the Dun Laoghaire seashore, is only one storey high at ground level so that views from the terraces above might not be obstructed. Beyond is one of the masterpieces of Dun Laoghaire, the Venetian-styled Town Hall (1880) now complemented by the adjoining new offices opened in 1997 for the Dun Laoghaire Rathdown County Council. Further up Royal Marine Road the steeple of St Michael's Church soars into the sky and is all that remains of the old church which was gutted by a fire in 1966. Lower down the road to the left and fronting Moran's Park is the Royal Marine Hotel unfortunately shorn, in the pursuit of modernisation, of its French Renaissance mansard roof and higher tower. Sweeping still further to the left you will see another church steeple, that of the Mariner's Church (1837) now, appropriately, the **National Maritime Museum**. Among its absorbing collections is a French longboat captured from an invasion fleet in 1796 and believed to be the oldest intact ship's boat in existence.

Lastly, before you move on, consider the building of the harbour itself. It had long been argued that ships arriving or waiting in the bay for safe passage in Dublin were in danger from unpredictable weather and were in need of an 'asylum' harbour. A Norwegian, Captain Richard Toutcher was the principal voice in the campaign and he was rewarded for his efforts when the foundation stone for such a harbour was laid in 1817. The East Pier, ³/₄ mile (1.1 kilometres) long, was finished in 1823 (the West Pier has already been mentioned above). Both piers enclosed 251 acres (102 hectares) of water, making it then the largest man-made harbour in the world. The granite for the piers was shunted down from Dalkey Common by funicular railway with the weight of the downward trucks pulling up the empty wagons.

Europe's First Lifeboat Service

Time now to continue along the Harbour Road passing a second Yacht Club, the Royal St George, founded in 1845. The obelisk on the right, at street level, is the George IV Obelisk and commemorates the officials associated with the harbour's construction. The Royal National Lifeboat Institution Station is next. The first lifeboats for Dublin Bay were organised in about 1800 and this service is regarded as Europe's first co-ordinated lifeboat service. The RNLI took over in 1862.

The National Yacht Club is Dun Laoghaire's third yacht club. You have now reached the East Pier and you may walk down its length if you wish and return on the alternative level. Either way, when you are ready, walk to the higher promenade wall and continue this walk down by the steps to the sea pathway (ignore this route if it is windy and waves are crashing on to the path). At the end of the pathway you will have to ascend some steps on to the roadside pavement. Known orig-inally as the Victorian baths, the public baths on your left use sea water and were once famous for the curative powers of one pool which was filled with heated water and seaweed. Now just enjoy a bracing walk down past the car park and into the linear park. The terraces of houses are typical of a Victorian upmarket seafront. At the end of the park follow Otranto Place into Sandycove Avenue West.

For Gentlemen Only
Ahead is tiny Sandycove harbour where swimmers, just like at Seapoint, brave the chilly waters all year round. At the top of this road you will come to a little path which leads down to a Gentlemen's Bathing Place – a former gun battery – not that the fair sex can be legally banned any more but they usually prefer to leave the men, who often bare all to the water's embrace, in peace. This is the famous Forty Foot (most likely named after the 40th Foot Regiment who did a stint of duty at the bat-tery and Martello tower) where a celebrated mass swim takes place every Christmas Day. Your last port of call is the nearby Martello Tower now housing the **James Joyce Museum**. Joyce himself stayed there for six days in 1904, stomping out after a row with his hosts. A month later he eloped to Europe with Nora Barnacle. He immortalised his short stay in the tower in the opening chapter of *Ulysses*. The tower, managed by Dublin Tourism, contains first editions of Joyce's works, trans-lations of his books, personal possessions, correspondence, a death mask, pho-tographs and many other items of interest to Joyce fans.

You can return to base now or visit the town of Dun Laoghaire itself to shop, browse or find something to eat.

The Forty Foot

115

Dalkey and Killiney Hill

Summary: Up to the building of proper port facilities in the 17th century Dublin relied on the deep-water harbour at Dalkey for the handling of larger ships. Because Dalkey was close to rebel territory a large number of castles and tower houses ringed the little town. In recent years the spectacular setting of Killiney Hill has attracted the rich and famous to live there.

Arguably the *crème de la crème* of all the southside walks, this peregrination will unfold some of the most magnificent coastal, hill and inland scenery that you will find in Ireland or indeed, in the whole of Europe. The sights, including small medieval castles, a cosy little town that time has gently glided over, a tiny harbour that was once an important port for Dublin, prehistoric and early Christian remains, granite headlands with private mansions hugging their slopes and hill climbs where there is a surprise around every corner; all will combine to an intoxicating whole even before you visit any drinking establishment! This walk alone is justification enough for visitors to stay an extra day in Dublin. The 14-km coastal journey to Dalkey, especially by DART, is also a pleasant experience.

Start and Finish:	Dalkey Village (Deilig Inis = Thorn Island). Bus: 8. DART Station: Dalkey. Car parking at the DART Station or along roads.
Length:	3 miles (5 kilometres).
Time:	2–4 hours (depending on the number of stops you make to take in the views or seek refreshment.
Refreshments:	Dalkey's pubs, Dalkey Island Hotel, Fitzpatrick Castle Hotel, and picnic areas along the route.
Pathway Status:	Roadside and parkland paths and hilly tracks.
Best Time to Visit:	A clear, sunny day is obviously the best time to enjoy the panoramic views but these same views are often enhanced by the changing moods of the weather and the seasons.
Route Notes:	There are no difficulties as such on the walk. Comfortable flat shoes will normally be sufficient but some of the hill tracks can be a bit muddy if it has recently rained. Also, you will need to be moderately fit as you will encounter modest climbs and at various stages no fewer than a grand total of 509 steps. The walk is unsuitable for wheelchairs. If you can, bring a pair of binoculars.

Connecting Walk: Continuation from the Dun Laoghaire walk (see page 110). Walk from Sandycove via Bullock Harbour and join this ramble at Coliemore Road in Dalkey.

Alight from the DART at Dalkey Station and reflect on that great day on 29th March 1844 when the world-acclaimed Atmospheric Railway, which connected Kingstown (Dun Laoghaire) with Dalkey was inaugurated. The upkeep of the vacuum-operated line became too expensive and too difficult and was replaced

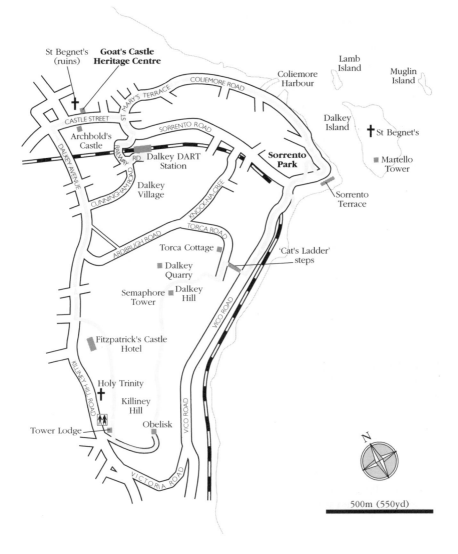

ten years later by a conventional steam-driven service. Head downhill towards the centre of the village and savour the old-world ambience that Dalkey has thankfully managed to preserve. It is now largely a Victorian township that grew, with the coming of the railroad, into a dormitory suburb of Dublin. However, its first inhabitants had settled here as far back as probably 8,000 years ago and Neolithic (Late Stone Age) remains have been unearthed in the area. But it was as Dublin's chief port in medieval times that the then walled town achieved its fame and fortune.

Coliemore Harbour
Go around St Mary's Terrace and immediately turn right into Coliemore Road. Turn right again at the gateway of the Sue Ryder Foundation (sheltered housing on part of the lands owned by the Loreto Abbey Schools) and notice, set into the wall beside the entrance pillar, a post box embossed with the insignia VR which signifies that it dates from the reign of Queen Victoria. Many of the houses from here on can only be described as mansions as they graciously stand side by side with less pretentious abodes. On the left side you will soon encounter two fine examples of flamboyant 19th-century residences, one a mock castle, the other a Tudor-style stone manor. Next to appear along the seafront are the gardens of the former Dalkey Island Hotel now being rebuilt as apartments and a restaurant. Enjoy the stunning views of Dalkey Sound and Dublin Bay from the seating area just beyond this development. Enjoy watching the small lobster boats or pleasure craft plying the Sound or the huge container ships and ferries gliding past distant lighthouses on their way to and from Dublin Port.

Because of the sand bars and the shallow, tidal water of the River Liffey, the larger medieval ships sought the deep water anchorage of Dalkey Sound. From the 15th century a spacious harbour, with piers built from 2.5-tonne blocks of granite, replaced Wood Quay in Dublin as the principal port of the capital city. The name of the harbour, Coliemore, is derived from the Irish Calladh Mór or Large Harbour. Part of the old harbour can still be seen underneath the foundations of a house called Rocksborough. Goods were offloaded at Coliemore and transferred to barges or carts for delivery to Dublin. The tiny but attractive harbour today services the lobster boats and day trips to Dalkey Island.

Dalkey Island
Craggy and uneven Dalkey Island lies about 980 feet (300 metres) off Coliemore Harbour. First settled thousands of years ago (parts of it are quite fertile and it has at least six fresh water wells), it also supported an early Christian community. The substantial ruins of an oratory, dedicated to a 7th-century holy woman, St Begnet, can easily be seen from the mainland. During the ninth century the Vikings settled here while they launched their plundering strikes at the mainland. They gave it the name Dalkey by taking the Irish name Deilig Inis and suffixing Deilig with the Norse word Ey, meaning island. A Martello tower (see page 112) and its dismantled gun battery stand at the southern tip of the island. A few wild goats are the only inhabitants today. Over the island and its rocky outposts a mock king and his burlesque of a court do reign. In a ceremony first instituted in the second half of the

Dalkey Island

18th century, later abandoned and revived in 1935, an individual with great ceremony is comically proclaimed 'His Facetious Majesty, the King of Dalkey, Emperor
of Muglin, Elector of Lambay and Ireland's Eye, Defender of his own Faith and
Respector of All Others and Sovereign of the Illustrious Order of the Lobster and
the Periwinkle'.

The Vico Road

Now continue along Coliemore Road until you reach Sorrento Terrace, a road
lined on one side by a very elegant row of large Victorian terraced houses. Enter into
Sorrento Park, which was a gift made to the public by one Lady MacDonnell in
1894. It is a small park built around a solid granite outcrop with a geological age of
more than 400 million years. Set into the rock face along the right-hand ascending
path is a restored mosaic honouring the great Elizabethan poet and lute composer,
John Dowland (1563–1626), who had associations with the area. Dowland was a
friend of William Shakespeare and it is said that his description of the locality was
used by the dramatist to describe the scene for Elsinore in Hamlet. From the summit of the park there is a marvellous view of Dalkey Island and the hill-hugging vil-
las along the Vico Road, home to many celebrities. The view to the south-west
takes in Killiney Hill topped by an obelisk, the high point of our walk.

Take the next exit at the bandstand end of the park, turn right then next left
to join the Vico Road, keeping to the seaward side. Many of the road and house
names around here are in Italian such as Vico itself, Sorrento, Nerano, Torca, La
Scala, Milano, Mount Etna, San Elmo and so on, reflecting the oft-made com-
parison between this sweep of coastline and the Bay of Naples. A gap in the railway wall will lead you down via steps and a sloped path to the beach but if you
decide to go down you will have to retrace your steps to regain the road.

To the Hills

When you come to a sign pointing to the Dun Laoghaire and Dalkey Ways (at an Italianate-style house called Strawberry Hill) cross the road and start the climb up a series of zig-zag steps called the Cat's Ladder. This is a fairly long climb; if you have children with you keep them amused by asking them to count the number of steps (there are 238 in all). Turn right at the top into Torca Road and the second house on the left is Torca Cottage, the boyhood summer residence of George Bernard Shaw from 1866 to 1874. The plaque proclaims Shaw's love for Dalkey, 'Irishmen are mortal and temporal, but her hills are eternal'.

Return to the top of the Cat's Ladder and continue to the very end of Torca Road and enter a very narrow track on the right which is separated from a neighbouring private driveway by a wire fence. This is a public right-of-way to Dalkey Hill and for most of the climb the path hugs a low stone wall. The panoramic views, revealing themselves one by one, are breathtaking: the bay, the surrounding townships and the capital city itself. Nearing the top of Dalkey Hill you can look down into Dalkey Quarry where, from 1817, the granite was blasted, hewn and transported by private railway to Dun Laoghaire to fashion the great piers of the new harbour. The precipitous granite walls are now the training ground for mountaineers and offer more than 200 short climbs on grades from difficult to extreme. From here the low wall climbs steeply to a castellated structure on the summit, reminding one of a mini Wall of China. This building is an old telegraph or semaphore tower erected at the time of the Napoleonic Wars to send messages to ships out at sea. Close by is a more recent communications tower, an aircraft navigational radio beacon.

On the far side of the semaphore tower head downhill in the direction of the obelisk on Killiney Hill. After you pass a wooded area on your right you will come to the dip between the two hills and to where another path intersects at right angles. You can pause here in the open parkland for a picnic or a rest or indeed, if you are too tired to go higher, leave the hill and make for the Fitzpatrick Castle Hotel (to the right and downhill). The reward for undertaking the next stage of the journey will make the effort worthwhile.

Killiney Hill

Go straight up a path that is interspersed with steps until you reach the obelisk and from various standpoints around the monument you will be able to obtain a magnificent 360-degree view of practically the whole of south Co Dublin. To the east lie Sorrento Point, Dalkey Island and the open sea. Beyond, and visible on a clear day, are the mountains of Wales. To the south is the curve of Killiney Bay ending with the jagged Bray Head and the soft outlines of the Wicklow Mountains behind and to the west, the hinterland of urban sprawl that seems somehow to melt into the natural landscape of the bordering Dublin Hills. Finally, to the north, are the enfolding arms of Dublin Bay, the city centre and the Howth Peninsula. The obelisk itself and the walls surrounding the hills were built by the former owner of these lands, John Mapas, in 1742, to give employment to destitute families who had lost their crops following an exceptionally harsh winter. The second, smaller obelisk is known as Boucher's Obelisk and the stepped monument, dated 1852, is known as the Wishing Stone – walk around each level, stand on the top facing Dalkey and make a wish.

Tower and Castles

When you are ready to descend take the south-facing path down into **Killiney Hill Park** proper (known originally as Victoria Park, it was first opened in 1887) which will bring you past the main entrance gates and the tower lodge. Opposite the entrance is a two-tonne bronze sculpture entitled *Thus Daedalus Flew* by Niall O'Neill and it symbolises the human search for ever higher levels of consciousness. Stay on the parkland path passing the Protestant church of the Holy Trinity (1858) on your left and entering a wide expanse of grassland and the public car park.

If you cut across the grass you can quickly reach Fitzpatrick's Castle Hotel either just to view over it or to rest any weary bones. Dating from 1741, it was then known as Killiney Castle and is now Dublin's only luxury castle hotel.

Emerge into Killiney Hill Road, turn right and head down into Dalkey Avenue. Just before the junction with Cunningham Road, a laneway with a steep incline appears at an angle on your right. This is the course of the old quarry railway which ran to Dun Laoghaire Harbour. A raised bank just off Dalkey Avenue is the remains of the town's rampart fortification. At the end of the avenue turn right into Castle Street, noting the narrowness of the streets, a legacy from the confinement of the town walls. In the 15th century there were seven castles in and around Dalkey. These were not large, garrisoned installations but tower houses used by the merchants to safeguard cargoes from Coliemore Harbour. Two examples still remain and both are situated in Castle Street. The first, on your right, is Archbold's Castle, recently restored by Dun Laoghaire Corporation. Note a bartizan, or murdering hole, a projecting turret used for pouring boiling oil or water on the heads of attackers. Immediately across the road are the ruins of another church dedicated to St Begnet. First founded in the ninth century, the present building dates from the Anglo-Normans and was abandoned for worship in 1689. Beside the church is the second castle, Goat's Castle, named after the goat in the coat-of-arms of the Cheevers family of Monkstown who had 16th-century connections with the building. The castle has been refurbished as the town's **Heritage Centre**.

The importance of Dalkey as a harbour town vanished when Ringsend, a locality much nearer to Dublin, was opened as the city's new deep-water port in the 17th century. A subsequent decline was only arrested with the arrival of the railway in 1844 which brought in new residents and day-trippers to savour the delights of the beaches and the hills. The electric tramway in the 1880s also aided communication and some of the tracks can still be seen on a cobbled entrance road beside the Tramshed Shop. Complete the walk by turning right up Railway road which leads back to the DART Station.

Bray to Enniskerry

Summary: Many years ago Bray was only a small fishing village but a century ago it was known as 'The Brighton of Ireland', which at that time meant that it must have been a very stylish and upper-class seaside resort indeed. From the 1820s and especially after the arrival of the railway in 1854 until the period after the Second World War, it enjoyed the patronage of the titled and wealthy. The great promenade was built and grand hotels, guesthouses and residences sprang up. In the 1960s the visitor profile changed completely. People no longer came in large numbers on holiday but preferred instead to visit on day trips and the town took on more of a Blackpool image and lost some of its grandeur.

With the convenience of the DART railway and an improved road network, the town then developed into a dormitory suburb for Dublin, being situated only 12 miles (20 kilometres) to the south of the city. Bray, while technically in Co Wicklow, actually straddles the border with Co Dublin. The 1990s have brought a real resurgence of local pride and a new appreciation of Bray's rich heritage and the town, in all its aspects, is enjoying something of a renaissance.

If Bray has changed enormously over the last hundred years its neighbour, Enniskerry, 3 miles (5 kilometres) to the west, in the foothills of the Wicklow Mountains, has hardly altered at all. Its timeless charm and the spectacular formal landscaping of the Powerscourt Demesne are the *pièce de résistance* of this walk.

Start:	Bray DART Station (Bré or Brí = Hill). Buses: 45, 84 from Dublin and 45A from Dun Laoghaire. Parking around DART Station.
Finish:	Enniskerry (Áth na Sceire = Ford of the Reef). Bus: 44 to Dublin or 185 to Bray DART Station. Roadside parking in the village or Powerscourt usually available.
Length:	Walking distance is 4 miles (6.5 kilometres) as the middle section is by bus (see route note).
Time:	2 hours plus bus time.
Refreshments:	The Royal and Esplanade Hotels in Bray, as well as many restaurants, pubs and coffee shops. Enniskerry has a couple of nice coffee shops and two hotels, the Powerscourt Arms and the Summerhill House.
Pathway Status:	Roadside paths, esplanade walk and a right-of-way clay track which can be muddy, so wear trainers or boots.

Best Time to Visit: In easterly winds the esplanade might be unpleasant with the addition of sea water splashing over it. Enniskerry has an atmosphere on even misty days but Powerscourt looks its best in the sunshine.

Route Note: It will be necessary to connect the main elements of the walk, Bray and Enniskerry, by bus. This is because, at the time of writing, there are no plans to build a footbridge across the motorway and it is simply too dangerous to walk across.

Connecting walk: This walk is in sequence to the Dalkey and Killiney walk if you use the DART link.

Start this walk from Bray's atmospheric mid-Victorian railway station, which you will obviously be doing anyway if you have arrived by DART. Before you leave the station forecourt check the times of the 185 bus to Enniskerry as you will be taking one in about one hour's time from now.

On 8th July 1854 the first train to reach Bray puffed into the flag bedecked station where a celebratory tea party was held on the spacious platform. The same venue saw a dance that evening with music provided by a military band. The town had good reason to rejoice as the railway had taken nearly 20 years, several railway companies, the services of the renowned British engineer, Isambard Kingdom Brunel and the final intervention of the Irish railway magnate, William Dargan, to bring it to completion.

Leave the station, cross over the tracks at the level crossing and proceed down towards the seafront and turn right again to walk along by the long row of large terraced houses and hotels, staying on this side until you reach the end of the road.

The Brighton of Ireland

Up to the early 1800s people thought it an eccentric and risky operation to bathe in the sea but the supposed curative properties of salt water and the new-found respectability of bathing among the English royalty and the nobility who aped them, brought fashionable society to the beaches. This was strictly a pursuit for the gentry and the upper classes and every amenity was laid on for them; luxury hotels, entertainments, changing booths on the beach, excursions and whatever other facilities that might be required were obsequiously made available. The arrival of the railway certainly brought much more of this kind of traffic to Bray and day visitors were not yet encouraged. Bray's response to its new-found popularity resulted in huge development along the seafront and the town boomed until at least the turn of the century. The buildings on your right are the legacy of this period. Their glory began to fade from about the 1950s or so when overnight guests, lured away to overseas destinations or more sophisticated Irish resorts, grew scarce and day trippers brought business only to the amusement arcades and the sweet shops. However, there is evidence once again of a revival in local tourism and the people of Bray themselves are taking a keen interest in their own rich heritage.

Ahead of you is Bray Head, a massive rock conglomeration dating from the Cambrian Period more than 500 million years ago. In the decades from the 1950s

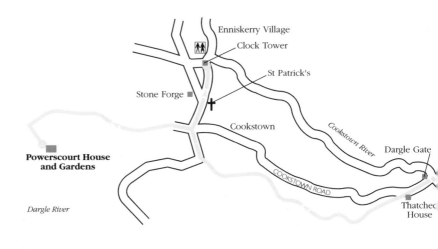

to the 1970s a chair lift, of happy memories to this author, used to swing its way from the end of Strand Road to its 653-foot (199-metre) summit. Nos 1 to 4 Esplanade Terrace (now partly occupied by Kinvara House Nursing Home) and a single house, Elsinore (now the Strand Hotel), were built as an investment by Sir William Wilde, the father of Oscar Wilde, and the family lived in one of the houses for a while in the 1870s. When you reach the end of Strand Road make your way over to the Esplanade and begin your return journey. In 1859, Dargan, at his own expense, laid down a grass esplanade. He had recently bought property in the town and developed what is now Duncairn Terrace along Quinsborough Road. Dargan was convinced Bray had a future and was prepared to invest his not inconsiderable energy and money into the township. His esplanade proved to be no barrier to stormy winter seas and between 1860 and 1877 serious flooding breached it five times. The present esplanade, which was opened in 1886 along with a further extension four years later, offered a successful bulwark against all but the most ferocious seas. Victorian and Edwardian society loved to promenade along this wall to take the sea air and, more importantly, to be seen. Fishing boats could now no longer use the beach to land their catch so a harbour was opened at the mouth of the Dargle in 1897. Coal and grain and wood colliers also sailed from here. The esplanade kiosks were erected by the Urban District Council in 1935.

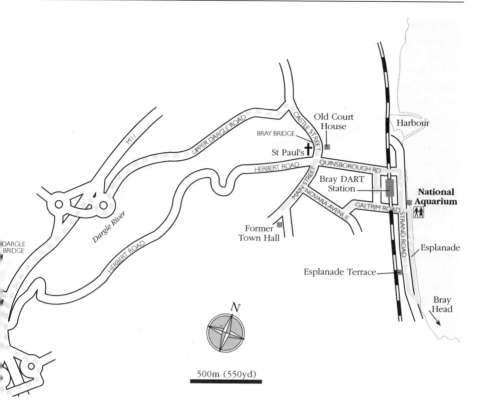

500m (550yd)

From Hamlet to Township

At the **Marine Aquarium**, turn off the esplanade and make your way up Albert Avenue, Galtrim Road and suburban Novara Avenue which will bring you into Main Street. On the left is the former Town Hall and Market, now a restaurant. This gem of a Tudor-style building designed by architects Newenham Deane & Son, was erected in 1881 at the sole expense of the local big landowner, Reginald Lord Brabazon, 12th Earl of Meath. The Town Commissioners and later the Urban District Council held their meetings in the first-floor Chamber Room. The stone fountain in front is surmounted by a Wyvern – a mythological half dragon and half viper, a wyvern being part of the Earl of Meath's coat of arms. There was a church opposite Florence Road from about the 18th century but it fell into disuse and was not replaced until Father James Doyle began work on the new church of the Most Holy Redeemer in 1824. In 1961 the facade and bell tower were totally refashioned into a modern but pleasing, pyramid-like shape.

Continue along Main Street, crossing Quinsborough Road and stopping beside the obelisk monument. From this vantage point several features of note can be easily viewed. Below is the River Dargle which separated Little Bray, for centuries the Irish part of the town housing poor Catholic workers (many of them living in wretched hovels), and Old Bray, the town of the gentry and the better-off. Until

125

1666 there was no bridge and when the river was in spate travellers from Dublin had to make lengthy diversions. The present bridge dates from 1856. Directly across the road is St Paul's Church, built in 1609 and further enlarged in 1859 and 1892. Behind the church, but out of view from here, is the firm of Kenneth Jones Pipe Organs Ltd who manufactured the excellent organ in the National Concert Hall. This is approximately the site where Sir Walter Ridelsford built his castle in 1174 and around which the first little hamlet of Bray grew up.

The obelisk itself is dedicated to the memory of Dr Christopher Thompson who volunteered to look after the cholera victims of 1876 and died himself of the disease. Beside the monument is the Old Court House (1841) which now serves as the wonderful **Heritage Centre** and tourist office – well worth a visit. Lastly, in this historic spot, is the Royal Hotel, a successor to Quin's Hotel, first opened in 1776. John Quin ran a very upmarket establishment and William Makepeace Thackeray described the hotel's cuisine as the best in Ireland. Quin even then saw the potential of Bray as a

Memorial Obelisk

tourist resort and gateway to the wonderful scenery of the Wicklow Mountains. What is now Quinsborough Road was originally the hotel's private path to the sea. It was opened and developed as a link to the railway station by Dargan in 1854.

You will now go down Quinsborough Road on your way back to the station. Outside the Carlisle Grounds (Bray Wanderers Football Club) there is a Celtic Cross which commemorates the citizens of Bray who died in both World Wars. Now cross over to the bus stop in front of the station and wait for the next Enniskerry bus.

Into the Hills

While you are waiting for or travelling on the bus you might like to know that apart from yourself other famous people down the years visited or lived in Bray and Enniskerry. We have already mentioned the Wildes. Others included poet and novelist Sir Walter Scott; the creator of Sherlock Holmes, Sir Arthur Conan Doyle; dramatist and editor, Lennox Robinson; short story writer, Mary Lavin; 'The Informer' writer, Liam O'Flaherty; playwright John Millington Singe; novelist, Alistair MacLean and poet and supernatural horror writer, Joseph Sheridan leFanu. Political life was represented by 18th-century parliamentary leader, Henry Grattan; the patriot executed for his role in the 1916 Easter Rising, Sir Roger Casement; former Taoiseach (Prime Minister) Garret Fitzgerald and the fifth President of Ireland, Cearbhall Ó' Dálaigh.

Ask the bus driver to let you off at the Dargle Gate on the far side of the motor-way about 2¹/₂ miles (4 kilometres) away to start your walk to Enniskerry. At the nearby Dargle Bridge two mountain rivers meet together; the Dargle itself and the Cookstown River. From the bus stop take the road to the left away from the bus route – this is the Cookstown Road, walk up about 300 yards (300 metres) until you reach a newly thatched building on the left. The art of thatching – in this case carried out by Kyran O'Grady who is responsible for many of the country's larger commissions – is still very much alive and other examples can be seen on the out-skirts of the city (see also page 160).

At this point, there are old gates set in off the road and you should now enter the open pedestrian gate which will bring you to an extremely pleasant right-of-way along by the Dargle Glen. There are marvellous scents in the air from a huge vari-ety of shrubs and trees and for most of this part of the walk the only sounds you will hear are the birdsong and the water of the Dargle far below crashing over the rocks and rapids. For the first half of the journey the climb is uphill and then it levels out. The approximate halfway stage is marked by a large outcrop of rock but keep chil-dren away as there is a very steep drop from it. Now you can close this book until you reach the road in about 30 minutes.

Resplendent Gardens and a Quaint Village
When you arrive at the public road (Henry Grattan lived in Tinnahinch House down this road to the left) turn right and you will quickly come to a crossroads. To the right lies the Summerhill House Hotel and a little further down was the home of *The Day of the Jackal* author, Frederick Forsyth, who lived for a few years in Kilgarron House. At the end of the short road to the left stands the impressive eagle-topped entrance to **Powerscourt Demesne**. During opening hours visitors are welcome to the exquisitely laid-out gardens of Powerscourt, with their formal Italian-style landscaping, statuary, lakes and fountain. There are also picnic spots, children's play areas, tea rooms and a Visitor Centre.

For those of you who choose to visit Powerscourt, here is a brief description of what awaits you. Leading down from the mansion is a stepped terrace with inlaid paving. The mansion itself, however, one of the most palatial in Ireland, and mod-elled on the Villa Pisani near Venice, was overwhelmed by fire in 1974 and only now is partially rebuilt. It was originally erected between 1731 and 1740 for Richard Wingfield, 1st Viscount of Powerscourt. His descendant, Richard, 6th Viscount, had the plain terraces, the amphitheatre of grass and a lake (known as Juggy's Pond) totally transformed, work which was continued by Mervyn, the next succeeding Viscount. Designed by Daniel Robertson, the upper terrace was based on another Italian house, the Villa Butera, near Butera in Sicily. Work was halted in 1844 when Richard died and only continued in fits and starts in the 1860s. The centre terrace was planned by Sir Francis Penrose, at that time architect to St Paul's Cathedral in London, and features a patterned design using black and white pebbles gathered on the beach at Bray.

The statues on the upper terrace are winged Figures of Fame and Victory (craft-ed in 1866 in Berlin) and a copy of the Apollo Belvedere purchased in Italy by the

6th Viscount. On the mid terrace are a pair of figures representing Aeolus, the God of Winds and some urns copied from originals at Versailles. The Aeolus figures were rescued from the burned palace of Prince Jerome Napoleon, nephew of Napoleon III, during the aftermath of the Franco-Prussian War. To complete the international flavour of the furnishing, the protective wrought-iron railings were purchased from a castle near Hesse, in Germany. Always a noble scavenger, Lord Powerscourt also found a use as a highly decorative gate for part of a screen discarded from Bamberg Cathedral in Germany. At the pool level there are two winged horses or pegasi (from the family coat of arms). The fountain in the pond is based on Bernini's model in the Piazza Barberini in Rome.

On leaving Powerscourt turn left and head down past St Patrick's Church, in the graveyard of which lies the painter Paul Henry (died 1958), well known for his billowing clouds and rugged landscapes of the West of Ireland. He tragically went blind 13 years before his death. At the fork in the road you keep to the right but you will just see to the left the disused old stone-built forge and its horseshoe-shaped doorway. When you reach the village you will be immediately struck by the homely arrangement of the period houses gathered around the clock tower which was built in 1843 by Lord Powerscourt. In fact the whole village was built to house workers of the Powerscourt Demesne. Backdropping Enniskerry is the Great Sugarloaf Mountain 1,644 feet (501 metres) high. You now have a couple of coffee shops (Poppies is long-established and has the atmosphere of an Alpine mountain restaurant), a hotel and several craft and design shops to choose from before you board a 44 bus to the city or the 185 back to Bray DART Station.

The Old Forge

Phibsborough to the National Botanic Gardens

Summary: It is said that Dublin is made up of a series of villages where communities are closely knit and have their own individual identity. These villages have of course been swallowed up in the spread of the greater metropolis but they have never quite lost their own distinct sense of neighbourliness, history and topographical uniqueness. Phibsborough is just such a place and one very close to my heart, having been born, reared and educated there. A mid- to late-Victorian creation, it was until fairly recently in the main bypassed by property speculation and development, despite its proximity to the city centre. Some of the country's most famous institutions such as Mountjoy Prison, the Royal Canal, Glasnevin Cemetery and the National Botanic Gardens are within the ambit of this walk. Phibsborough is a mere 1 mile (1.5 kilometres) north of O'Connell Street.

Start: St Peter's Church, Phibsborough (Baile Phib = The Town of Phipp). Buses: 10, 22, 38, 120. DART Station: none. Car parking difficult and available only on nearby residential streets.

Finish: National Botanic Gardens (Garraithe Náisiúnta na Lus = National Garden of Plants). Buses: 13, 19, 134. DART Station: none. Car parking only a little less difficult than Phibsborough.

Length: 2 miles (3.2 kilometres).

Time: 1¹/₂ hours.

Refreshments: There are many pubs, which also serve food, along the route. The Addison Lodge Hotel is located at the route terminus.

Pathway Status: Roadside and parkland paths. Low-heel shoes would be best if you want to pick your way across cemetery plots crowded with headstones arranged in an irregular manner.

Best Time to Visit: Obviously, only undertake this walk during the opening times of both the cemetery and the Botanical Gardens. The gardens themselves reflect a seasonal character but for blooms the summer is the high point.

Route Notes: This is a very easy walk and is also suitable for wheelchairs. The overall gradient is downhill with only a small uphill section at the Royal Canal.

Connecting Walk: From The Phoenix Park walk (see page 75) take Bus 10 from Infirmary Road.

Take the bus to **St Peter's Church** and, as it is usually open, pay a visit to view its elegant neo-Gothic interior. Administered since 1838 by the Vincentian Community, this particular edifice replaced most of an earlier structure. It dates from 1902–11 and, amazingly, was built solely from charitable donations of suffi-cient quantity that left the parish with no debt on its completion. The spire at a height of more than 200 feet (61 metres) is the tallest in Dublin. G.C. Ashlin, the famous ecclesiastical architect, designed the church. Cross the road to your left and walk in the direction of Doyle's Corner (named after one of the pubs standing at this crossroads). In contrast to the magnificence of St Peter's is the tiny former Baptist church which has now been converted into offices. The laneway encoun-tered almost immediately to the left leads to Dalymount Park (opened 1901), the home of the Bohemians Football Club, a foremost team in the Irish soccer league. Bohemians, so named because they had led a wandering life until settling in Phibsborough, was founded in 1890. Beside the Post Office is the grandly named Phibsborough Avenue, in effect what must be one of the narrowest and shortest avenues in the city. The name Phibsborough itself is likely to have been derived from the Phipps family who acquired land here in the late 18th century.

The Royal Canal

The Oul' Triangle

Pause for a moment at Doyle's Corner. There was a tram depot beside the present Irish Permanent Building Society offices which is still remembered by the term, the 'Tramway End' of Dalymount Park. The bulk of the buildings are late Victorian and some carry fine embellishments. The Hut Bar still has its curious circular window mirror which reflects upside-down images. Proceed again across the road until you reach the opening, just before the library, which leads downwards via a flight of steps. Before descending, note directly opposite the statue of a kneeling soldier on Blacquiere Bridge which commemorates the Dublin Brigade of Irish Volunteers formed in 1913. Behind the statue is the linear park laid out when a spur of the Royal Canal was filled in during the 1930s.

The large building to the right of the statue is the former State Cinema, a place in which, along with the library, I received much of my early education. Walk down the steps (wheelchairs can go around the other side of the library) coming out into Royal Canal Bank, the northern half of the linear park. Here you are confronted with Mountjoy Prison and its towering walls. The prison is named after Luke Gardiner, Lord Mountjoy, who would have built in its stead a radius of

boulevards issuing from a circus of stately mansions (from where the Mater Hospital now stands) had he not stopped a bullet to his head in the Insurrection of 1798. The jail was opened as a model prison for its time. Brendan Behan, a one-time inmate, immortalised the jail in his play *The Quare Fellow* with the lines:

> *The oul' Triangle,*
> *Goes Jingle Jangle,*
> *Along the Banks of the Royal Canal.*

(The triangle sounded the signal for unlocking time.)

Canals, Railways and Aeroplanes

The road now reaches those same banks of the Royal Canal. Opened in stages between 1790 and 1815 as a rival to the Grand Canal, the Royal never prospered and was eventually closed in 1961. Now it is being rehabilitated by voluntary effort and by the Office of Public Works and will soon again be a navigable waterway from the Liffey to the Shannon. Ahead, on your left, is a large stone building now converted into apartments but founded as Robert Mallet's Iron Works (the firm built the railings around Trinity College and they still exist on the Nassau Street side). Flour milling succeeded iron manufacture in 1860. The level of the ground along this stretch of canal rises quite perceptibly and numerous lock gates have had to be employed to surmount the height.

Cross the iron canal bridge (known as Cross Guns Bridge) and then the railway bridge noting in the right distance the imposing new stand in Croke Park, the headquarters of the Gaelic Athletic Association (GAA). The building at the corner was originally a garage owned by Hugh Cahill, who, in 1930, founded Iona National Airways, Ireland's first operational passenger airline. Continue along Prospect Road, passing another railway line and the Brian Boru pub which externally displays a stirring painting of the Gaelic Chieftain blessing his troops before the Battle of Clontarf in 1014. At a fork in the road cross to the high railings of Dalcassian Downs, a residential complex built on the grounds of the demolished St Vincent's' Orphanage and Schools.

Glasnevin Cemetery, Where Heroes and Heroines Rest

In a short while you will see the boundary wall of **Glasnevin Cemetery**. These walls are punctuated by no fewer than seven watchtowers built to prevent bodysnatchers from stealing freshly interred bodies for sale to surgical students. At the traffic lights cross over the Finglas Road into the cemetery. Up to the 1820s Roman Catholics could only be buried in Protestant-controlled cemeteries where their families often could not afford the charges. By 1828, Daniel O'Connell (1775–1847) and the Catholic Association achieved the right for Catholics to open their own graveyards. Glasnevin Cemetery conducted its first interment on 22nd February 1832 and for its part has always been non-denominational. Now more than a million people have been buried here, most of whom have lived hidden but nonetheless, in their own way, heroic and distinguished lives.

From an historical perspective Glasnevin Cemetery is an extraordinary place where so many prominent personages of the last century and a half lie gathered in one location often under grandly sculptured monuments. The tour suggested here can only take you around a small representative number of the more eminent residents – a more complete guide is available from the cemetery office. Start your tour by following the descriptions in the numbered sequence on the enlarged map before returning to the office to take the path as indicated on the main map.

A short tour of Glasnevin Cemetery in the immediate vicinity of the O'Connell Monument

This little tour will meander around the final resting places of clerics, lawyers, trade unionists, nationalists, revolutionaries, writers, poets, actors, soldiers and entrepreneurs (the year of their death is given in parentheses).

1. William J. Walsh, Archbishop of Dublin and Primate of Ireland (1921).
2. Cardinal Edward McCabe, Archbishop of Dublin and Primate of Ireland, and strong opponent of political change (1885). Monument designed by Sir Thomas Drew and sculpted by Sir Thomas Farrell who is himself laid to rest nearby.
3. Antique cart for bearing coffins.
4. Cemetery Chapel based on the design of Cormac's Chapel on the Rock of Cashel.
5. The 168-foot (51-metre) high Daniel O'Connell Monument. Based on the ancient Irish monastic round tower, this memorial (1861) rises above the crypt

of one of Ireland's foremost political leaders who consistently fought for social reforms and religious and political liberties in Ireland and abroad (1847).

6. Barry Sullivan, actor, widely known for his Shakespearean roles (1891).
7. Jack Cruise, popular comic actor and theatrical impresario (1978).

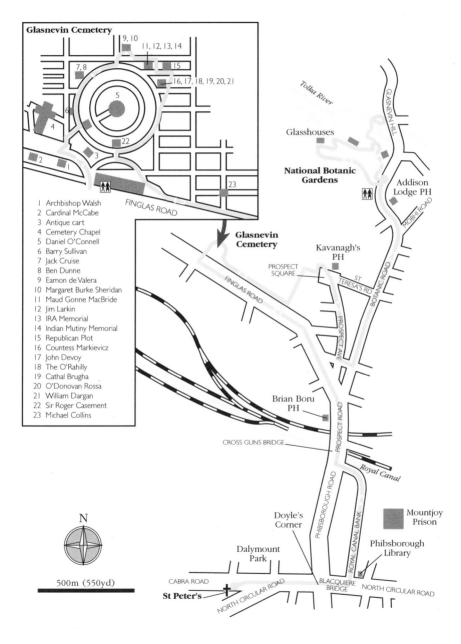

Glasnevin Cemetery

9, 10
11, 12, 13, 14
7, 8
15
16, 17, 18, 19, 20, 21
5
6
4
22
2
3
1
23

FINGLAS ROAD

1 Archbishop Walsh
2 Cardinal McCabe
3 Antique cart
4 Cemetery Chapel
5 Daniel O'Connell
6 Barry Sullivan
7 Jack Cruise
8 Ben Dunne
9 Eamon de Valera
10 Margaret Burke Sheridan
11 Maud Gonne MacBride
12 Jim Larkin
13 IRA Memorial
14 Indian Mutiny Memorial
15 Republican Plot
16 Countess Markievicz
17 John Devoy
18 The O'Rahilly
19 Cathal Brugha
20 O'Donovan Rossa
21 William Dargan
22 Sir Roger Casement
23 Michael Collins

Tolka River

GLASNEVIN HILL

Glasshouses

National Botanic Gardens

Addison Lodge PH

MOBHI ROAD

Glasnevin Cemetery

Kavanagh's PH

PROSPECT SQUARE

FINGLAS ROAD

ST TERESA'S RD

BOTANIC ROAD

PROSPECT AVE

Brian Boru PH

PROSPECT ROAD

CROSS GUNS BRIDGE

Mountjoy Prison

Royal Canal

PHIBSBOROUGH ROAD

ROYAL CANAL BANK

Phibsborough Library

Doyle's Corner

Dalymount Park

N

500m (550yd)

CABRA ROAD

St Peter's

BLACQUIERE BRIDGE

NORTH CIRCULAR ROAD

NORTH CIRCULAR ROAD

8. Ben Dunne, retailer and owner of Ireland's largest retail multiple, Dunnes Stores (1983).
9. Eamon de Valera, revolutionary, politician, a central figure in modern Irish history, Taoiseach and President of Ireland (1975).
10. Margaret Burke Sheridan, Ireland's first international soprano, sang at La Scala, Milan and with Count John McCormick (1958).
11. Maud Gonne MacBride, famed revolutionary, actress, natural beauty, human rights campaigner and romantically admired by W.B. Yeats (1953).
12. Jim Larkin, charismatic trade union leader and indefatigable defender of workers' rights (1947).
13. I.R.A. Memorial, to various members of that organisation.
14. Indian Mutiny, to those that were involved in the Connaught Rangers Mutiny of 1920.
15. Republican Plot, Republicans killed in both the War of Independence and the Civil War.
16. Countess Markievicz fought in the 1916 Easter Rising and became the first woman to be elected to the British Parliament.
17. John Devoy, Fenian leader, later based in America where he attempted to organise help for the Easter Rising (1928).
18. The O'Rahilly, a founder of the Irish Volunteers, who died leading a charge at British Army barricades in the Easter Rising (1916).
19. Cathal Brugha, prominent member of the Irish Volunteers, involved on the Anti-Treaty side in the Civil War, killed in O'Connell Street (1922).
20. O'Donovan Rossa, Prominent Fenian revolutionary at whose burial Patrick Pearse delivered his famous speech signalling the coming Rising (1915).
21. William Dargan, builder of Ireland's first and several subsequent railways. Organised a major industrial exhibition which included an art exhibition that led to the inaugural collection of the National Art Gallery. Died bankrupt (1866).
22. Sir Roger Casement, knighted for his service on behalf of human rights in the Congo and Peru. His efforts to obtain German help for the Rising of 1916 led to his execution by hanging in London's Pentonville Prison. His body was returned to Ireland in 1965 (1916).
23. Michael Collins (see main text) (1922).

Drive a Coach and Six

The path to the left of the main office will bring you past the plots dedicated to members of the Irish Army who died in the Civil War, on home duties or serving overseas with the United Nations. In the centre is the memorial to Michael Collins, revolutionary leader and commander-in-chief of the Government forces during the Civil War in which he was killed in an ambush in 1922. Continue past graves mostly dating from the end of the 19th century and whose headstones are inscribed with an all-too-brief synopsis of life and death. The high child mortality rate in the 19th century is often sadly portrayed on headstone inscriptions such as on Alderman Farrell's: '...his children Patrick 6 years, Anna Teresa and Josephine who died young, grandchildren Michael who died young and Desmond aged 9, his son

Patrick 33 years.' The Alderman himself, however, died at the ripe old age of 98! At the end of this path is a large open space known as the Angels Plot where infants were once buried. Turn left with the path skirting the horticultural nursery beside which the 'Unknowns' and the 1872 cholera victims were interred.

Leave the cemetery by the two World War memorials and Prospect Gate into Prospect Square (if this gate is closed return to the main entrance and use the map to reach this point). This was the original entrance into Glasnevin Cemetery (until 1879) and Prospect Avenue, which leads directly to it, was opened by Daniel O'Connell to avoid mourners having to pay tolls at the turnpikes on Finglas Road. His success in outflanking the toll gatherers led to his famous promise that he would next 'drive a coach and six' through the Act of Parliament (his attempt to repeal the infamous Act of Union). Kavanagh's Pub, now a trendy place in its own right, was in those early days a most popular rendezvous for post-funeral liquid commiserations.

Lush Green and Exotica

Follow Prospect Avenue into Botanic Road. Built to manufacture Players cigarettes, the premises of Smurfit Web Press is a good example of the eloquent industrial architecture of prestigious 19th-century firms. The Sunnybank Hotel used to be a nursing home and as such was the first place this author saw the light of day. The road of red-bricked assorted suburban houses now approaches Mobhi Road, a reminder of the sixth century monastery and school of St Mobhi whose scholars included St Canice and St Columcille. Stay on Botanic Road until it reaches the entrance gates to the **National Botanic Gardens**. In the 19th century this part of Glasnevin became a fashionable retreat for the wealthy and several notable demesnes were laid out. One such demesne was owned by the poet Thomas Tickell (1686–1740) who was often visited by distinguished fellow literati including Thomas Addison, Jonathan Swift, Sir Richard Steele and Thomas Parnell. Part of Tickell's estate was purchased in 1795 by the Royal Dublin Society with the support of the Irish Parliament to provide a place to advance the study of botany.

In 1877 the Gardens were placed under direct government control and since extended to cover 48 acres (19.5 hectares), they contain more than 20,000 plant species and cultivars. If you wish to explore the gardens more fully than is outlined here you can consult the available maps on site. The walk here invites you to start via the Thomas Moore Rose (*Rosa chinensis*) raised from a cutting which inspired the immortal song *The Last Rose of Summer* and on past the various flower beds to the Great Palm House and the Orchid House. The Botanic Gardens reputedly carried out the world's first attempt to raise orchids from seed to the flowering stage (1844). Other firsts include the hybridisation of the insectivorous pitcher plants and the introduction to European gardens of pampas grass.

From these glass houses go across to the magnificently restored Curvilinear Range Glasshouse built by Dublin ironmaster, Richard Turner between 1843 and 1876. Turner also designed the large glasshouse in London's Kew Gardens. Make a side trip to the Rose Gardens beside the River Tolka before finally entering the Cactus, Aquatic and Fern houses. When you leave the gardens cross the road to either a city-bound bus or relax for a while in the Addison Lodge Hotel.

Griffith Avenue to
Clontarf Castle

Summary: What was once the land of country estates started to be developed in the 1920s to urgently rehouse people living in insanitary or unsafe city-centre dwellings. The land is now covered in a kaleidoscopic carpet of suburban public and private housing. Dublin is still a city where most people seem to prefer their own house with a front and rear garden rather than an apartment although the latter option is appealing to a growing sector. However, many interesting vestiges of past glories and wide open spaces still remain and the itinerary offers an opportunity for a brisk and engaging walk. The district is situated on the Northside only about 1³/₄ miles (3 kilometres) from the city centre (12 minutes by bus).

Start:	Institute of Adult Education, Griffith Avenue (Ascal Griofa = Griffith Avenue). Bus: 123. Car parking available along Griffith Avenue. DART Station: Clontarf Castle.
Finish:	Clontarf Castle (Caisleán Cluain Tairbh = Castle of the Meadow of the Bulls). Bus: 130. DART Station: Clontarf Road 1 mile (1¹/₂ kilometres) walking distance. Car parking on roads in the vicinity.
Length:	6 miles (9.6 kilometres).
Time:	2¹/₂ hours.
Refreshments:	Pubs along the route. Full facilities at end of the walk in Clontarf Castle Hotel.
Pathway status:	Roadside and parkland paths.
Best Time to Visit:	Any time. Try to complete your tour of St Anne's Park in daylight as there are no public lights within.
Route Notes:	No difficulties and except for a gradual and minor incline along the Malahide Road the route is ideal (but perhaps too lengthy) for wheelchairs.
Connecting Walk:	From this walk take Bus 130 to start the following walk, Sutton Coastal.

Get off the bus at the Charlemont housing estate and enter past the landscaped gate pillars. After the first row of houses turn right but stop before the entrance gates to the **Marino Institute of Education**. The gates have survived being relocated twice. They were first erected in Fairview as the imposing entrance gates to Lord Charlemont's Estate in the mid 1750s. Lord Charlemont named his estate Marino (small sea) as a memory of his Grand Tour to Italy. In 1925 the gates were moved to the site of the modern entrance pillars you just passed and a few years ago they were moved again to their present location. The family motto carved on the piers, *Deo Duce, Ferro Comitante* means 'With God as my Guide, my Sword by my Side'. The Institute itself was previously the Headquarters and Missionary College for the Irish Christian Brothers who were founded in 1802 by Kilkenny-born Edmund Ignatius Rice who was beatified in 1996.

Retrace your steps back to Griffith Avenue and its glorious double row of trees. Begun in 1924 and finished four years later, it was Dublin's first all-concrete road. Named after Arthur Griffith, founder of Sinn Fein and President of Dáil Éireann in 1922, it is considered to be one of the most elegant and picturesque avenues in the city. It stretches from here for a further 1³/₄ miles (3 kilometres) in the opposite direction to our itinerary. The church of St Vincent de Paul, parish church of Marino, was opened in 1928 to accommodate the mushrooming population of the area. It is flanked by primary schools on both sides including, on the left, Scoil Mhuire (Mary's School) which was opened by the Christian Brothers to help in the training of their novices.

Vampires and Turnpikes
Cross the pedestrian lights and walk down St Declan's Terrace and turn left into St Declan's Road and Carleton Road. These roads are part of Marino, a vast and imaginatively laid out housing estate built in the 1920s by Dublin Corporation to start the relief of Dublin's chronic housing shortage. When you reach the busy Malahide Road cross at the lights to the far side. The large green area to your right is Fairview Park, a land fill area where once the sea washed up to the roadside. Enter Marino Crescent, built in 1792 by a painter named Folliot who, bearing a grudge against Lord

Marino Crescent

137

Charlemont, erected the charming terrace of houses to deny the earl a view of the sea from his Marino House. Its a far cry from the chilling Transylvanian world of the tormented undead to the agreeable ambience of Marino Crescent where probably not even a harmless bat ever bothered to venture but it was at No. 15 that Bram Stoker, author of *Dracula*, was born. Emerge into the Howth Road and turn up Copeland Avenue to arrive again at the Malahide Road.

In 1786, in order to earn money to maintain the surface of the Malahide Road, turnpike gates were erected at several points to collect tolls ranging from one penny to a shilling. These tolls lasted well into the 19th century and evidence of the turnpike system is still to be found in the milestones placed at intervals along the road. The great red-bricked facade standing behind some playing fields on the left was built as the O'Brien Institute in 1882, a specialised school run by the Irish Christian Brothers. It closed in 1972 and ten years later it was converted into the training headquarters for the Dublin Fire Brigade. It also houses the intriguing **museum** of a fire service that, in its time, led the world in its firefighting techniques.

Mount Temple Comprehensive School, famous as the birthplace of the rock group, U2, was once the site of a quarry for a black stone and was known as The Black Quarries. Also in the grounds is a man-made mound thought to be a prehistoric tumulus. The land became an estate in the mid 1700s and the present red-bricked building dates from 1862 and was erected by Sir Calvert Stronge, Chief Magistrate of the Dublin Metropolitan Police.

Architectural Miniatures and Mammoths
Cross the pedestrian lights and head into Casino Park, a finely designed public housing estate. Turn left and walk through a couple of gateways until you arrive at the **Casino**. Built by James Caulfield, the first Earl of Charlemont, between 1758 and 1776, this charming garden temple is considered to be among the finest examples of 18th-century classical architecture in Europe. In the distance it looks small but close-up its equivalent four-storey height becomes more evident. It is also built over underground rooms and passages. No expense was spared in its construction (costing more than £6 million in today's values) and the building is very cleverly designed. The roof urns serve as chimneys, the outer columns are hollowed to act as drainpipes and the 16 rooms, many exquisitely decorated, have a central heating system built into the walls. The architect was William Chambers and the work was supervised by Roman sculptor Simon Vierpyle. The ornaments were carved by the famous Dublin sculptor, Edward Smyth.

Return to the Malahide Road and cross back again to the other side. The Clontarf Golf Clubhouse was formerly the home of Alex Thom, the well known 19th-century printer and originator of *Thom's Dublin Directory*, which is still published annually to this day. Seven terraced cottages on the left are a reminder of when Donnycarney was just a tiny village. Like Marino, it grew when Dublin Corporation selected the district to resettle people from the appalling tenements in the city centre. Tradition points to St Patrick as the founder of a chapel in Donnycarney but there are no remains of any pre-Norman church in the area. Today there is the huge church of **Our Lady of Consolation**, dating from 1969,

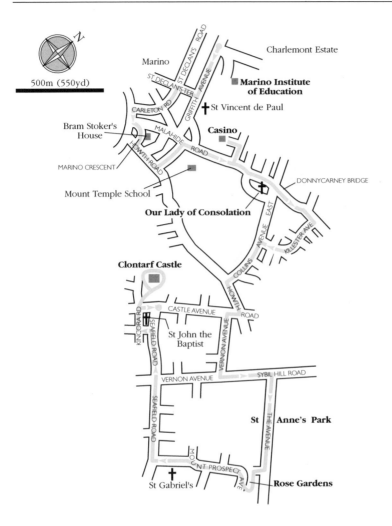

which was built from the voluntary contributions of parishioners to replace a temporary tin structure.

Cross the junction with Collins Avenue – in its less grand days it was known as Pukstown Lane and it is now named after Michael Collins (see page 134). At a self-hire shop there is the short red-bricked parapet of Donnycarney Bridge (1896) which spans the now culverted Wad River (formerly called the Holly Brook). Further up the road, behind the trees and houses, can be seen the grey exterior of St David's Secondary School, home to the nationally famous Artane Boys' Band (founded 1872) and formerly the Artane Industrial School (1870–1969), a corrective institution for boys. The stone used in the building came from the medieval Artaine Castle, home to the Hollywood family, sadly demolished in 1825. The

Castle was the scene in 1534 of the murder of Archbishop John Allen, a friend of King Henry VIII, by the soldiers of Silken Thomas Fitzgerald (see page 72).

A Demesne and a Bounty of Roses

Turn right into Killester Avenue (named after Cill Easra or the Church of Easra) following the map until you reach the Howth Road, turning first left then right into Castle Avenue (the medieval road connecting Artane with the sea) followed by a first left again into Vernon Avenue. The hospital on your right is the Central Remedial Clinic, a rehabilitation centre offering advanced treatment and training for people with disabilities. At the end of this road, turn left into Sybil Hill Road – Sybil was a daughter of the Guinness family (see below) – and halfway along cross over to and enter **St Anne's Park**, a 484-acre (196-hectare) park run by Dublin Corporation since 1939. In 1835 the demesne was purchased by the Guinness family from the Vernons of Clontarf Castle. Originally a smaller holding, the estate was expanded and beautified by Benjamin and Elizabeth Guinness and today it is an extensive park with playing fields, hidden walled gardens, tree-lined walks, an ornamental lake area and the renowned Rose Garden. Dublin Corporation operates a large nursery here which helps to supply the average of 15,000 new trees planted throughout the city every year. Altogether the Corporation tends to more than 100 parks of varying sizes (the Phoenix Park and St Stephen's Green are both in the care of the Office of Public Works and the outer suburban parks are looked after by one of the three county councils). To reach the Rose Garden follow the main road and take the second main turn on the right.

Exit the park into Mount Prospect Avenue, past St Gabriel's Catholic Church and turn right into Seafield Road. This road cuts through the centre of Clontarf, a highly sought-after suburb of Dublin. Clontarf is best known as the battleground on which the Irish High King, Brian Boru, resoundedly defeated a coalition of Vikings and rival Irish troops in 1014 thus ending two centuries of Norse domination. The actual location of the main battle was nearer to Fairview and Drumcondra. Continue across Vernon Avenue until you almost reach the graceful church of St John the Baptist (opened in 1866) with its 150-foot (45.7-metre) spire and an outstanding east window representing, in stained glass, the 12 apostles. A left turn into a pedestrian lane will give a good view of the church and bring you to Kincora Road where you will turn right. The road is named after Brian Boru's reputed birthplace in Co Clare.

Clontarf Castle

At the roundabout, head over to the castellated entrance to the grounds of **Clontarf Castle**. First founded in 1172 by the Norman Adam de Phepoe, the castle formed part of an inner ring defence around Dublin. When Oliver Cromwell arrived in 1649 the castle was granted to his quartermaster general, John Vernon. The Vernons were to remain until the 1950s. The old castle had fallen into decay and was totally reconstructed by architect William Morrison in 1835. An attempt had been made to preserve the Norman tower but faulty foundations frustrated this endeavour. In any event the 70-foot (21-metre) tower was rebuilt in the fashion of the original keep and the rest took the form of a Tudor Revival style. The heraldic badge over the front entrance carries the Vernon motto, *Vernon Semper Viret* – 'Vernon Always Flourishes'. The interior has several noteworthy features including timber beams, stained glass windows and a great hall, gallery and sweeping staircase. Also provided are the refreshments you may need after your exertions.

Just behind the castle is the old **graveyard** which contains the ruins of a 17th-century church and may even be the site of an early Christian monastery of St Comgall (517–603). It also holds the remains of many prominent personages who have given their names to several of Clontarf's roads. It can be accessed from a gate at the terminus of the 130 bus, your transport to the city.

Clontarf Castle

Sutton Coastal

Summary: This is a pleasant seaside walk starting at North Bull Island, an island which is barely 200 years old, and ending at the isthmus of Howth Peninsula, a land mass of 500 million years antiquity. On the way you will pass an area that supports an incredible array of birdlife and other flora and fauna. In fact Bull Island was declared a UNESCO biosphere reserve in 1981, a unique privilege for an urban location (Dublin's O'Connell St is only 3 miles [5 kilometres] away). In 1988 it was designated as a National Nature Reserve. An Interpretative Centre is open to the public on the island. Much of this itinerary is along a newly developed walkway and cycle path where you will most likely encounter scores of Dubliners taking exercise and the sea air. Dollymount is located to the north-east of the city centre and is only about 15 minutes away by bus.

Start:	Bull Bridge, Dollymount (Baile na Gcorr = Town of the Herons). Bus: 130. DART Station: none. Car parking scarce except along side roads or at the car park on Bull Island itself.
Finish:	Sutton Cross (Suí Fhiontáin = Fintan's Seat). Buses: 31, 31A, 31B, (102 to Malahide). DART Station: Sutton. Parking on side roads or in the Marine Hotel but only if you intend to patronise the hotel.
Length:	5^1/$_2$ miles (8.8 kilometres).
Time:	2^1/$_2$ hours.
Refreshments:	Picnics or a portable snack will have to suffice until you reach Sutton Cross where you can visit either Coffey's Coffee House or the bar and restaurant of the Marine Hotel.
Pathway Status:	Roadway paths, wooden bridge, sandy beach, sand dunes and dedicated pedestrian walkways. Wheelchairs should keep to the roadside for the whole journey. Binoculars useful to view the birdlife but telescopes are available at the Interpretative Centre and on the Causeway.
Best Time to Visit:	Any dry day would be ideal providing it is not too windy, which might make it a little unpleasant to walk along the beach and sand dunes. To observe the migrant seabirds from the Arctic the winter months are the best.

Route Notes: No difficulties but wear shoes suitable for walking on sand.
Connecting Walk: From the previous walk, Griffith Avenue to Clontarf Castle via a short bus ride on Bus 130. This walk also connects with the following walk, Howth.

Dollymount, the start of the excursion, appears to have got its name in the 1830s from Dollymount House which in turn was named in honour of Dolly Vernon, wife of the local major landowner. Your first task is to cross Bull Bridge, a delightful wooden structure originally built in 1819 to facilitate the construction of the North Bull Wall. Thankfully, proposals over the years to replace it with a concrete bridge were all discarded. The present crossing over the creek, known as Crab Lake Water, dates from 1907 and was refurbished in the mid 1980s. Both the bridge and causeway are owned by the Dublin Port and Docks Board and to maintain their private status they are closed to the public one day a year (usually in February).

Rocks and Sandy Places
You can now get a good view of Dublin Harbour with its large cranes and docking facilities and the distant soaring chimneys (680 feet [207metres] high) of the Poolbeg Generating Station. The causeway you are now entering is the North Bull Wall, built between 1820 and 1825 to help keep the entrance to Dublin Harbour clear of sand bars. The work was undertaken following a survey taken on behalf of the Ballast Board in 1800 by Captain William Bligh, of 'Mutiny on the Bounty' fame. You can only walk to about two thirds of its $1^3/_4$ miles (2.7 kilometres) length – the rest of the breakwater is below high tide level. At the end of the public way stands a statue of Our Lady known as the Realt na Mara (Star of the Sea) Memorial erected in 1972 through monies collected by port workers (the sculptor was Cecil King). Beyond the statue is the Bull Lighthouse dating from 1880. Along the wall are the separate ladies' and gents' bathing shelters, a flashback to the time of old decency.

Bull Bridge

143

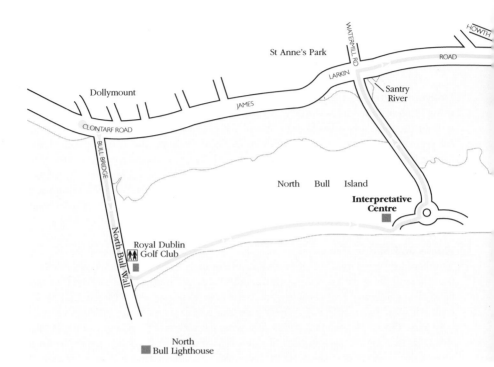

The Royal Dublin Golf Club was founded in 1885 but during the First World War it had to surrender the course to the Army for use as a firing range. When handed back in 1919 it was found to have been pummelled out of all recognition but within three years it had been redesigned and laid out by the famous golf course architect, E.S. Colt. The present club house dates from 1943.

Leave the causeway just beyond the golf club, taking the descending road which leads to the beach car park and the sandy beach itself. If you are lucky, the tide will be coming in showing off its ranks of white breakers, if not, the low tide waters will seem a long distance off. You are now walking on remarkable territory. Around 200 years ago this was open sea but with the building of the South Wall in the 1700s small sandbanks began to emerge from the sea, a process which was accelerated by the construction of the North Bull Wall. The isolated sandbanks became interconnected and with their dunes held by marram grass (it has 16-foot [5-metre] long roots), red fescue and yellow ragwort the whole evolved into one island. Bull Island is still growing and is now approximately 3 miles (5 kilometres) in length.

Birds of a Feather

Enjoy the walk along the beach and, depending on the weather, perhaps indulge in a foot paddle. The flanking sand dunes and their surrounds support an ecosystem of great international importance and they form one of only a couple of natural vegetation areas in greater Dublin. A host of very rare plants grows here including

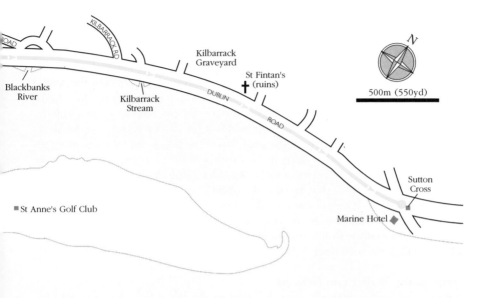

orchids such as early purple, pyramidal, bee and autumn lady's tresses. The insect wild life is abundant and mammals such as mountain or blue hares, rabbits, mice, rats and foxes all contribute their share. Birds of prey, among them kestrel, merlin, peregrine falcons, short-eared owls and occasional buzzards keep the ground population in check. In the sea common and grey seals are plentiful. When you reach the red and yellow lifeguard huts (about halfway along the beach) turn inland and climb through the sand dunes (or use the road further along the beach) until you reach the **Bull Island Interpretative Centre** (opened 1986), which is run by Dublin Corporation. The Centre and its helpful staff provide information brochures, displays, slide shows and viewing areas to help you to more fully appreciate the abundant and varied flora and fauna of the island.

North Bull Island and its highly specialised habitats was first recognised as a bird sanctuary in 1931. The combination of sand dunes, tidal mud flats, fresh water creek and salt marshes has attracted several species of birds not found in the same numbers per hectare anywhere else in Ireland. The normal resident summer population of little tern (they come just for the summer from Africa), some curlew and oystercatchers who often stay over from a previous winter, herring gulls and others is massively increased by the incoming migration of wintering birds, a process which starts in late October. Most renowned are the 3,000 or so Brent geese who fly in from Arctic Canada via Greenland and Iceland. Joining them will be 30,000 wading birds (lapwings, dunlins, curlews, redshanks, etc.) and 15,000 ducks (widgeon, shelduck, mallard, etc.). This book is not the adequate place to describe in detail the wonders of Bull Island but the Interpretative Centre should fill this need.

When you can finally tear yourself away from the Interpretative Centre head for the adjoining roundabout and the causeway road passing another Golf Club, St Anne's, founded in 1921. The location of the Interpretative Centre was the original site of St Anne's clubhouse but it has since been moved further up the island. The wide causeway was opened in 1965 to remove the intolerable volumes of traffic on the old wooden bridge. The journey down the causeway gives an excellent view of the salt marshes and then the mud flats if the tide is out. A coin-operated telescope is available half way along the footpath. On the far right, alder trees have begun to establish themselves naturally in the alder marsh. These trees are likely to be followed by Scots Pine showing that the island is discernibly evolving in the span of a single lifetime. The causeway road comes out on to the James Larkin Road beside St Anne's Park (see the previous walk) at the bottom of Watermill Road. The latter gets its name from a watermill that was once worked by the Santry River which parallels the road until it disgorges into the lagoon beside the causeway.

Invigorating Walk to an Isthmus

A quickened pace is probably now the order of the day if full advantage is to be taken of the good surface and the sea air. It will be sufficient to note only a few items as you approach the wonderful setting of the Howth Peninsula. The pathway you are on is, by the way, designated as a Slí na Sláinte (literally Way of Health) one of a number of such walks designated by the Irish Heart Foundation in conjunction with the local council. Watch out for fast-moving roller bladers, though. As you approach the converging Howth Road, the houses on the hill above are part of Bettyglen, named after Betty, one of the daughters of the Guinness family who resided at St Anne's Estate. A culverted river called the Blackbanks, which gives its name to the district where the two roads join, empties into the lagoon at the junction. More than a century ago, before the tramline to Howth was built, this part of the old road was called 'The Whip of the Water', a reference to where the incoming tides from both ends of the islands met with some violence (that was before the causeway blocked off the southern flow). The same tramway, built in the 1880s, helped to end the isolation of Howth and brought many new residents, holidaymakers and day trippers to the area.

Along this stretch of coastline you will often notice a type of tree which has the appearance of a palm but it is not. It is the Cordyline, an Australian plant, but now ubiquitous along Ireland's East Coast. Next to pass by is the square block of the Kilbarrack Sewage Pumping Station. It stands where the Kilbarrack Road joins the Howth Road which from here becomes the Dublin Road. Yet another culverted river, the Kilbarrack Stream, meets the lagoon at this point. Kilbarrack Graveyard contains the ruins of St Fintan's Church, a structure which dates, in part, from the 9th century. The belfry was built in the Middle Ages. Adjacent to the church is St Fintan's Holy Well whose waters are said to have curative powers. Just beyond Baldoyle Road and before Binn Eadair View stands an old house which was once a lodge to Warren Villa Estate, former home of the McDowells, the well known jewellers and owners of Caughoo, the 1947 winner of the Aintree Grand National. The lodge was once a post office, hence notice the wall-mounted post box.

Sutton

The pathway now rejoins the roadside path which swings away from the coast and arrives at a crossroads on the 1,312-foot (400-metre) wide isthmus known as Sutton Cross. It was from here that the famous Hill of Howth Tramway commenced its circuit until the line was closed down in 1959. It is some consolation, thanks to Jim Kilroy, a tram restoration expert and a local legend, that one of the tramcars has been fully rehabilitated and may soon be working again from the National Transport Museum in Howth (see the following walk). Sutton is one of the earliest prehistoric sites around Dublin and 5,000-year-old middens (refuse dumps) have revealed polished stone axe heads among other items. The advent of the train and tram turned Sutton and its surrounding beaches into something of a seaside resort. The famous portrait artist, James Abbot McNeill Whistler (1834–1903) lived here for a while in 1900.

For historical as well as perhaps for refreshment reasons visit the Marine Hotel. Established in 1897 as the Golfers Hotel, it was renamed the Marine Hotel when it was rebuilt after a fire in 1932. The lobby contains some fine maritime paintings. Go through the hotel on to the rear lawns which overlook the sea and where in fine weather you can relax and sip a drink. The back of the hotel was built as the front originally and the rise in the ground level halfway down the lawn is the site of the old Sutton coast road. Now return home by DART or bus or resuscitate yourself for the next walk, the longest of them all!

Royal Dublin Golf Course

147

Howth

Summary: If Killiney is perhaps the most spectacular walk on the Southside of the city, on the Northside this honour has to go to Howth. Just as the climb around Dalkey and Killiney is over 'developed' land, the ascents and walks around Howth are over fairly rugged and natural terrain. Howth (from the Norse name Hoved, meaning a head) is of extremely ancient geological formation of quartz and slate and until comparatively recent times was an island until an isthmus of gravel formed, thus connecting it to the main land. More than half the total of Ireland's plant species can be found in Howth where an abundance of wildlife and seabirds have also found sanctuary. The walk is both bracing and breathtaking along routes varying from cliff-hugging pathways to exposed promontories, all ending in the cosiness of a charming fishing village. A transport museum and an inhabited ancient castle round off the excursion. Howth Peninsula, 10 miles (16 kilometres) from Dublin, is well served by public transport. DART is recommended for at least one side of your round trip.

Start: Sutton Cross (Suí Fhiontáin = Seat of Fintan). Buses: 31, 31A, 31B, 102 from Malahide. DART Station: Sutton. Parking available at Sutton Station (usually full on weekdays), Superquinn Shopping Centre and Marine Hotel (both exclusively for the use of their patrons).

Finish: Howth Village (Binn Eadhair = Eadhair's Hill). Buses: 31, 31B (indirect route departing from DART Station). DART Station: Howth. Parking available along Harbour Front.

Length: Full walk 8 miles (12.8 kilometres) but there are shorter options.

Time: 3^1/$_2$ hours. It might be best to allow for a full day, breaking the walk at some point near or in Howth Village for a meal and allowing enough time fully to explore the varied scenery.

Refreshments: At Sutton Cross there is a coffee shop (Coffey's Coffee House) beside the Shopping Centre or else try the Marine Hotel's budget lunch. Your next opportunity will be just beyond the halfway stage at the Summit Inn. Once you reach Howth there are four hotels, several pubs and restaurants ranging from the economic to the expensively chic.

Pathway Status: About half of the route is on roadside pathways or tarmacadam but the remainder is over rough trodden paths through gorse heather and open grasslands. Some of these paths can be muddy after rain or composed of loose stones. However, provided you wear trousers or jeans (to protect against the thorny bushes) and strong, flat and comfortable footwear and exercise due caution there is no special difficulty or danger. Take a walking stick if you want the support of one. Only average fitness is required to negotiate the steeper climbs.

Best Time to Visit: A warm, sunny day allows you the best environment to enjoy the natural surroundings and the panoramic views. I have travelled the route with snow and ice on the ground in a harsh easterly wind but the extreme weather only made the walk more bracing and the welcome of Howth's warming hostelries more inviting. Sunset views are beautiful from Howth Summit but abandon the subsequent cliff walk in the dark.

Route Notes: It is possible to cut out elements of the walk or terminate the walk at various stages where the path crosses a bus route. These are marked on the map. Bring a pair of binoculars if at all possible. Ad hoc picnic sites are available.

Connecting Walk: Directly from the last walk, Sutton Coastal. This also connects with the next walk, Malahide: take the bus or DART to Sutton Cross then a bus to Portmarnock.

Arriving at Sutton Cross take the road (Greenfield Road) which goes off to the left of the Marine Hotel. Your main objective rises up like a mini mountain range – Howth Summit. But first enjoy a pleasant coastal walk along the tidal shore. If the tide is out you can walk on the beach past stranded boats and people digging for fish bait. At the next junction keep to the coastal road (Strand Road) – rejoin the road if you have been on the beach. The road now narrows and the path disappears but hug the wall facing the on-coming traffic of which there is very little anyway. From here you will be able to appreciate the vast expanse of the Dublin and Wicklow mountains beyond the bay. Shortly after overtaking the Sutton Dinghy Club you will arrive at a group of houses with interesting architectural prominences, the very apogee of Victorian coastal design. Just beyond these houses where the road curves away from the strand and the first house on your right hand side appears, enter a well-trodden laneway which still skirts the coastline.

A Tower and a Rock

To the left of the rather flat terrain and in among the trees is the red-brick Sutton Castle Hotel which was built as a private manor in the 19th century. Ahead is a Martello Tower converted somewhat for domestic use but its rather forlorn look is emphasised by its desolate location. The rock foundations of the tower are impressive. Continue walking along what is now becoming a cliff walk. From here to the North East corner of the peninsula the cliffs and hidden coves provide shelter for an abundance of seabirds including herring gulls, kittiwakes, fulmars, razorbills, guillemots and the larger cormorants and kestrels. Offshore, two species of seal are fairly widespread, the common and grey seal.

A large clump of rock now appears ahead, its colour giving the district its name, Red Rock. Take the left track around the rock formation (at the sign announcing 'Warning No Through Path') and head towards the distant houses. At another sign, 'Warning Dangerous Cliffs', turn left again which will lead you through the shrub-

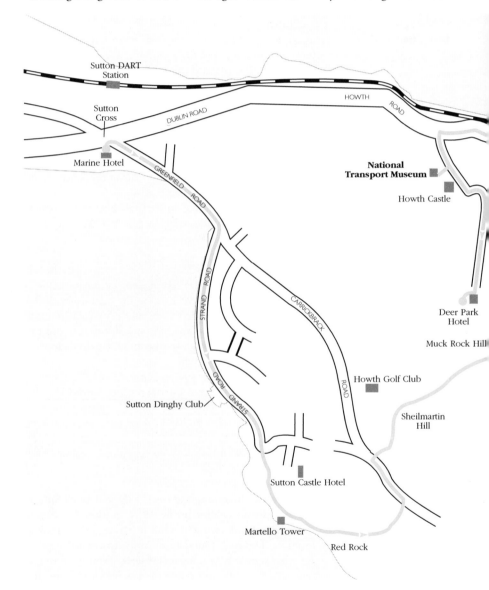

bery and a derelict metal gateway on to Carrickbrack Road. Carefully cross this road and head left until you encounter the unobstructed view of the next hill.

Hills and Valleys

At an open part of the low walls dividing the path from the hill begin your steepish climb to the top of Sheilmartin Hill, at 550 feet (168 metres) the tallest point in Howth. (There is a more gentle gradient path to the left which avoids the higher

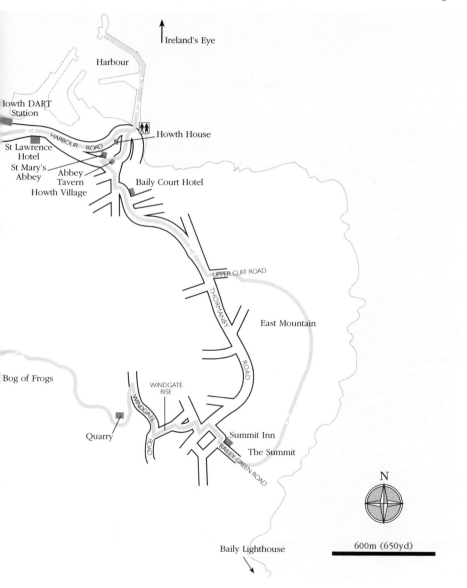

climb but our chosen route is more rewarding.) The path is stony so care is needed. This side of the hill is dominated by gorse showing off yellow, coconut-scented flowers. Beware of the vicious little spines of the plant stems. Pause from time to time to take in the panorama below and beyond from the patchwork of small farms and the sweeping expanse of the North Bull Island to the Bay, Dublin Harbour and city and the distant mountains. Much of this area is subject to gorse fires in the summer droughts (Howth is reputedly one of the driest parts of Ireland) but as far as the flora is concerned this is an entirely natural phenomenon to which the heathland plants have successfully adapted. Buried seeds quickly germinate with the added fertility of the nutrient rich ash. While the heather and gorse are struggling to re-establish themselves, the purple flowers of the tall rosebay willowherb predominate. About two thirds of the way up, way over to the right, is a mound of stone, a cairn under which is believed lie the remains of King Crimthan, a 1st-century monarch of Howth.

Bog of Frogs
On finally reaching the summit you can rest a while on the rocks taking in a breathtaking view. The by now familiar view of Dublin Bay is mirrored by the seascapes stretching away to the North. Immediately below Sheilmartin are the manicured fairways of the Howth Golf Club surrounded by a number of lower hills. Make your way down the path, this time through a carpet of heather which from July to September displays a profusion of crimson-purple flowers. The object of the exercise is to now get clear of the golf course as quickly as possible to avoid both being hit by stray balls and damaging the course itself. Follow the path outlined by white stones until you reach the Muck Rock Hill and keep to the northern edge of the Bog of Frogs, a valley peat bog. It is close to a group of four Scots pine trees and is raised slightly above the level of the surrounding ground. Typically a bog of this kind (and this is only a miniature example) is formed when dead vegetation accumulates in acidic conditions and when microscopic organisms who promote decay fail to survive and only partly decomposed material, i.e. peat, is left behind. Various sheltered spots around here are suitable for a picnic but be sure to take your rubbish away.

There are many paths and tracks in the area and it is easy to get confused but even if you take a wrong path head east all the time and you will re-emerge somewhere along Windgate Road. Your best route is to join the path near some high pylons that will take you between the Loughoreen Hills and Black Linn, past a quarry and out on to Windgate Road. Turn right, then left into Windgate Rise near the end of which is an exit covered by three bollards which will lead into Thormanby Road. A guiding light ahead is the Summit Inn where you may seek victuals and repose. Next continue up Bailey Green Road to the viewing area where there is a stupendous prospect that encompasses the whole bay area with its varied shipping and miscellaneous lighthouses and to the east, on a clear day, a glimpse of the Welsh Mountains is sometimes possible.

Far below, on the Dun Griffin promontory, is the Baily Lighthouse. The L-shaped bungalow on the top of the summit incorporates part of the first lighthouse

Plate 32: *Picturesque Coliemore Harbour at Dalkey services local lobster boats and is the starting point for day trips to Dalkey Island (see page 118).*

Plate 33: *Dun Laoghaire is the gateway to Ireland for many of the visitors who arrive from Britain by ferry (see page 110).*

Plate 34: *Beautifully landscaped Italianate gardens in the grounds of Powerscourt, near Bray (see page 127) stretch towards the distant hills.*

Plate 35: *The coastal walk from Sutton Cross to Howth (see page 148) offers spectacular scenery and an opportunity to enjoy nature at its best.*

Plate 36: *The delightful fishing village of Howth boasts one of Ireland's important harbours as well as a wealth of other attractions (see page 153).*

Plate 37: *The Jameson/Haig marriage plaque (see page 158).*

Plate 38: *The fine medieval Great Hall at Malahide Castle (see page 160).*

Plate 39: *Malahide Castle, on the coast north of Dublin, is the oldest continuously inhabited castle in Ireland (see page 160).*

Baily Lighthouse

built in 1667. The present lighthouse was erected in 1814. The light source then was no more than 250 candlepower but experiments to improve light and lenses, carried out at the Baily by John Wigham in the 1860s, were to revolutionise the efficacy of lighthouses around the world. The strength of the present light is more than 1.2 million candlepower and it can be seen from a distance of 26 miles (42 kilometres). Dun Griffin promontory is said to have been the site of King Crimthan's fort from where he made frequent pillaging attacks on Roman Britain. The Danes used the fort as a refuge of last resort following their defeat in 1014.

A Village with a Fishy Tale
Take the upper cliff walk which is a relatively wide and safe pathway swinging around East Mountain and leading eventually into Upper Cliff Road. Since 1996 this whole area, along with the cliff terrain to Red Rock on the south side, has been protected from further development by a special government order. From Upper Cliff Road move downhill along Thormanby Road into the fishing village of Howth, a place where, until recently, progress had passed by. The new buildings that are coming on stream are, by and large, in sympathetic agreement or contrast to the old and the village is taking on a more welcome sophistication.

Keep heading downhill until having passed the Baily Court Hotel choose the left hand road at the next junction. The parochial hall (1814) was the original church for the Roman Catholics until the present church (which you passed a few minutes ago) was opened in 1899. Straight ahead is one of the most important buildings in Howth, St Mary's Abbey with its graveyard and collegiate building.

Founded first by Norse King Sitric of Dublin in 1042 the present ruin dates from between the 13th century and the 15th century. The altar tomb in the Mortuary Chapel carries, among others, the arms of the St Lawrence family (see Howth Castle). Return to Abbey Street via the stone steps to your right coming outside beside the Abbey Tavern one of the best-known entertainment pubs in Dublin, where Irish ballads and so on may be heard. The castellated walls of the abbey merge into some apartment and retail complexes which, on the harbour side, have incorporated Howth House, a well-proportioned house with a facade of dressed granite. It was built around 1807 for Captain George Taylor, the engineer in charge of building Howth Harbour. The craggy looking island out to sea just beyond the harbour mouth is Ireland's Eye. The name is a corruption of Eria's Ey, *Ey* being the Norse for Island and Eria was confused with Erin, Irish for Ireland! It is possible to take a licensed boat out to the island to see its ruined Church of the Sons of Nessan and the Martello Tower.

Promenading

If you are not too tired (there is still more than a mile [1¹/₂ kilometres] to go) take a side trip down the east pier on the top deck and return by the lower level along the inner harbour. Stone for the piers was quarried locally and the work, to turn Howth into the main packet station between Dublin and Britain, was completed in 1812. More than adequate in size – it is 52 acres (21 hectares) in area – the harbour continually silted up and was abandoned in favour of Dun Laoghaire. It offers ideal berthage now to leisure yachts and fishing trawlers. The Howth Yacht Club has some good facilities here and an admirable clubhouse. Close by is the lifeboat station, an essential service in these parts.

The west side of the harbour is reserved for the Howth Fishing Fleet, one of the country's largest. Several fish shops will sell directly to the public offering you fresh cod, whiting, sole, prawn and many other varieties. Opposite the St Lawrence Hotel is the Ready Boat Pillar, a wonderfully crafted 13-foot [4-metre] high stone pillar sculpture with 15 panels depicting the Four Ages of Howth (sculptor, Sean O'Dwyer, 1996).

Old Transport and an Older Castle

A short walk out of the village by way of the St Lawrence Hotel and the DART Station will bring you to the entrance of the **National Transport Museum** and Howth Castle. The Transport Museum is packed (literally) with a huge range of vehicles from a fully restored Hill of Howth Tram to a humble horse-drawn delivery vehicle. Trams, buses, fire engines, military vehicles and commercial transport make up an extremely interesting and rare collection.

Further uphill from the museum is the venerable Howth Castle which owes its origins to the Norman knight St Almeric Tristam who wrested the peninsula from the Norsemen in 1177. Sir Almeric adopted the name St Lawrence in honour of the saint on whose feast day the victory occurred. Nothing remains of the original fortifications but the square gate tower is probably mid-15th-century. Down the following centuries more additions and embellishments were added including the

Howth Castle

Gaisford Library Building designed by the eminent architect, Sir Edwin Lutyens. The St Lawrence family still reside in the castle which is unfortunately not open to the public.

Rhodendron Gardens

The 16th-century pirate queen, Grace O'Malley, also known as Granuaille, landed in Howth in 1575 to avoid a storm and called to the castle for dinner. Her way was barred by closed doors and, taking severe umbrage, she kidnapped the owner's son. The young lad was only returned when his father promised never to close the door at dinner time again, a pledge that was faithfully kept for centuries afterwards. Make your way finally past the golf course to the Deer Park Hotel and to the famous **rhododendron gardens**. Nearby is a collapsed portal dolmen known as Aideen's Grave, whose quartzite capstone weighs an unimaginable 90 tonnes. Just how did they assemble and raise stones of this weight 4,500 years ago?

Congratulate yourself on finishing the longest and hardest walk in this book. You deserve a well-earned drink in the Deer Park Hotel or in one of the many other establishments in the village.

Portmarnock to Malahide

Summary: The coastline of Dublin Bay has been dotted for millennia with fishing communities and tiny harbours. At various times in history these small settlements rose in strategic or commercial importance in relation to the capital city only to fall again into obscurity and isolation. Portmarnock and Malahide could be said to fit into such a category but their star has ascended again, this time as dormitory towns and seaside resorts for Dublin. The walk is mainly an invigorating coastal one, taking in the Velvet Beach which is washed not only by high breakers but by a glorious aeronautical past. Towards the end of the walk a modern marina will give way to the longest inhabited castle in Ireland. Both towns are located about 9 miles (15 kilometres) north-east of the city.

Start: Country Club Hotel, Portmarnock (Port Mearnóg = Marnock's Harbour). Buses: 32, 32A. DART Station: none. Public car park next to the Country Club Hotel.

Finish: Malahide Castle, Malahide (Mullach Íde = Ide's Hilltop). Bus: 42. Railway Station: Malahide, offering direct services to city and connections to DART. Car park in Malahide Castle Park, off the Dublin Road or the Back Road.

Length: 4 miles (6.4 kilometres)

Time: 1¹/₂ hours.

Refreshments: In either the Country Club Hotel or the Coffee Shop and Restaurant in Malahide Castle. In Malahide itself there are many fine restaurants and cafés ranging through the whole price spectrum.

Pathway Status: All hard surface paths including some dedicated pedestrian walks unless you abandon them by choice.

Best Time to Visit: Anytime but it would be a shame to walk all the way to Malahide Castle and miss the visiting hours. Malahide Village and its marina also look delightful by night.

Route Notes: Take the right footwear if you want to walk on the beach. For views of the vast panorama, off shore islands or the bird life take a pair of binoculars. Malahide Castle grounds are very suitable for picnics as also are some of the beaches and rocky outcrops along the way.

Connecting Walk: From the previous two walks, Sutton Coastal and Howth by bus 102 from Sutton DART Station.

On arrival in Portmarnock (ask the bus driver to let you off at the Country Club Hotel) enter the front driveway of the Country Club Hotel. You will be struck by a number of competing views straight away. On the right is the 18-hole golf links spread over 180 acres (73 hectares) of undulating dune terrain. To date it is the only PGA European Tour golf course in the country. Its next-door neighbour, the Portmarnock Golf Links, has hosted the Irish Open, the World Cup and the Walker Cup. Many Neolithic artefacts have been found in the vicinity of the hotel links proving that Portmarnock has been settled for thousands of years. Some of these are on view in the hotel. A second- or third-century Ogham stone was found near the third green. Ogham was the earliest form of written language found in

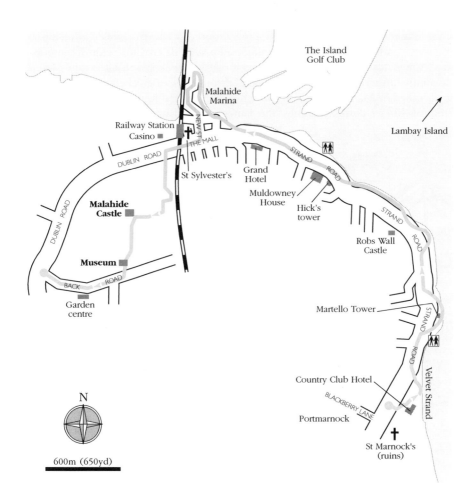

Ireland and consisted of a series of incised strokes along the edges of stone pillars. In an unique gesture to the past, each course marker has been hand-crafted in a manner similar to an ancient Ogham stone. Near where the Ogham stone was found stands the ruin of an early medieval Cistercian church and the site of a holy well, both dedicated to St Marnock, the man who gave his name to the region. Little is known of him except that he was a sixth-century sailor monk whose stories of fabulous lands across the ocean inspired fellow monk, St Brendan, to undertake his great voyages of discovery including, it is speculated, the first European contact with North America. In the adjoining cemetery a horde of 15th-century silver groats and fourpenny pieces were uncovered in 1948. They date from three reigns, Henry V, Henry VI, and Edward IV.

From Golf Links to Royal Links

So much for the golf links et al. Seaward are the great dunes over which you will later climb. To the left is the hotel and the path to the golf clubhouse. Proceed part of the way to the latter until you come to a group of walls which once formed part of a secret garden. Take note of a sculptured plaque dated 1907 with the inscription 'Amor' (love) and carrying carvings of the shamrock and thistle – more about this a little further on. Now enter the hotel through the original entrance of the old house called St Marnock's House and which was owned in the last century by the famous whiskey distilling family, the Jamesons. William George Jameson knew

Malahide Railway Station

how to live well and owned several fine racing yachts in the 1880s. He was on personal terms with the Royal Family and presented one of his yachts, *The Britannia*, to the Prince of Wales who renamed it *The Royal Britannia*, a name that was handed down to subsequent royal yachts. When the same prince became King Edward VII he paid several visits to the Jamesons. The plaque mentioned above was unveiled by the King to mark the nuptials between the members of two great distilling families, Jameson and Haig, hence the shamrock and thistle.

Pioneering Aviators and Weekend Sailors
From the hotel enter the car park and take a path over the dunes to reach the beach. The sudden noise of the breaking waves may be slightly startling, especially if the tide is in. You can continue along the beach or walk up to the roadway path. When the tide is out the 2-mile (3.5-kilometre) length of the beach, the Velvet Strand, is ideal as a smooth and firm runway and a number of early aviators took advantage of it. On 24th June 1930, the Australian Kingsford-Smith and his crew of three, including Dubliner Captain J. P. Saul as navigator, rolled their Fokker Tri-motor Southern Cross down the sand and lifted off for Newfoundland which they reached $31^{1}/_{2}$ hours later. Later the plane landed at Oakland finishing a marathon two-year journey and becoming the first plane to circumnavigate the world at almost its greatest circumference. The first successful solo east west flight across the Atlantic was achieved on 18th August 1932 when Jim Mollison left the Velvet Strand in a deHavilland Puss Moth for Newfoundland. Mollison was the husband of an even more famous aviatrix, Amy Johnson.

Out to sea you may be lucky enough to see a full-blown regatta skimming over the waves, otherwise content yourself with the odd yacht and sail board. Take the lower path around the converted Martello Tower, after which it rises again to meet the road. A large island to the north-east is Lambay Island, once populated by scores of people but now home to only a handful. Of volcanic origin, Lambay was called Limnos by the second-century cartographer Ptolemy. It comprises 1.371 acres (555 hectares) and has its own castle. Smugglers with waving lanterns use to lure unsuspecting ships onto the treacherous rocks, Cecil Baring, of the famous banking firm, bought the island in 1904 and Rupert Baring, Lord Revelstoke, is still resident there. It was the scene in 1854 of the terrible wrecking of the emigrant ship, the *John Tayleur* with the loss of 347 people, the majority of them being women and children.

Malahide Marina
The beach has by now given way to a rocky foreshore. You can lengthen your stride from this point as there are only a couple of distractions between here and Malahide. The first is a tower house which in times past was owned by Cistercian monks who levied fishing boats entering Malahide Harbour. It

is called Robs Wall Castle and for a short time it served as a lighthouse. The second building of interest is Hick's Tower, a very much altered Martello tower built in 1805. It is named after the architect who bought and converted the tower in 1910. A witch rides her broom on the roof apex.

Nearer the village is Muldowney House, home of the renowned 19th-century landscape painter, Nathaniel Hone II. Several of his works can be seen in the National Gallery. He also founded the Malahide Golf Club in 1892. Across the bay is a peninsula, simply but incorrectly known as 'The Island' which contains two further golf links – there is no dearth of golf opportunities along this walk! The Grand Hotel and Conference Centre started life in 1835 as the 'Pink Hotel'. In 1910 it was bought by Dr John Sidney Colohan who was the first person in Ireland to own a petrol-driven motor car. At this point join a narrow coastal path which goes down by the tennis club. Head towards the promenade and the Malahide Marina, a welcome new development which gives a decidedly continental air to the proceedings. The marina is designed to hold 300 boats and many of its clients live in the nearby apartments. At the tip of this little peninsula you will be able to see the railway viaduct, an immense engineering feat of the day although it has been substantially rebuilt a couple of times. Leave Marina Village by the entrance archway and continue up New Street to the cross-roads otherwise known as The Diamond.

A Thatched House and a Mighty Castle
Take a right turn along the Mall passing Old Street, which was the former Main Street of Malahide and was lined with thatched cottages. St Sylvester's Church (1837) at the corner is named after a well halfway down the street which provided a water supply to the medieval fishing settlement. The well has been restored by the Old Malahide Society who have been responsible for much good work around the town. Next is the well-preserved Malahide Railway Station (1904) nostalgically redolent of the steam era. The line was opened to Malahide in 1844. Beyond the station, in a dip on the right hand side of the road, is a thatched glory, the Casino, originally built in the late 17th century as a shooting lodge for the local ruling family, the Talbots. Speaking of the Talbots, now enter their former domain and demesne, **Malahide Castle** and its 268 acres (108 hectares) of leisure space including a magnificent playground, pitch and putt and golf courses, tennis courts, a cricket ground, football pitches and a plethora of walks. Central to the whole park is the castle and this is your first stop.

Malahide Castle is the oldest continuously inhabited castle in Ireland. In 1185 the Malahide lands of the last Viking king of Dublin, Hamund MacTurkill, were confiscated and granted to Sir Richard de Talbot, a knight in the service of Henry II. With the exception of only one interruption during the rule of Oliver Cromwell, the Talbots lived at the castle from the 12th century until the line died out in 1973 – almost 800 years of tenancy! Of course the present building is not the original – it has been greatly added to over the years – but it does include a very early tower. The outer walls and moat are long gone. The Great Hall, with its charming minstrel's gallery, dates from c.1487, the Oak Room, and the Library are 16th-century and the Drawing Rooms are 18th-century. In the late 19th century, the 5th Lord

Talbot married the great-granddaughter of James Boswell, biographer to Dr Samuel Johnson. The contents of the Boswell home came to Malahide c. 1914, including a cabinet in which the celebrated Boswell papers and journals were subsequently discovered. There is a rare collection of antique furniture throughout and the castle is also the home to the National Portrait Collection. If you think every castle should have its ghost then you will be spine-chillingly delighted with Malahide – it is reputedly haunted by no fewer than five spectres!

The World's Largest Model Railway

Situated around the outside of the castle are the 20-acre (8 hectare) botanical gardens featuring more than 5,000 plants from Chile, Australia, Tasmania, New Zealand, California and Africa. The last owner of the castle, Milo Talbot, planted the gardens between 1948 and 1973. At the back entrance to the castle is the ruined Abbey and Graveyard. Across from here, in a purpose-built complex is one of the world's largest model railway layouts, the **Fry Model Railway**. It is based on real scenes from Dublin incorporating many aspects of rail and other transport from all over the country on a track length of $2^3/4$ miles (4.5 kilometres).

Head down the central roadway to the main exit taking a backward look at the castle to see it in its full context. The extensive open grounds became a base from 1916–1918 for a blimp or airship squadron whose job it was to escort ships across the submarine infested Irish Sea. At the gate is a small cottage, which is, in fact, a packed little **museum** run by the Old Malahide Society and is well worth a visit. Turn right outside the gates and head for the bus stop on the Malahide Road passing a thatched roofed garden centre and some beautifully landscaped modern mansions. Alternatively, return to Malahide Railway Station.

Malahide Castle

Further Information

Opening times

Opening times are constantly changing, so telephone before a visit to avoid disappointment. Churches are open at service times as well as at times indicated.

Statutory bodies in charge of Dublin's parks and historical sites

(The international dialling code for Dublin from abroad is your own international access code + 353 1 + the local number).

Department of Arts, Culture and the Gaeltacht, 43 Mespil Road, Dublin 4.
Tel: 667 0788; Fax: 662 0198.

Dublin Corporation, Public Relations, Civic Offices, Wood Quay, Dublin 8.
Tel: 679 6111; Fax: 679 2226.

Fingal County Council, 46/49 Upper O'Connell Street, Dublin 1.
Tel: 872 7777; Fax: 872 5782.

Dun Laoghaire and Rathdown Council, Town Hall, Dun Laoghaire, Co Dublin.
Tel: 280 6961; Fax: 280 6969.

South Dublin Council, Town Centre, Tallaght, Dublin 24.
Tel: 462 0000; Fax: 462 0111.

Wicklow County Council, County Buildings, Wicklow, Co Wicklow.
Tel: (0404) 67324; Fax: (0404) 67792.

SOUTH CITY CENTRE
Tourism Centre, St Andrew's Centre, Suffolk Street, Dublin 2. Tel: 1550 1122 33 (calls charged at 58p per minute from anywhere in Ireland) or 605 7700; Fax: 605 7749.
E-Mail: Dublin Tourism@msn.com
Open 2 Jan–15 Jun and 15 Sep–30 Dec: Mon–Sat 9.00–17.30 (Tues open 9.30);
16 Jun–14 Sep: Mon–Sat 08.30–19.30; Sun 11.00–17.30. Public Holidays 11.00–17.30.

St Ann's Church, Dawson Street, Dublin 2. Tel: 676 2186.
Open during daytime hours and for services and concerts.

Civic Museum, South William Street, Dublin 2.
Tel: 679 4260. *Open* Tues–Sat 10.00–18.00, Sun 11.00–14.00.

St Stephen's Green, c/o Office of Public Works, 51 St Stephen's Green, Dublin 2.
Tel: 661 3111; Fax: 661 0747.
Open Mon–Sat 08.00–dusk; Sun 10.00–dusk.

Newman House, 85 St Stephen's Green, Dublin 2. Tel: 706 7422; Fax: 706 7211.
Open June–Aug: Tues–Fri 12.00–17.00, Sat 14.00–17.00, Sun 11.00–14.00 (closed Mon).
Outside these hours tours arranged by advance arrangement.

National Museum, Kildare Street, Dublin 2. Tel: 677 7444; Fax: 676 6116.
Open Tues–Sat 10.00–17.00, Sun 14.00–17.00. *Admission:* free.

Leinster House, Kildare Street, Dublin 2. Tel: 678 9911.
Groups and individuals may only visit on the invitation of a Public Representative, either a Member of Parliament (Teachta Daile, T.D.), or a Senator (Seanadóir).

National Library, Kildare Street, Dublin 2. Tel: 661 8811.
Open Mon 10.00–21.00, Tues and Wed 14.00–21.00, Thurs and Fri 10.00–17.00, Sat 10.00–13.00. Closed Sun. *Admission:* free but readers have to register.

Royal College of Physicians, Kildare Street, Dublin 2. Tel: 661 6677; Fax: 676 3989.
Visit by advance arrangement is preferable.

Genealogical Office and Heraldic Museum, Kildare Street, Dublin 2. Tel: 6614 877.
Open Mon–Fri 10.00–12.30 and 14.00–16.30.

Trinity College, College Green, Dublin 2. Tel: 677 2941; Fax 677 2694.
Old Library and Book of Kells *Open* Mon–Fri 09.30–16.45, Sat 09.30–12.45. *Admission:* charge. There are also individual museum collections belonging to various departments such as Engineering, Geology, Zoology and Biblical Antiquities. Visits should be arranged with specific departments. The college itself is open during daytime hours (entrances from College Green, Nassau Street and Lincoln Place) and most evenings through the main entrance on College Green only.

TEMPLE BAR
Irish Stock Exchange, 28 Anglesea Street, Dublin 2. Tel: 677 8808.
Open Mon–Fri 09.30–10.30 approx. and 14.15 to 15.15 approx.

Temple Bar Information Centre, 18 Eustace Street, Dublin 2. Tel: 671 5717; Fax: 677 2525.
Open Jun–Aug: Mon–Fri 09.00–18.00, Sat 11.00–16.00, Sun 12.00–16.00. Sep–May: Mon–Fri 09.00–18.00.

Irish Film Centre, 6 Eustace Street, Dublin 2. Tel: 679 5744; Fax: 677 8755.
Offices and shop open during normal office hours. Cinemas and bar open until late evening.

House of Lords, Bank of Ireland, College Green, Dublin 2. Tel: 677 6801.
Open Mon–Fri 10.00–16.00; Thurs 10.00–17.00.

VIKING AND MEDIEVAL DUBLIN
Dublin's Viking Adventure and Feast, Essex Street West, Temple Bar, Dublin 2. Tel: 679 6040; Fax: 679 6033.
Open Mon, Thurs and Fri 10.00–16.30, Sat, Sun and Public Hols 11.00–17.30. *Admission:* charge. Advance booking for feast (held in the evenings) Tel: 605 7777.

Dublinia, St Michael's Hill, Dublin 8. Tel: 679 4611; Fax: 679 7116.
Open Apr–Sep: 10.00–17.00, Oct–Mar: Mon–Sat 11.00–16.00, Sun 10.00–16.30.
Admission: charge.

Christ Church Cathedral, Christchurch Place, Dublin 8. Tel: 677 8099; Fax: 679 8991.
Open daily May–Sep 09.30–17.00, Oct–Apr 09.30–16.00. Tours 11.30 on Wednesdays.
Donation requested.

Mother Red Caps, Bar, Restaurant and Market, Back Lane, Dublin 8. Tel: 453 8306
(Bar and Restaurant only).
Open afternoons Fri, Sat, Sun.

Iveagh Markets, Francis Street, Dublin 8. Tel: 454 2090.
Open Mon–Sat 09.00–17.00.

St Patrick's Park, Patrick Street, Dublin 8. Tel: 454 3389.
Open daily during daylight hours.

St Patrick's Cathedral, Patrick Street, Dublin 8. Tel: 475 4817; Fax: 454 6374.
Open Tues–Fri 09.00–18.00, Sat 08.30–17.00. Closed daily 13.00–14.30. Afternoon service
on Sundays at 15.00. Donation requested.

Marsh's Library, St Patrick's Close, Werburgh Street, Dublin 8. Tel: 454 3511.
Open: weekdays 10.00–12.45, 14.00–17.00, Sat 10.30–12.45. Closed Tues, Sun and Public
Hols.

St Werburgh's Church, Werburgh Street, Dublin 8. Tel: 478 3710.
Open Mon–Fri 10.00–18.00, by appointment only. Entrance 8 Castle Street. Morning service on Sundays at 10.30.

Dublin Castle, Dublin 8. Tel: 677 7129; Fax: 679 7831.
State Apartments and Undercroft *Open* Mon–Fri 10.00–12.15, 14.00–17.00; Sat, Sun and
Public Hols 14.00–17.00. *Admission*: charge.

City Hall, Cork Hill, Dublin 8. Tel: 679 6111.
Open during office hours.

Chester Beatty Library, Dublin Castle, Dublin 8. Tel: 677 7129; Fax: 679 7831.

GEORGIAN DUBLIN
St Andrew's Church, Westland Row, Dublin 2. Tel: 676 1270.
Open daytime and during Mass in the evening.

Archbishop Ryan Park (Merrion Square Park), Merrion Square, Dublin 2. Tel: 661 2369.
Open daily 09.00–dusk.

Number 29, Lower Fitzwilliam Street, Dublin 2. Tel: 702 6165.
Open Tues–Sat 10.00–17.00, Sun 14.00–17.00. Closed 2 weeks prior to Christmas.
Admission: charge.

Irish Architectural Archive, 73 Merrion Square, Dublin 2. Tel: 676 3430.
Open reading room Tues–Fri 10.00–13.00, 14.30–17.00.

The National Gallery, Merrion Square, Dublin 2. Tel: 661 5133; Fax: 661 5372. *Open* Mon–Sat 10.00–17.15 (Thurs until 20.00), Sun 14.00–17.00.

The Natural History Museum, Merrion Street, Dublin 2. Tel: 677 7444. *Open* Tues–Sat 10.00–17.00, Sun 14.00–17.00.

The National Concert Hall, Earlsfort Terrace, Dublin 2. Tel: 671 1533; Fax: 671 2615. *Open* for buffet lunches and evening meals. Lobby and booking office open 10.00–19.00. Concerts most evenings and often at lunchtime.

Royal Hibernian Academy, Gallagher Gallery, Ely Place, Dublin 2. Tel: 661 2558; Fax: 661 0762. *Open* Mon–Sat 11.00–17.00 (Thurs until 20.00), Sun 14.00–17.00.

National Museum of Ireland, Merrion Row, Dublin 2. Tel: 660 1117; Fax: 662 2674. *Open* Tues–Sat 10.00–17.00, Sun 14.00–17.00.

CUSTOM HOUSE DOCKS
Connolly Station, Amiens Street, Dublin 1. Tel: 836 3333; Fax: 836 9760.

Harbourmaster's Bar, Custom House Docks, Dublin 1. Tel: 671 1688. *Open* pub hours.

Custom House Visitor Centre, Custom House Quay, Dublin 1. Tel: 878 7660; Fax: 874 2710. *Open* Mon–Fri 10.00–17.00, Sat and Sun 14.00–17.00. *Admission*: charge.

THE GRAND CANAL
Waterways Visitor Centre, Grand Canal Quay, Dublin 2. Tel: 677 7510; Fax: 677 7514. *Open* daily Jun–Sep 09.30-18.30, Oct–May: Wed–Sun 12.30–17.00. *Admission*: charge.

Sisters of Mercy International Centre, Baggot Street, Dublin 2. Tel: 661 8061. Tours Mon–Fri 10.30–14.30. Donation of £3.00 requested.

THE LIBERTIES
Kilmainham Gaol, Inchicore Road, Dublin 8. Tel: 453 5984. Access to cells etc. by guided tour only. *Open* Apr and Oct: Mon–Fri 13.00–16.00, Sun 13.00–16.00, May–Sept 10.00–18.00. Closed Sat. *Admission*: charge.

Irish National War Memorial Park, Islandbridge, Dublin 8. c/o Office of Public Works, Tel: 661 3111; Fax: 661 0747. *Open* daily all year during daylight hours.

Royal Hospital Kilmainham, Military Road, Kilmainham, Dublin 8. Tel: 671 8666; Fax: 671 8695. *Open* Tues–Sat 10.00–17.30, Sun 12.00–17.30. Closed Mon. Coffee Shop *open* Mon–Sat 10.00–17.00, Sun 12.00–17.00. *Admission*: charge for exhibitions.

Guinness Hop Store, Crane Street, Dublin 8. Tel: 453 6700 ext. 5155; Fax: 454 6519. *Open* all year Mon–Sat 09.30–16.00, Sun 12.00–16.00. *Admission*: charge.

NORTH CITY CENTRE
The National Wax Museum, Granby Row, Dublin 1. Tel: 872 6340.
Open Mon–Sat 10.00–18.00, Sun 12.00–18.00. *Admission*: charge.

Hugh Lane Municipal Gallery of Modern Art, Parnell Square North, Dublin 1. Tel: 874 1903; Fax: 872 2182.
Open Tues–Fri 09.30–18.00, Sat 09.30–17.00, Sun 11.00–17.00. Closed Mon. Most Sundays at 12.00 there is a free concert in the Gallery. *Admission*: free to all Gallery events. Guided tours should be arranged two weeks in advance.

Writers' Museum, 18/19 Parnell Square, Dublin 1. Tel: 872 2077.
Open mid-Mar–Oct Mon–Sat 10.00–17.00, Sun and Public Hols 11.30–18.00. Nov–Mar telephone for details. *Admission*: charge.

Garden of Remembrance, Parnell Square East, Dublin 1.
Open daily 09.00–dusk or until 18.00.

Rotunda Hospital Chapel, Parnell Square South, Dublin 1. Tel: 873 0700.
Open during office hours.

OXMANTOWN
Chapter House, St Mary's Abbey, Meeting House Lane, off Capel St, Dublin 1. Tel: 872 1490.
Open Jun–Sep: Wed only 10.00–17.00.

Fruit and Vegetable Markets, St Michan's Street, Dublin 7.
Open 08.00–17.00 approx.

Four Courts, Inns Quay, Dublin 7. Tel: 872 5555.
Open 10.00–16.00 approx. The public may attend most court cases.

St Michan's Church and Vaults, Church Street, Dublin 7. Tel: 872 4154.
Open Mon–Fri 10.00–17.00, Sat 10.00–13.00. *Admission*: charge.

Irish Whiskey Corner, Bow Street, Dublin 7. Tel: 872 5566.
Open daily 10.00–18.00. Last conducted tour at 17.00. *Admission*: charge (but this includes a glass of whiskey or two!). No alcoholic beverages to under 18s.

Arbour Hill 1916 Memorial, Arbour Hill Cemetery, Dublin 7.
Opening times slightly erratic – the middle of day is the best time.

National Museum of Ireland, Collins Barracks, Benburb Street, Dublin 7. Tel: 677 7444; Fax: 677 7828.
Open Tues–Sat 10.00–17.00, Sun 14.00–17.00. Closed Mon.

THE PHOENIX PARK
General Office, Phoenix Park, Dublin 8. Tel: 821 3021; outside office hours: 677 2210.
All gates to the park are open during daylight hours but at night only the main gates remain open.

American Ambassador's Residence, c/o American Embassy, 42 Elgin Road, Dublin 4. Tel: 668 8777; Fax: 660 8469.
Visits by groups only by a few months' advance arrangement.

Áras an Uachtaráin, Phoenix Park, Dublin 8. Tel: 677 2815.
Visits by groups by advance arrangement only.

Ashtown Castle Visitor Centre, Phoenix Park, Dublin 8. Tel: 677 0095.
Open mid Mar–Oct: daily 09.30–17.00, except Jun–Sep: 09.30–18.30, Nov–mid Mar: Sat and Sun 09.30–16.30. Also opens other days for groups if arranged in advance. *Admission*: charge. Coffee Shop open daily all year, Mon–Fri 10.00–16.00, Sat and Sun 10–16.30.

Zoological Gardens, Phoenix Park, Dublin 8. Tel: 677 1425.
Open daily mid Mar–mid Oct: Mon–Sat 09.30–18.00, Sun 10.30–18.00; mid Oct–mid Mar: Mon–Fri 09.30–16.00, Sat 09.30–17.00, Sun 10.30–17.00. *Admission*: charge

Gárda Museum and Archive, Gárda Headquarters, Phoenix Park, Dublin 8. Tel: 677 1156 or 679 5677.
Visits by advance arrangement only.

ULYSSES WALK
James Joyce Centre, 35 North Great George's Street, Dublin 1. Tel: 878 8547; Fax: 878 8488.
Open Oct–Mar: Tues–Sat 10.00–16.30, Sun 12.30–16.30. *Admission*: charge.

St Andrew's Church, Westland Row, Dublin 1. Tel: 676 1270.
Open daytime and for evening Masses.

Sweny's Chemist, 1 Lincoln Place, Dublin 2. Tel: 676 2055.
Open Mon–Sat during office hours.

Davy Byrne's, 21 Duke Street, Dublin 2. Tel: 671 1298.
Open Mon–Sat 10.30–11.30 (11.00 in winter). Sun 12.30–14.00, 16.00–23.00.

FAMOUS DUBLINERS
The Shaw Birthplace Museum, 33 Synge Street, Dublin 8. Tel: 475 0854.
Open May–Oct: Mon–Sat 10.00–18.00. Sun and Public Hols 11.30–18.00 (closed 13.00–14.00). Nov–Apr: open for groups by request; Tel: 872 2077. *Admission*: charge.

Jewish Museum, 4 Walworth Rd., Dublin 8. Tel: 453 1797.
Open May–Sep: Sun, Tues and Thurs 11.00–15.30, Oct–Apr: Sun 10.30–14.30 (closed Jewish holy days).

Alex Findlater Wine Vaults and Museum, Harcourt Street, Dublin 2. Tel: 475 1699.
Open daily Mon–Fri 10.30–18.00, Sat 10.30–17.30. Groups welcome by prior appointment. Wine appreciation evenings are a regular feature.

Our Lady of Mount Carmel Church, Aungier Street, Dublin 2. Tel: 474 8821; Fax: 478 5525.
Open daily 08.00–18.30; Tues open until 21.00; Sat and Sun open until 19.45.

LEAFY SUBURBS

Radio Telefís Éireann Studios, Donnybrook, Dublin 4. Tel: 208 3111; Fax: 208 3080.
It is possible to walk into the complex but usually invited audiences only may view the
studios and vacancies for the more popular shows are booked up months in advance.

Royal Dublin Society, Ballsbridge, Dublin 4. Tel: 668 0866; Fax: 660 4014.
Visits can usually be made only during public occasions (see public advertisements).
Facilities such as the library and dining rooms are open to members only.

The American Embassy, 42 Elgin Road, Dublin 4. Tel: 668 8777; Fax: 660 8469.
For security reasons visits are only available to people on legitimate business.

ST ENDA'S PARK TO MARLAY PARK

St Enda's Park, Rathfarnham, Dublin 16. C/o Office of Public Works, 51 St. Stephen's
Green. Tel: 661 3111; Fax: 661 0747.
Open 09.00–dusk.

Pearse Museum, St Enda's Park, Rathfarnham, Dublin 16. Tel: 493 4208; Fax: 493 6120.
Open daily Nov–Jan: 10.00–16.00, Feb, Mar and Oct: 10.00–16.30, Apr and Sep:
10–17.00, May–Aug: 10–5.30. Closed daily 13.00–14.00 all year round. *Admission*: free.
Guided tours of house and park on request.
Café open with museum except during winter months when it is only open Sat and Sun
11.00–16.00.

Marlay Park, Rathfarnham, Dublin 16. C/o Dun Laoghaire and Rathdown County
Council, (see above). Park office Tel: 493 4059.
Open daily 09.00–dusk. Craft Centre and Coffee Shop. Tel: 494 2083. Craft Centre shops
open during office hours and some weekends, especially in the summer. Coffee Shop open
10.00–17.00 or until 21.00 depending on the season.

HELL FIRE CLUB

Hell Fire Wood, Managed by Coillte, The State Forestry Board, Leeson Lane, Dublin 2.
Tel: 661 5666; Fax: 678 9527.
Open during daylight hours. Barrier to car park locked at 16.00.

Sean Doherty's Pub and Restaurant, Rockbrook, Rathfarnham, Dublin 16. Tel: 493
1495; Fax: 493 0531.
Open lunch 12.00-14.30, dinner à la carte 18.00–21.30. Pub open 10.30–23.30 (23.00 in
winter). Sun 12.30–14.00 and 16.00–23.00.

DODDER RIVER WALK

Rathfarnham Castle, Rathfarnham, Dublin 16. Tel: 493 9462.
Open daily Apr–Oct: 10.00–18.00. Tea rooms open daily all year.

Herbert Park, Ballsbridge, Dublin 4. Tel: 668 4364.
Open daily 09.00–dusk.

DUN LAOGHAIRE COASTAL

Blackrock Park, Blackrock, Co Dublin. c/o Parks Superintendent, Tel: 284 8080.
Open during daylight hours.

Tourist Office, Stena Terminal, Dun Laoghaire Harbour.
Open daily 10.00–21.00 subject to ferry arrivals.

National Maritime Museum, Haigh Terrace, Dun Laoghaire, Co Dublin. Tel: 280 0969.
Open May–Sep: Tues–Sun 13.00–17.00. *Admission*: charge.

James Joyce Tower, Sandycove, Co. Dublin. Tel: 280 9265.
Open Apr–Oct: Mon–Sat 10.00–13.00, 14.00–17.00, Sun and Public Hols 14.00–18.00.
Nov–Mar by appointment only (Tel: 872 2077). *Admission*: charge.

DALKEY AND KILLINEY HILL
Sorrento Park, Sorrento Park, Sorrento Road, Dalkey, Co Dublin. C/o Dun Laoghaire
and Rathdown County Council (see above).
Open during daylight hours.

Killiney Hill Park, Killiney Hill Park, Killiney, Co Dublin. C/o Dun Laoghaire and
Rathdown County Council (see above).
Open during daylight hours.

Dalkey Heritage Centre, Goat's Castle, Dalkey, Co Dublin. Tel: 205 4745; Fax: 284
3141. Opening Spring 1998.
Open Tues–Sun 09.00–17.00 (closed Mon). (Provisional hours.)

BRAY TO ENNISKERRY
National Aquarium, Strand Road, Bray, Co Wicklow. Tel: 286 4688.
Open daily 10.00–18.00. *Admission*: charge.

Bray Heritage Centre, Old Court House, Bray, Co. Wicklow. Tel: 286 6796.
Open Mon–Fri 09.30–16.30, Sat 10.00–16.00. Closed daily 13.00–14.00.

Powerscourt Demesne, Enniskerry, Co Wicklow. Tel: 286 7676; Fax: 276 6054.
Gardens and Visitor Centre open daily Mar–Oct 09.30–17.30. Waterfall daily all year
09.30–19.00 (summer), 09.30–dusk (in winter). *Admission*: charge.

PHIBSBOROUGH TO THE NATIONAL BOTANIC GARDENS
St Peter's Church, Cabra Road, Dublin 7. Tel: 838 9708.
Open from early morning until after evening Mass.

Glasnevin Cemetery, Finglas Road, Dublin 11. Tel: 830 1133; Fax: 830 1594.
Open daily 08.00–16.00. View O'Connell Crypt by advance arrangement. *Admission*: free.

National Botanic Gardens, Botanic Road, Dublin 9. Tel: 837 7596; Fax: 836 0080.
Open weekdays 09.00–18.00 in summer, 10.00–16.30 in winter. Sun 11.00–18.00 in
summer, 11.00–16.30 in winter.

GRIFFITH AVENUE TO CLONTARF CASTLE
Marino Institute of Education, Griffith Avenue, Dublin 9. Tel: 833 5111; Fax: 833
5290.
Visit the courtyard gardens and other facilities by advance arrangement.

Fire Brigade Museum, Malahide Road, Dublin 3. Tel: 833 8313; Fax: 679 2226.
Visit by advance arrangement.

Casino, Marino, Malahide Road, Dublin 3. Tel: 833 1618; Fax: 661 0747.
Open daily Jun–Sep: 09.30–18.30, Oct–May: Wed and Sun only, 13.00–16.00.

Church of Our Lady of Consolation, Donnycarney, Dublin 5. Tel: 831 6016.
Open mornings until 12.00 and during Mass times.

St Anne's Park, Rose Gardens, Dublin Corporation Parks Department, Civic Offices,
Dublin 8. Tel: 679 6111; Fax: 679 2226.
Open all year during daylight hours.

Clontarf Castle, Castle Avenue, Dublin 3. Tel: 833 2321; Fax: 833 4549.
Keeps hotel hours.

Castle Avenue Cemetery, Castle Avenue, Dublin 3, c/o Dublin Corporation
Environmental Health Department, Civic Offices, Wood Quay, Dublin 8. Tel: 679 6111;
Fax: 679 2226.
Open during daytime hours.

SUTTON COASTAL
Bull Island Interpretative Centre, Dollymount, Dublin 3; (Managed by Dublin
Corporation). Tel: 833 8341.
Admission: free but telephone in advance for groups so special facilities can be laid on.
Open Mon–Fri 10.15–13.00, 13.30–15.30, Sat and Sun 10.00–13.00; 13.30–16.30.

HOWTH
National Transport Museum, Howth Castle Demesne, Howth, Co Dublin. Tel: 847 5623.
Open Sat, Sun and Public Holidays, 14.00–17.00. *Admission*: charge.

Rhododendron Gardens, Howth Castle Demesne, Howth, Co Dublin. Tel: 832 2624.
Open daily until sunset all year. Best seen in May and June.

PORTMARNOCK TO MALAHIDE
Malahide Castle Park, Malahide, Co Dublin (c/o Fingal County Council). Tel: 846
2456.
Open daily 10.00–17.00 or until 21.00 depending on the season.

Malahide Castle, Malahide, Co Dublin (in the care of Dublin Tourism). Tel: 846 2184.
Open Apr–Oct: Mon–Fri 10.00–17.00, Sat 11.00–18.00, Sun and Public Holidays
11.30–18.00, Nov–Mar: Mon–Fri 10.00–17.00, Sat , Sun and Public Holidays
14.00–17.00.

Malahide Castle Botanical Gardens, Malahide, Co Dublin (c/o Fingal County
Council–for contact details see above).
Open May–Sep: daily 14.30–17.00. Guided tours Wednesdays at 14.00.

Fry Model Railway, Malahide Castle, Malahide, Co Dublin (c/o Dublin Tourism). Tel:
846 3779.
Open Apr–Sep: Mon–Thurs 10.00–18.00 (closed Fridays), Sat 11.00–18.00, Sun and Public
Holidays 14.00–18.00. Jun–Aug: Fri: 10.00–18.00, Oct–Mar: Sat, Sun and Public Holidays
14.00–17.00.

Old Malahide Society Museum, Malahide Castle, Co Dublin.
Open daily 10.00–13.00 and 14.00–17.00.

Bibliography

Bennett, D. *Encyclopaedia of Dublin*, Dublin, Gill and Macmillan, 1991.

Costello, P, Farmer, T. *The Very Heart of the City*, Dublin, Clery & Co. 1992.

Cowell, J. *Where They Lived in Dublin*, Dublin, O'Brien Press, 1980.

deBreffny, B., *Ireland; A Cultural Encyclopaedia*, London, Thames and Hudson, 1983.

deCourcy, J.W., *The Liffey in Dublin*, Dublin, Gill and Macmillan, 1996.

Gardiner's Dublin, Dublin, N.C.E.A., 1991.

Gillespie, E., *The Liberties of Dublin*, Dublin, E & T. O'Brien, 1973.

Gilligan, H.A., *A History of the Port of Dublin*, Dublin, Gill and Macmillan, 1989.

Hart C, Knuth L., *A Topographical Guide to James Joyce's Ulysses*, Colchester, A Wake Newsletter Press, 1981.

Illustrated Road Book of Ireland, Dublin, The Automobile Association, 1970.

Joyce, J., *Ulysses*, London, Chancellor Press, 1993.

Mac Thomáis, E., *Me Jewel and Darlin' Dublin*, Dublin, O'Brien Press, 1980.

MacLoughlan, A., *A Guide to Historic Dublin*, Dublin, Gill and Macmillan, 1979.

McCarthy, J., *A Walking Guide to Ulysses*, Dublin, Wolfhound Press, 1986.

McCready, C.T. *Dublin Street Names*, Dublin, Carrig Books, 1994.

Moriarty, C. *On Foot in Dublin and Wicklow*, Dublin, Wolfhound Press, 1989.

Mulligan, F., *One Hundred and Fifty Years of Irish Railways*, Belfast, Appletree Press, 1983.

Neary, B. *A History of Cabra and Phibsborough*, Dublin, Lenhar Publications, 1984.

Nicholson, R., *The Ulysses Guide*, London, Methuen, 1988.

O'Donnell, E.E., *The Annals of Dublin*, Dublin, Wolfhound Press, 1987.

Pearson, P., *Dun Laoghaire*, Dublin , O'Brien Press, 1981.

Rathfarnham, Dublin, Irish Countrywomen's Association, 1991.

Some Dublin Writers, Dublin, Dublin Corporation Public Libraries, 1988.

Sommerville-Large, P., *Dublin, The Fair City*, London, Hamish Hamilton, 1979.

St. John Joyce, W. *The Neighbourhood of Dublin*, Dublin, Hughes & Hughes, 1994.

Wrenn, J. *The Villages of Dublin*, Dublin, Tomar Publishing, 1982.

Index